M000237424

ONE DAY AS A TIGER

ONE
DAY AS
A TIGER

JOHN PORTER

RMB

Copyright © 2016 by John Porter
Originally published in the UK by Vertebrate Publishing in 2014

All rights reserved. No part of this publication may be reproduced, stored in a retrieval system, or transmitted in any form or by any means – electronic, mechanical, audio recording, or otherwise – without the written permission of the publisher or a photocopying licence from Access Copyright. Permissions and licensing contribute to a secure and vibrant book industry by helping to support writers and publishers through the purchase of authorized editions and excerpts. To obtain an official licence, please visit accesscopyright.ca or call 1-800-893-5777.

RMB | Rocky Mountain Books Ltd.
rmbooks.com
@rmbooks
facebook.com/rmbooks

Cataloguing data available from Library and Archives Canada
ISBN 978-1-77160-166-5 (paperback)
ISBN 978-1-77160-167-2 (electronic)

Cover photo: Alex at first light after our all-night singsong without food or sleeping bags.

Printed and bound in Canada by Friesens

Distributed in Canada by Heritage Group Distribution and in the U.S. by Publishers Group West

For information on purchasing bulk quantities of this book, or to obtain media excerpts or invite the author to speak at an event, please visit rmbooks.com and select the "Contact Us" tab.

RMB | Rocky Mountain Books is dedicated to the environment and committed to reducing the destruction of old-growth forests. Our books are produced with respect for the future and consideration for the past.

We acknowledge the financial support of the Government of Canada through the Canada Book Fund and the Canada Council for the Arts, and of the province of British Columbia through the British Columbia Arts Council and the Book Publishing Tax Credit.

Canada Council
for the Arts

Conseil des arts
du Canada

BRITISH COLUMBIA
ARTS COUNCIL
An agency of the Province of British Columbia

To Jean and Libby MacIntyre, Sarah Richard
and the mountains that owned him.

CONTENTS

FOREWORD

It was John Porter who introduced me to the bakery with the best doughnuts in Chicken Street. I was on my first expedition and had just arrived in Kabul after a four-week bus journey from London, thrilled at last to be getting close to the mountains of the Hindu Kush. John was already on his way home, dealing masterfully, between doughnuts, with the Byzantine process of obtaining exit visas to leave Afghanistan – a process made doubly complicated for him because he was part of a large Anglo-Polish expedition travelling through the Soviet Union.

This was 1977 and the world was still a long way from the end of the Cold War. Getting a large team of Polish and British climbers to Afghanistan and back required a determined blend of diplomacy, skulduggery, luck and creative wheeler-dealing. Later that day in Kabul I met the expedition leader – the hugely charming and persuasive Andrzej Zawada – who struck a deal to sell his leftover expedition food to our team. He had just made an impressive first ascent of the north face of Kohe Mandaras with the British actor and climber Terry King. But it was John Porter's buccaneering splinter group that made the biggest impression.

We didn't meet their Polish guru, Wojciech Kurtyka, but we did meet Alex MacIntyre, and I can still picture the wild gleam in his dark eyes as he and John gabbled manically about the gigantic east face of Koh-i-Bandaka. It was a tale of crumbling rock walls and towering ice-fields, of cataclysmic rockfalls, of cyclopean seracs, of bridges burned repeatedly. And the climax of the tale was the great central chimney, raked by falling stones, which they nicknamed the cyclotron – the Atom Smasher.

Heady stuff. Suicidal, some might think. Except that the bravura was underpinned by years of alpine experience and lots of canny calculation. And, in case anyone thought that Koh-i-Bandaka was a one-off lucky escape, the same trio returned to the Himalaya the following year, with the addition of Krzysztof Zurek, to pull off an even more accomplished coup on the south face of Changabang. By which time Alex MacIntyre had already mapped out his future journey up the biggest unclimbed faces on the very highest peaks – a journey that progressed according to plan, until it was brought to a sudden and brutal end in October 1982, by a single deadly stone on the south face of Annapurna.

Apart from a few chance encounters like the one in Kabul, I did not know Alex MacIntyre. But I read and enjoyed the few articles he wrote, and I have quoted from them in my own books. He was articulate, witty, self-confident and brazenly honest about his ambition. He showed what was possible on the world's highest mountains and although few of his contemporaries could – or even wanted to – match his single-minded boldness, he influenced all of us. So, having followed his career from a distance all those years ago, it is fascinating now to read this book by someone who knew him so well. However, John's book is not simply a biography of Alex MacIntyre. There is a lot about John in it, too. But nor is it an autobiography. Nor is it a mountaineering history. Nor is it a conventional travel book. It has elements of all those genres, and a lot more besides, bravely defying glib categorization.

Early in the book, John mentions how his friend predicted that one day they would hang up their boots and become commentators. For Alex, that never happened. But John has now, at last, written that commentary, combining the wisdom of hindsight with the immediacy of great days recalled with detailed intensity. From 1977 to 1982 he was at the heart of what really was a golden age of Himalayan mountaineering, when the whole notion of what was possible changed radically. He gives us vivid narrative accounts of some of those climbs, but he also puts them in perspective, looking back to Edward Whymper and forward to Ueli Steck. Best of all, he gives us many of the previously unpublished back stories of a wild bunch going on wild adventures and generating some very funny stories. What a wonderful antidote to

Photo: Bernard Newman

Alex MacIntyre

1954–1982

today's regime of sponsored athletes, Seven Summiteers and Everest package tours!

However, the golden age was tarnished with a tragic roll call of names of the fallen, including Peter Boardman, Joe Tasker, Roger Baxter-Jones, Georges Bettembourg and, of course, Alex MacIntyre, the key figure in the book, who emerges from this affectionate portrait as an altogether more sensitive, generous and ultimately troubled figure than his brash public persona. Climbers tend to shy away from serious discussion of death, but John recalls movingly the anguished conversations with sisters, mothers and girlfriends – the ripples of grief emanating from a falling stone. He also gives a moving first-hand account – the first to be published, I think – of that final, ill-fated, expedition to Annapurna.

Stephen Venables
June 2014

PREFACE

While writing this book, I realized that the retelling of Alex's life also included my own very personal "take" on the climbing scene in those days. No doubt some of the characters in the book will have different memories of Alex and of those times. There are many people who I wish I had found time to see and record their thoughts, but I could have done that forever. In the end, I had to be selective, and back up my memory with taped interviews of those who were part of our close circle of friends at that time. But there were many more conversations with old friends, often through chance encounters and email exchanges. I also had a wealth of articles from climbing media to research. Over the years, as the 1970s and 1980s receded as though seen through the wrong end of a telescope, I began to realize how difficult it was to get a true picture of everything that happened. There came a moment when I felt there was more than enough material to pull together into something like a coherent whole.

It must be remembered that most of the action takes place in a time nearer to the end of the Second World War than it is to the current era. Originally, I tried to take myself completely out of the book, writing as if I was Alex (on Ken Wilson's suggestion), but that proved impossible, in part because the intensity of our times and climbs together was best described in my own voice, and in part because there was no way I could match Alex's inimitable style of writing. So, as a result, this story of Alex is not in any sense of the word a pure biography.

There are far more people to thank than I have capacity to remember. Firstly, I thank everyone who knew, loved and climbed with Alex and made a contribution to his life and story. Most importantly, Alex's mother Jean, whose insights into Alex and his friends remain the central contribution to the book around which everything else revolves. Without Jean's early support for the book, it would never have been written. The same is true of Alex's sister Libby, and Sarah Richard. I would not have written about Alex without their sanction. They suffered his loss more than the rest of us can imagine.

In August last year, just as I realized I finally had enough material to finish the book, I was selected to join the Mountain and Wilderness Writing Program at the Banff Centre in Alberta. The intensity of this program forced me to make the most of the many hours spent writing in my personal studio folded into the snowy mountain woods. It provided the space and time to complete the core of the book, so thank you Banff Centre, and especially the Arts Faculty, for that opportunity. The critical insights of the two tutors from the program – Tony Whittome and Marni Jackson – directed me toward the structure that (hopefully) holds the different levels of the book together. And, of course, I was not alone; the encouragement and critical friendship from the rest of the program members – Jack Tackle, Rebecca Loncraine, Sarah Johnson, Aaron Spitzer and Lyndsie Bourgon – made me more determined than ever to finally get it done. Back home over recent weeks, thanks to Ed Douglas for copy-editing and all the team at Vertebrate Publishing, especially John Coefield and Jon Barton.

For their contributions of stories, photos and words of encouragement and advice, thanks to John Powell, Maria Coffey, Bernard Newman, Colin Brooks, Nick Colton, Tim Jepson, Brian Cropper, Dennis Gray, Roger Martin, Leo Dickinson, Doug Scott, Chris Bonington, Tut Braithwaite, Brian Hall, Guy Lee, René Ghilini, Wojciech Kurtyka, Anna Milewska and all my Polish friends. Bernadette McDonald, Judith Brown, Chris Bonington and Doug Scott all made constructive suggestions to improve the writing and corrected facts that I got wrong. Jon Popowich reminded me of a long forgotten article in *Mountain Review* in which I quote from Novalis. Pete Woolaghan asked the difficult question to which no mountaineer can provide a complete answer. I resurrected that quote to help shape my view of fate and Alex's character. And, of course, I'm very grateful to Stephen Venables, whose foreword puts the climbs and the times into context.

And, lastly, thanks to everyone who over 15 years has asked, "how's the book going?" – words that made my stomach churn. I heard those words most from my wife Rose and my daughters Sarah and Laura, who endured my angst and gently encouraged me to find my way through to completion.

John Porter
Cumbria, July 2014

1

STAIRWAY TO HEAVEN

A steady breeze flows down from unseen peaks, easing the discomfort of the strong sunlight and noonday heat. The wind ripples through fields of ripening barley and peas, the long stems flexing and rebounding in harmony. The intense greens of the fields seem to shine with an internal light. Mountains of dull brown deeply scored by *nullahs* tilt up from the edge of the plain like rusting sheets of corrugated iron. Their flanks rise from the fertile valley into an arid landscape of spiny scrub trees and rocky towers toward the snows of the Hindu Kush.

We are camped where four valleys meet on the plain of Zebak. This is the entrance to the Wakhan Corridor in the far northeast of Afghanistan. It is just past midday on an August afternoon in 1977. I doze in a state of semi-exhaustion and deep contentment. This is a magical place, filled with dazzling light and verdant growth in the middle of a desert.

It isn't much of a camp. The gales of the previous night have nearly destroyed our single tent. It is torn down one side, exposing an assortment of clothes and gear scattered inside. We make no effort to stitch the tent or pick up the mess or wash the pots. At this moment, nothing seems to matter. A hoopoe flits toward the river, the splash of colour on its wings accentuated by the blinding sun. All is calm. Being alive, still existing, is all that matters.

Alex is visible through the ripped side of the tent, dozing on top of his sleeping bag. His exposed ribs and wasted arms and legs speak of weeks of hard effort and not enough food. His face is framed by a mop of hair, part vagrant part rock star, like Marc Bolan with a stubbly beard. A battered copy of *The Magus* by John Fowles lies tipped on its side next to him. A half-drunk cup of tea has upended onto my sleeping bag.

It doesn't matter. The sun dries things within minutes. The world around us is a slow cycle of time and colour. The only sounds are the rush of the distant river, the wind in the grain and the occasional call of a bird of prey circling high above. We have enough to eat. Within a few days, the expedition will come to an end and new journeys will begin.

But for the moment, we are still in Afghanistan, miles from our friends and with no idea as yet how we will get home. We have to find our way back to Kabul by truck. Maybe six days? Then the big question: Will the Russians let us cross the Amu Darya to retrace our train journey across the Soviet Union? The Poles smuggled us here with false papers, so going back is a problem. If they grant us permission in Kabul, maybe ten more days to get to Warsaw, then three days to England. It is only time and we have plenty of that. I drift off again.

As if from a dream, the distant sound of engines gathers strength. Beyond the fields, at the base of the hills to the north, lies a rough road that links Faizabad with the upper reaches of the Wakhan and then on to the smuggling route into Soviet Asia across the Amu Darya. Could this be Wojciech Kurtyka – known as Voytek – and the rest of our expedition returning from the Mandaras valley? Voytek has been gone two days. I make a quick calculation – no, that is not enough time to get there and back. We follow the plume of dust rising from the road half a mile away as it grows in size to reveal a military jeep and a truck half-full of soldiers heading west.

The vehicles stop at the nearest point on the road to us, about a quarter of a mile away. Three men get out and set out at a fast march across the fields in our direction. We have camped far enough from the road to give ourselves a chance to run if required. A threatening encounter at Bandikan a week ago is still fresh in our memory. We have no official permission to be here, which in the eyes of bandits is as good as not being here at all. We have no choice now but to wait and see what unfolds. In any case, these men are clearly military. We can tell by the height and sweep of their peaked caps that two of them are officers. By his braids, one appears to be a colonel. Perhaps a cell in a military camp won't be too bad.

As the men approach, Alex sits up to have a better look. We can see clearly that Voytek is not with them.

"What do you think? Are these guys going to arrest us, shoot us or are they just stopping by for a brew?"

"Hopefully just checking us out, but maybe they will do all three."

I stand up to greet them, while Alex does his best to bring order to our possessions. First priority, get our British passports ready to wave if required. Being "*Inglestani!* London!" has proven to be one of our strongest cards during our entire illicit time in this region.

The colonel covers the last yards with grace and authority.

"Hello, where are you from?"

Around forty years old and with 1950s movie-star looks, he is clearly the senior man here. His Horse Guards moustache dates from the era of the British Army's fatal retreat from Kabul. It suddenly occurs to me to question how the English military of past centuries developed the fashion for moustaches.

"*Inglestani!* London," I reply like an obedient dog.

"Ah, where in London do you live? I love the West End. I did my masters at the London School of Economics."

I am about to relax and mumble something about actually being from Cumbria when to my horror I see that the junior officer and his driver are rifling through the contents of the tent and that Alex is powerless to stop them. The next question from the colonel takes me totally by surprise.

"How much do you want for your tent, for your equipment, anything else you want to sell?"

I look around, and then turn back to him in astonishment. The tent is clearly in ruins. The sleeping bags and clothing are patched and filthy with sweat and grime. Everything else including our stove and nesting pots are battered and barely usable. Only the pile of nuts, pitons, ice axes and crampons, already used before this expedition, re-tain something of their original condition.

The activity of barter in Afghanistan is highly complex, and potentially dangerous. On the first day of the walk-in, a village elder tried to buy Alex's boots. Alex explained that his boots were worth more than the village bull. For the local people, that suddenly made us seem incredibly wealthy. Everything is relative. This entire trip from the time we arrived in Warsaw to this very moment had been a masterpiece of turning pennies into goods to barter and the resulting dollars into summits. The Poles have taken a huge risk smuggling us across the Soviet Union to get us here. Now I must find an answer to this man's offer to trade that will not insult him and, perhaps, save us the need for any further explanations. My boy scout's sense of honour comes to my rescue.

"I'm afraid we are not in any position to sell our equipment. You see it all belongs to the High Mountain Club of Poland, which makes it all the property of the Peoples' Republic of Poland. It has been loaned to us and is in our care."

Now it is the colonel's turn to stare incredulously at me. There is a short pause.

"Ah well," he says, "in that case we must be on our way. It is so hard to find good equipment for use in the mountains. That is a pity."

And with that, they turn and begin to leave, but then the movie-star colonel stops and turns round.

"Oh, I must tell you that all your Polish and English friends are well and send their regards. We met them two days ago and they, quite happily, sold us equipment. I guess that must have been their private property? *Inshallah*, they will find you in one or two days at the most. In the meantime, I'll make sure you are sent some trout and bread from the village – it looks like you could do with some food. Goodbye. And may Allah protect you."

The men float away. Alex and I stand in the sweltering sun and breathe freely again. Life is direct and immediate. No one needs to know where we are, who we are. We are no longer sure ourselves. We are just travellers in the middle of a story from another world. When the engines start and the convoy heads out, we laugh until near to tears and only stop when two men from the village arrive with a massive trout and some cold *naan*. Ramadan has clearly finished. We offer the men a handful of small denomination Afghanis and ask them to join us. We brew tea, fry the trout and watch shadows move down into the valley as though the mountain is the gnomon on a sundial. We finish our simple meal and the men leave, their curiosity diminished by the chill mountain air that fills the valley each evening.

Waking midway through the night, I see through the tear in the tent a dazzling array of stars illuminating the black sky. The Milky Way seems like all that is good and safe in life. I remember childhood nights spent secretly with my small homemade telescope on the roof in Massachusetts while my parents slept. The sky is so incredibly clear above me now, I can see nebulae, and areas where opaque clouds of gas obscure what lies behind, like the impenetrable darkness that looms in the soul even when it is most content.

2

PUBLIC IMAGE

In the middle of the afternoon on 15 October 1982, Alex MacIntyre and the French/Italian climber René Ghilini reached a steep rock band at around 7200 metres on the south face of Annapurna. The south face is one of the great walls of the Himalaya, a complex assortment of buttresses and steep couloirs three miles wide and a mile and a half high. Of the fourteen peaks over 8000 metres, Annapurna has claimed the most lives for each attempt. Alex and René were trying a new route, a diagonal line starting from the right side of the face that would eventually lead them to the central summit. If successful, it would be the fourth route on the face. The three main buttresses had already been climbed by large "national" expeditions. In 1970, a British team led by Chris Bonington climbed what was then the most difficult route on an eight-thousander. It went directly up the far left buttress to the highest of Annapurna's three summits. The Poles climbed the central buttress in May 1981 and the Japanese the right pillar in October 1981. All three of these expeditions comprised many members and climbing the mountain took months, with fixed ropes and permanent camps. Alex and René planned to climb the face in three days with two more in descent, just the two of them. If they failed on this attempt, they would be back to try again.

Together they surveyed the possibilities for climbing the 30-metre wall that now blocked their progress. From base camp it seemed inconsequential, the width of a pencil set against a two-storey house. A tempting snow ramp led left, perhaps all the way to open snow slopes on the other side, but after 60 metres, the ramp narrowed to a thin smear of ice and then there was just a sweep of compact rock. It was impossible. They retreated to a crevasse at the start of the ramp and prepared to bivouac. Climbing safely down the 800-metre couloir to the foot of the face, they would have to start at dawn, while the mountain was still frozen. Brewing drinks, they discussed what equipment they would need to get past this band of rock on the next attempt.

It was after dawn by the time they started down. They were slowed by the initial difficult descent into the couloir. The sun reached the top of the face and slowly descended in a yellow veil toward them, growing stronger. At around 10 a.m., the two men were about halfway down the couloir. From below, where I sat watching them, they were two tiny specks in a sea of snow and rock. Then, in a moment, fate rushed to meet Alex in the form of a fist-sized stone accelerating from half a mile above. It smashed into his helmet with the accuracy of a sniper's bullet. He crumpled then fell the remaining 400 metres down the couloir.

René clung to his ice axes, stunned for a moment, and then called Alex's name. When there was no response, he descended as quickly as possible in a semi self-arrest, kicking his crampons into the softening snow while jabbing his axes above his head in a controlled fall. When he reached Alex's lifeless body, he understood death had been almost certainly instantaneous. There was nothing he could do. He forced himself to be calm, to control his own shock and continue his retreat alone. He placed the body in a recess just above a crevasse and marked the spot with Alex's ice axes holding him to the face. Then he raced the remaining four hours toward base camp on the opposite side of the glacier.

I met him halfway across. I had been watching from the lateral moraine just above base camp and seen the accident through the lens of my camera. All we could do that day was return to the tents; it was too late to go up. That night, René told me the story, about being stopped by the rock step, the conversations they had during the bivvy the night before, how they hoped I would have recovered and with extra equipment we would return and succeed. The evening before, as they descended, I thought my luck had changed. Feeling fit again after a bout of diarrhea, I hoped we could still climb the face together. Now this.

The evening before, as I watched them prepare to bivouac through my zoom lens, a sudden burst of intense red filled the viewfinder. My heart missed a beat, but then I realized what I had seen. It was Alex shaking out the bivvy tent.

The morning after the accident, René and I started to pack up to return to the face and recover the body, but cloud descended before we set off and it began to snow lightly. A storm was brewing. We waited another day in a state of uncertainty. Our liaison officer said he would leave immediately to get news back to Kathmandu. I thought of his mother Jean, and Sarah, his girlfriend, and the need to speak to them. We could stay and try to recover Alex's body, but what would that achieve? It was clear Annapurna would be Alex's tomb.

There is now a memorial stone for Alex at Annapurna base camp with an inscription that reads: "Better to live one day as a tiger than to live for a thousand years as a sheep."* Had René and Alex managed to overcome the short section that stopped them, there would have been few difficulties between them and the top. In 1984, two Spaniards, Nil Bohigas and Enric Lucas, climbed the line Alex and René had tried. It was a brilliant ascent, but their success was testimony to Alex's vision. Luck had been with them. A narrow runnel of ice led steeply up and over the buttress that had stopped Alex and René.

Alex was 28 when he died, so young his life was little more than a preface, but a preface to what? Alex thought he knew. Just before we left Kathmandu to go to Annapurna, he completed an article for the *Karrimor Technical Guide* for 1983 – Karrimor then being among the leading outdoor brands. I have a picture of Alex sifting through the many sheets he had written by headtorch during a power cut at the Lhotse Hotel. He was doing a final "cut and paste" of the article, which meant just that, cutting bits out and sticking them at a more

* "Better to live one day as a tiger than to live for a thousand years as a sheep" was chosen by Alex's mother Jean for the memorial stone that she erected, accompanied by his sister Libby, his girlfriend Sarah Richard and his good friend Terry Mooney, the season after his death. Some years later it was smashed by an avalanche. In November 2012, I walked in with Pete and Diane Clark to replace it. The south face and the enclosing cirque of peaks still towered high and serene above the sanctuary, but the development of hotels complete with Internet connectivity throughout the region shocked me; Alex would have welcomed it. In 1982, there was only one lodge on the walk-in, and that was the Captain's Lodge at Chamlang. Otherwise, we camped or stayed in shepherd's huts.

appropriate place in the text, or writing a new paragraph by hand and gluing it over the old one.

With uncanny foresight the equal of anything in H.G. Wells, he predicted changes in modern mountaineering and a revolution in worldwide communications. Here is the first of his predictions, right at the beginning of the article: "As we pack our gear for our attempt on Annapurna south face, we do so in the sure knowledge that one day, in the not too distant future, some lad will be packing half as much or less and setting off to climb the wall in a time beyond our comprehension, backed by a methodology and an understanding of the environment that we do not have today. Our lightweight sacks will be like dinosaurs. The Himalaya will, for a few at least, become an alpine playground, while the waiting millions watch!"

In 2013, the Swiss alpinist Ueli Steck soloed a significantly more difficult line to the right of the British buttress directly to the summit on the south face, up and down in 28 hours. Steck, dubbed the Swiss Machine, sets speed records on routes almost every time he steps on a mountain, and millions really do watch films of these ascents on YouTube and television. Such an ascent would have been impossible in 1982 with the equipment of the day. And Steck has achieved the highest standards of modern athletic fitness. There are no Olympic events for climbers, but he is the only gold medallist when it comes to soloing eight-thousanders. Even by the generally very high standards of modern mountaineering, active climbers today find Steck's achievements amazing.

The gap between a very good climber and an exceptional climber like Steck is much greater today than it was in the 1970s and 1980s. Back then, climbers soloed routes in the Alps to improve their skills and efficiency. It was training to learn to move fast on similar ground in the Himalaya. Setting a speed record wasn't part of the equation. Now speed has become almost a separate sport within mountaineering. It puts the experience into a new dimension. There is little to reflect on when writing about a two-and-a-half-hour ascent of the Eigerwand. Stopwatches and sponsors dilute the mystique. And yet what does Steck himself say about his achievement? "I am not a better climber than Anderl Heckmair.* This is just a different style in a different era."

The other remarkable prediction in the article foreshadows the coming of the Internet. "One day, in the not too distant future, we may be sitting in our base camp trying to choose between *Dallas* and some lad soloing Makalu's west face live, while trying to keep in touch with the progress of other expeditions by the press of a button. But perhaps by then, René, John and I will have jobs as commentators! Yours, Alex."

You might say that in writing this book I am proving him right.

When Alex had finished cutting and pasting his article that September day in 1982, he shoved it into an envelope, addressed it to Karrimor's owner Mike Parsons and walked a mile into town through the monsoon rains, along teeming, muddy streets to the post office. Fortunately, the letter reached Mike some weeks later.

Alex MacIntyre's short but brilliant climbing career spanned barely a decade, from early 1972 until the autumn of 1982. By the end of that decade, he was known internationally for his audacious ascents in the Alps, the Andes and the Himalaya. Reinhold Messner described Alex as "the purest exponent of the lightweight style now climbing in Himalaya." Around the same time, Alex said of Reinhold Messner, "He had some interesting projects until he took up peak-bagging and became more interested in number-crunching."**

This impertinent response was recorded in an interview with Ken Wilson for *Mountain* magazine in 1982, during the summer before Alex's death. Wilson purged it from the final printed version, fearing Messner would take offence. But the comment was typical of Alex – provocative, some might say offensive given the great man's contribution to mountaineering, and yet, in truth, one way of looking at the facts. Alex, after all, had graduated with a top honours degree in law. There was no malice intended in his comment. Alex respected Messner.

---

* The Eiger Nordwand was first climbed in July 1938 by Anderl Heckmair, Ludwig Vörg, Heinrich Harrer and Fritz Kasparek. The Germans, Heckmair and Vörg, caught up with the Austrians who started a day earlier. Heckmair led the team up the final pitches in appalling weather.

** By this he meant the race to become the first to climb all 14 peaks over 8000 metres. Messner was the first; it has now been achieved by over 30 people and the number grows annually.

He considered his traverse of Nanga Parbat a model for the light-weight style:

"Reinhold is very fit when he arrives and does not, by my standards, do a lot of acclimatisation. He is an athlete and his approach is to take the peak very fast, spending an absolute minimum period of time at altitude ... but [the approach] only works where there are few techni-calities. Once you have technical problems, you need to arrive at them fully acclimatised, strong, and with enough supplies to be able to spend a few days on them. Good acclimatisation and the weight of your gear thus become critical."

Like Messner, Alex had a desire to conceive bold projects above and beyond the ordinary. Ueli Steck continues that tradition today with a different mindset and for far greater commercial reward. Alex lived in a time when equipment was relatively primitive compared to today. Scientific training regimes for high altitude had yet to be fully devel-oped. To reach the base of the biggest mountains took weeks not hours. Would Alex have been like Ueli Steck had he lived today? Possibly. The only certainty is that the best mountaineers of any age would always agree that "when the chance is there, take it."

Alex had a nickname in university – Dirty Alex. It was not entirely fair. We were all a pretty grubby bunch, but it stuck. His dishevelled appearance contrasted sharply with his bold good looks, constructed around inquisitive, intelligent and somewhat mocking eyes. He was certainly not, as has been suggested, a product of the flower power generation. Like many sportsmen of the 1970s, Alex styled his appear-ance with a mix of punk and glam rock. His appearance was both a statement and a challenge to draw out any ambivalence others might have from first impressions. Like most climbers in the 1970s, he smoked pot occasionally and used to joke that drinking was good "brain training" for the Himalaya. But Alex was not a late-night boozer like many leading stars of those days, including the mercurial genius John Syrett and the American Henry Barber, who enjoyed legendary pub crawls.

Alex's vision of the possible was backed up with an unnerving intel-lect and a wicked perversity to provoke and toy with other people's emotions. He was also a pragmatist. His approach to lightweight alpinism was well thought through; his aspirations were matched by his own designs for equipment that were often developed.

"Alex was in many ways unique," said Maria Coffey, the author of *Fragile Edge* and other books about the psychological and emotional implications of climbing. "He stood out from everyone else. He definitely had a glimmer." Maria knew Alex as well as anyone, having been his landlady for a year and a half while she was teaching in Manchester and Alex was working for the British Mountaineering Council. After Alex's death, Maria said those climbers who knew of her friendship with Alex would often ask about him. "Mark Twight and Tomaz Humar were in awe of him. His uniqueness sprang from his karma and charisma, generated from a sense of purpose, not just ambition."

I climbed with Humar a few times at Paklenica on the Dalmatian coast of Croatia. Alex was indeed one of his heroes. Tomaz was like Alex in many ways, enthusiastic, bold and brash and scoffed when warned he might share the same fate. Tomaz, like many climbers, had a spiritual connection with the mountains. For Tomaz, it was manifested through his Catholic faith and the mystical connection of his nation, Slovenia, to its highest mountain – Triglav – on which it was founded. In Alex, it was harder to detect, but it was there. Alex had a true love for the mountains and an imagination that allowed him to seek out new approaches. But he was also an enigma. Even good friends today say they really knew very little about Alex.

"He was hard work much of the time when we first started climbing together," said John Powell, his roommate and early climbing companion at university. "He didn't have much to say about things. He spent most of his time weighing things up but, eventually, when he did make a comment, it was usually pretty accurate. When, just occasionally, he was well off the mark, he would never admit defeat in an argument. He would resort to sarcasm when required as a way of wearing you down."

By the time he got to the south face of Annapurna, he had taken the idea of lightweight to extremes. He and Ghilini carried only one ice screw, two rock pegs, one rope and the sheath of another to use for abseiling, light sleeping bags, a bivvy tent, and food and gas for four days. Some have suggested that Alex broke his own rules going this light on such a massive face where the technical difficulties were unknown.

Style is a balancing act between the audacious and the acceptable. Alex's wiry stature hid an immensely strong will, but he hated heavy loads. He never planned to carry more than 18 kilos to the base of any unclimbed route on an 8000-metre peak. On Annapurna, he tried to get this down to less than that. In theory, by going light, your speed increased and thus reduced your exposure to danger. It was a simple theory; in speed lay safety. But the desire to make first ascents of great, unclimbed routes on the highest peaks was an ambition fraught with exposure to incalculable dangers. Very few climbers have got away without sustained good fortune if they continued to climb at the highest standard. Many had the sense to retire, or at least climb on lower peaks where the risks were more manageable.

"Good acclimatisation and the weight of your gear thus become critical," Alex had proclaimed as the golden rules of high-altitude climbing. These two elements were among the keys to any successful expedition. But what else was needed? The right team, of course, unless you were soloing. For exponents of lightweight style, that usually meant just two members, and never more than four. Roger Baxter-Jones, one of the leading and strongest British alpinists of the 1970s and 1980s, summed up the essential dynamics of teamwork on a Himalayan climb:

1. Come back
2. Come back friends
3. Get to the top

Roger, with Alex and Doug Scott, achieved all three goals while making the first ascent of the giant southwest face of Shisha Pangma in the purest style possible, but the climb tested their friendship to breaking point. The hardest of the three dictates is to come back friends. Other members of the team not capable of the climb were discarded at an early stage of the expedition and there was considerable resentment from those members left behind.

The final and least predictable requirement for success in the big mountains was – and still is – good luck. Alex knew full well he could not control objective dangers and so set out to manage his own luck by developing his concept of lightweight style. Safety came through speed, and speed was gained by stripping out much of the traditional safety net: camps, support, spare food and fuel, equipment and so forth – what Alex described as "the umbilical cord." And the need to reduce weight wasn't just about paring back on the amount of stuff. Lightweight style required lightweight gear and that meant new designs and new materials.

In the 1970s and 1980s, Himalayan climbing was still an adventure pursued by very few people, but in the lower ranges of North America and Europe, alpine climbing was a fast-growing sport, becoming socially acceptable and even fashionable. The growth in participation drove a growth in demand for equipment that would not only reduce the risks but also make the experience more enjoyable. There are very few people, even among the most hardened mountaineers, who actually find pleasure in carrying huge weights of gear in lumpy rucksacks.

Established companies and innovative new businesses set up and run by climbers responded to these new markets with lighter and better-designed products. The development of new equipment required investment in expensive research and technology. Specialist manufacturers worldwide vied to produce the best aluminum karabiners, hollow ice axes, lightweight crampons, high-altitude tents, waterproof nylon clothing and plastic boots, and they provided products to leading climbers to test. Anyone climbing in the 1960s and 1970s will remember the moment they clipped their steel karabiners for the last time, replaced pegs and knotted slings with lightweight nuts and tapes and condemned their uncomfortable canvas rucksacks – like carrying a potato sack – to the attic.

Alex had good contacts with many equipment manufacturers. In those days, they were mainly climbers and, therefore, likely to be friends. Through strength of personality, Alex often convinced them to develop new equipment made from the latest lightweight fabrics for clothing, rucksacks and tents that might be used on one expedition only and so would never be of commercial value unless modified. Necessity really was the mother of invention. Most climbers had little money and lived on thin air. Obtaining free equipment in exchange for bright suggestions on innovative and saleable products was an essential part of almost every Himalayan expedition. From the manufacturer's point of view, the development of lightweight equipment was often somewhere between an act of faith and a sign of friendship.

The right people and good gear meant nothing unless you were properly acclimatized for high-altitude climbing. Alex was clear that for most climbers this could only be achieved with the culmination of years, if not decades, of time spent in the mountains. He believed that good performance at high altitude was not simply a matter of the body physically adapting. The mind also had to adapt. It had to learn to accept everything encountered on the mountain as perfectly normal, including extreme danger. This, he argued, could only be achieved after thousands of hours of living in that environment. There were no shortcuts to mountain success. You needed to be "time served." He hounded one teammate on Shisha Pangma until he agreed to drop all thoughts of going onto the mountain with the rest of them.

"Fundamentally, Nick has not logged enough hours slogging through Scottish bogs in winter blizzards, lumbering through the frantic, non-stop twenty-four-hour exhaustion of the Alps ... like a pack of pursued wolves with a badly wounded mate, the experienced climbers smelt the inevitable."

Climbers have long debated whether mountaineering is a lifestyle or a sport. In the 1950s, it was more of a lifestyle, in part because there was little chance of making a living from it and, in part, because it demanded so much of your life to serve a full apprenticeship. Alex certainly served a full apprenticeship. Before the widespread popularity of climbing walls, sport climbing* and commercial mountain tourism, the formula for an apprenticeship in Britain more or less followed the sequence set out below. (For North America, replace the Alps with Rockies, Sierras, Cascades or Tetons.)

1. Walk in the hills and dales – observe mad people climbing rocks.
2. Read books about climbing, get inspired.
3. Decide you are also mad, and find someone with whom to go climb a rock.
4. Climb ice in winter, get thoroughly miserable and thoroughly hooked.
5. Go to the Alps in summer, learn to function in thin air, to move fast.
6. Climb in the Alps in winter, have miserable epics and taste the joy of hard-fought success.

If, after five to ten years, you were still alive and climbing, you graduated to the Greater Ranges. That was where being "time served" mattered most. (Scottish climbers had the only possible variation allowed in this classical apprenticeship. In the Scottish version, Step 5 was seen as a requirement before you attempted Step 4 in the Scottish hills. Anyone who has spent a few weeks climbing in full winter conditions in Scotland will have some sympathy for this view.)

After his ascent of Shisha Pangma, Alex was asked in an interview if the time was coming when climbers might go straight from Scottish training to the big problem faces of the Himalaya. He responded: "I am not sure about that. I wrote an article for a Japanese magazine recently where I pointed out the advantages that British climbers enjoy, having been able to learn their trade through five or six alpine seasons. There are an awful lot of tricks of the trade you can perfect only on alpine terrain. Himalayan trips are still pretty cumbersome and I can't really see anyone going there and operating safely without

---

* The advent of sport-climbing destinations around the world, from Spain to Thailand, has made rock climbing a massive holiday market. It is made relatively safe by having fixed-bolt protection and sometimes "pre-clipped runners" for the rope in place. If you fall, you generally do not hurt yourself. For the best rock athletes, the hardest climbs may take weeks of effort and dozens of falls before success. The only difference with indoor wall climbing is that it is just that, indoors.

having a good alpine training somewhere. We might get a lad who misses out the summer alpine season, does some good routes in winter, then goes to Alaska, then goes straight to the Himalayan twenty-thousanders. If he is intelligent, talks to the right people, does his homework, not so much to be influenced but to acquire tips for staying alive, then yes, I can see that sort of person developing in the future."

This balanced and thoughtful response is typical of Alex's lawyer's training. It is clear but also leaves the question hanging and for the unaware could easily be misinterpreted. His answer is really "no." There is no replacement for the full alpine apprenticeship, but you might accelerate it by having nasty winter and 6000-metre peak experiences. Some very good British climbers with little experience at altitude tried to advance straight to the Himalaya, but returned humbled. Most had nothing worse than some bad experiences with altitude sickness. Ueli Steck's phenomenal solo ascents in the Alps and the Himalaya were the result of thousands of hours of hard training and climbing. His ascent of the south face of Annapurna was his third attempt, so he knew a lot about the terrain. Professional mountaineers climb day in day out to achieve in a few years what used to take a decade.

Until around 1980, Alex had no particular ambition to be famous or known outside of his own circle of friends. He showed little interest in writing reports and articles for magazines. It was part of his vision for himself, to be one of the boys and to be a purely amateur climber, uncontaminated by outside pressures. His attitude and ambition would change.

Upheaval in the world's post-war political makeup was still some way off, however. It is difficult today to picture countries divided into the "free world" and the "communist bloc," but it is relevant to Alex's story on several levels. The 1970s generation more than half-expected that one side or the other would push the button and civilization would end in a series of big bangs. Taking possibly fatal risks did not seem such a bad gamble. That was a view shared by some, including Ken Wilson, the editor of *Mountain* magazine. Wilson believed having adventures in the high mountains was a means of escape from both the real and perceived threats of the Cold War.

Alex also had a dark and fatalistic side that revealed itself – only occasionally – in his morbid fear of rock fall. Anyone who has climbed big mountains knows the feeling of instinctively cringing beneath your rucksack, like a tortoise withdrawing into its shell, when the air fills with the whine and whoosh of falling rocks. Your heart stops as stones explode around you. But in my years climbing with Alex, I noticed that in him it was something deeper, so much so that I wonder if he had a premonition about his fate.

3

NO MORE HEROES

"It's frightening that despite everything we are becoming a British institution, but all institutions deserve to be questioned and knocked down."
Jean-Jacques Burnel, The Stranglers

When Alex graduated from Leeds University in 1976, British mountaineering was in transition. It wasn't simply a case of the older generation passing the flame to the new one; it was a time when climbers of different eras came together. Younger climbers were emerging, but at the same time older, successful climbers such as Chris Bonington, Doug Scott and Don Whillans were still climbing at a high standard. Most serious alpinists of either generation saw the Himalaya as the place where the real challenges were to be found. Lower costs and rising incomes meant the Greater Ranges were becoming more accessible. A growth in climbing media, particularly *Mountain* magazine, meant there was much more information on the biggest unclimbed challenges.

Bonington and Scott, in particular, were still very much in the game of raising standards and trying the "last great problems."* These were the unclimbed faces and difficult ridges of the 8000-metre peaks, since almost all the major peaks over 7500 metres in the Himalaya and Asia had been climbed. Attention had shifted from the highest to the hardest.

Initially, these new challenges were attempted by national siege-style expeditions, a hangover from the earlier rush to be the first on

---

* In 1974, there were still many of these: the southwest face of Everest, the south face of Lhotse, the east face of Dhaulagiri, the (direct) west face of Makalu (still unclimbed) and the west ridge of K2 to name a few. As these were climbed, other "last great problems" soon emerged, like the Kangshung Face and northeast ridge of Everest.

top of one of the 14 8000-metre peaks. (There was a neocolonialist angle to this earlier phase; the planting of flags on the world's highest peaks being a feather in the cap of whichever nation first claimed each small patch of snow in the Himalayan sky. Just one of the eight-thousanders was climbed by a truly international expedition* and the race was concluded with the Chinese first ascent of Shisha Pangma in 1964.**)

These large-scale, well-organized and business-like expeditions – the "professionals" – were joined in the mid-1970s by smaller, less formal and less well-funded teams of climbers, who were more like privateers – fairly disorganized and impecunious in comparison and made up of ambitious types fighting their way to the top despite their lack of resources.

In the 1970s, it was much harder to make a living from climbing than it is now. Mountaineering had a small following; media interest was limited. Chris Bonington was then the only true professional climber in the country. His first British ascent of the north face of the Eiger in 1962 with Ian Clough propelled him into the media spotlight. "Our ascent of the north wall got the biggest press coverage I've ever had," he told me. "I had no prior concept of just how great it would be; my decision to snatch the route had been just that of the opportunist climber – it was something that had exercised a whole host of climbers back in the early 1960s."

A few more climbers like Doug Scott scraped a living from climbing by writing and lecturing, but for Doug climbing was very much a way of life than a serious occupation, at least in his early years. It certainly wasn't easy for any climber to survive by climbing alone in the 1960s. Bonington's first few years were very thin, lecturing to ladies' luncheon clubs and the Women's Institute for £10 a time and running three years over the deadline on his first book. He worked hard to make his way of living a profession, working at his various crafts: lecturing, writing and photography. There was no such thing as a sponsored athlete.

* Dhaulagiri I in 1960.

** As with the Chinese claim to have climbed Everest from the north in 1960, this was initially doubted by Western authorities.

Being linked to a manufacturer meant little more than being loaned equipment to test and endorse.

These things would change dramatically over the next decade or so, but it was only after the south face of Annapurna expedition in 1970 that Bonington began to earn a proper living. To remain a professional, he had to work extremely hard, finding new climbing and adventure objectives each year, and then pitching them to sponsors, publishers and the media. The new generation of privateers, which included Alex, was more lackadaisical when it came to the business side of climbing. To complete the maritime parallel, the difference was between official endorsement for the exploits of Sir Walter Raleigh and the daring deeds of the self-financed Captain Hawkins. Climbing privateers were private in two senses. They were relatively secret about their aims, and their impoverished lifestyles meant financing trips required some creative deals.

Over time, the boundaries between the two groups became blurred. As lead climbers in Bonington's circle died or were discarded, others were given the opportunity to move up; it was a bit like promotion in the military during a war. If you climbed at a high standard and were safe, no one really cared much about your background. Climbing is inherently competitive, but the community is generally respectful of climbing achievements, although wickedly satirical of class and status.

The impact and influence Chris Bonington had at the time was huge but often derided and even misrepresented. Chris unashamedly acknowledged he wanted to make a living by climbing as a writer, photojournalist and lecturer. Others had done this in the past – Frank Smythe for example – but Bonington proved especially successful. Unlike many climbers, he has the communication skills to put a complex mountain story into language understood by the general public. He had the ability to catch the media's interest, gain financial backing and lead a successful expedition. Most importantly, he climbed at a high standard. Now in his 80s, he is still star billing for festivals and corporate speaking engagements.

Success brings scrutiny, and sometimes envy; Bonington was often characterized as someone who put his career ahead of his climbing and everyone else. When it came to deciding who would join his trips and who would be the lead climbers, Chris knew the qualities he wanted, choosing people on their merit as climbers or organizers and how they would work in the team. He had loyal friends around him: Nick Estcourt, Ian Clough, Dougal Haston and Doug Scott. One or two, like Martin Boysen, felt their loyalty to Bonington went unrewarded; others were better described as ambitious colleagues, most obviously Don Whillans.

"I never had an easy relationship with Don," Chris said. "There was no give and take but he was a brilliant climbing partner. Dougal was a very close friend on and off the crag though there was an element of mutual convenience in our expedition relationship. I think Dougal took it for granted that I'd put him in the position to make the summit bid because he knew that he was the best qualified to do so and I wanted to use him in that role because I shared that view. The important thing was that he was liked and respected by the other members of the team, whilst Don created tension."

Managing a large team of successful climbers all eager to reach the top was a challenge that melted away with the advent of alpine-style climbing in the Himalaya. Bonington's decision making was focused on one thing: success. He was not there to satisfy all the personal ambitions of all his climbers. He was able to make unpopular decisions in what he felt were the best interests of the team's common objective. (Whillans famously said after being excluded from the 1975 Everest expedition that Chris was "without Ruth," meaning ruthless. For his part, Bonington said he "left Don out because none of the Annapurna team, including Dougal, wanted him along, though Doug and Hamish [MacInnes] would have.")

To be invited on a Chris Bonington expedition was a good start on the road to becoming a professional climber. Most of the climbers on Bonington's teams were there for the usual reasons – to have fun and accept a challenge. But there was a difference in terms of what was expected of you. If you were invited on a Bonington trip, you were asked to take a professional approach, understand your responsibilities and, in some instances, sign a contract. That probably meant giving up some of your rights to write independently about the trip or use photographs without Chris's permission.

There were good reasons for this, inextricably linked to a problem all climbers face, whatever style they choose – money. The problem for the leader of a big expedition is that you need much more of it. For the 1970 Annapurna expedition, the Mount Everest Foundation took a big gamble and underwrote the entire expedition, which saved Bonington the hassle of finding a sponsor. As a result, this highly successful expedition brought a very healthy profit back into the coffers of the MEF.

On the first of his expeditions to the southwest face of Everest in 1972, Bonington hoped the MEF would underwrite this trip as well, but this time it was not so keen. Strong expeditions had failed in 1970 and 1971 and it was felt to be too big a risk. So the only way to finance the expedition was through a mix of corporate and personal finance. Chris took a gamble and it made sense that these financial risks were shared, just as the climbing risks were. To hedge that risk, team members took part in joint lectures and contributed to the expedition books as part of their contract. When the 1972 expedition failed, the team returned to a huge debt. To pay it off, every member chipped in and did a series of lectures for expenses only until the debt was repaid. It was a truly corporate approach to climbing mountains. (They had to do the same when Nick Estcourt died on K2 in 1978 and the climb was abandoned.)

Fortunes change. For the 1975 Everest South West Face expedition, Bonington managed to raise the necessary finance with one letter to Barclays Bank, promoting the Everest expedition as the "hardest" route up the highest mountain. Barclays agreed to underwrite the bulk of the expedition's cost by a contribution of £100,000. In return, any profits from books, films and lectures went back to the bank. Surfing the huge wave of public interest after the ascent, almost all the team were engaged to lecture around the country. Chris was given a budget for the expedition book and lecture series and most of the members took part. Those who contributed were paid by the word for the book and given a set fee and expenses for taking part in a lecture. There was even a management committee, to make sure it was all done fairly. It was an important opportunity for younger members like Peter Boardman, who were keen on developing their professional skills as writers and presenters.

After Everest, Chris drafted more young climbers like Pete onto his expeditions: Joe Tasker, Dick Renshaw and Alan Rouse, who were all from the privateer tradition. By bringing in climbers from this new generation, Chris was taking a risk, but two things happened as a result. First, it helped Chris return to a more individualistic and lightweight approach. And for the privateers, it meant exposure to the professionalism and commercial potential of sponsored expeditions, which in turn impacted on their own attitudes and career opportunities.

Until invited on a Bonington trip, the independently minded climber thought his management style dictatorial and corporate. But most came to recognize that Bonington's style was broadly consensual; he may have taken the final decisions, but without such an approach, he knew his expeditions would fail. It was good business; good leadership was the way Bonington could gain the confidence of sponsors and raise finance. The summit was the product the sponsor was buying to add value to their brand.

Of course, he needed to manage the story for the media as well, whether the news was good or bad. This management was not just external; it also applied to team members. His anxiety about presentation could backfire at times. While I was working for Ken Wilson at *Mountain*, we published an article by Mike Thompson called "Out with the Boys Again." It was a genuinely funny, alternative look at the workings and dynamics of Bonington's 1975 Everest expedition by one of its members. Thompson was known for his wry humour and his attitude that climbing should be something unfettered and independent of any bureaucratic or authoritative control.

In the article, he describes how two groups formed during the expedition's walk-in to base camp. The first group includes the managers of the expedition, those close to Bonington running base camp and logistics, the media representatives, doctors and so forth. The second group – the "lads" – included more raucous and anarchistic individuals like Jim Duff, Braithwaite, Scott and, of course, Thompson himself. Bonington was described as the leader glimpsed in his tent typing out orders for the day on a porridge-encrusted computer. Peter Boardman, the newly appointed national officer of the BMC, was also targeted for ridicule as a climbing bureaucrat working on the seventeenth floor of the BMC's headquarters. It is a seminal piece of satire that captured the changing face of British mountaineering.

The morning after *Mountain* hit the shelves, Ken answered the phone to an outraged Bonington shouting at him down the line about misrepresentation. As soon as Ken had regained his composure, he went on the offensive, talking about freedom of the press but, more importantly, pointing out that the Thompson story carried a second underlying theme that was, in fact, a homage to the organization of both people and materials on the expedition. Thompson may not have entirely accepted his role as a high-altitude porter for the summit teams, but he appreciated the planning that made it so successful. Chris soon calmed down and both Thompson and Wilson were once again friends. Just as his team eventually realized the value of Chris's leadership, Chris now sees Mike Thompson's article as a "brilliant yet witty study of the expedition – a true social anthropologist's view."

Bonington's professional approach may not have been the model others wanted to emulate, but his record of success was one with which many aspiring climbers wanted to be associated. An endorsement from Chris could make all the difference when seeking sponsorship. Although selective, Chris was generally very generous when it came to allowing his name to be used as patron for privateer trips, as he did for our Anglo-Polish Changabang climb. An association with his professionalism gave credibility without impinging in any way on the lightweight approach to the highest peaks.

The public had become captivated by Chris Bonington's brand of patriotic adventure in the 1960s and 1970s and this gathering interest in climbing, promoted through live broadcasts on the BBC and climbing films for independent networks such as Thames Television, created public interest that Boardman, Tasker and others exploited through writing and lecturing. (They were also very good at it; their books are still in print and their names associated with the leading mountain literature prize in English.)

There were other, less high-profile ways to make a living from this growing interest in climbing. There were already a handful of guides and professional outdoor instructors, and their numbers grew as outdoor education became fashionable. Climbers from this generation also proved technically curious and entrepreneurial, men like Denny Moorhouse, Tony Howard, Mike Parsons and Pete Hutchinson, who all played a part in growing the outdoor industry. It was even possible to make a living from publishing, as Ken Wilson did at *Mountain* and then with his book imprint Diadem. All of these provided career models for young climbers.

Although Thompson's "Out with the Boys Again" was a humorous take on Bonington's management style, it hid his ability to manage individuals. This may seem obvious, but knowing the individuals involved, it must have been like herding cats. Strong teams led by Alan Rouse failed on Everest in winter in 1981 and on the northwest ridge of K2 in 1986 because the individuals in the team tended to do things their own way. There was no coordinated plan. Huge pressure was brought to bear both on friendships and the logistics of these trips.

Privateers saw planning as a burden and secondary to all other concerns. Enjoying the experience came first and foremost; trips seemed to happen spontaneously, planned in bars at events like the BMC's Buxton Conference or at Alpine Climbing Group discos, or in the backrooms of pubs. Privateers seemed to gravitate toward one another over beers, rather than be formally chosen as part of a team. "Get there and have a go" was the creed at least in the early days of the movement. Only a minimum amount of everything was required to achieve this – anything on top was a bonus. This would change as reputations grew, but while Bonington could cash a cheque for a hundred grand, we were happy with a trolley full of groceries from the local supermarket.

There was no point in taking more than was required. Western goodies were needed mainly for higher altitudes, with just enough at base camp to add variety to local staples of rice, lentils, tsampa and noodles. Days on the mountain were calculated and soup, cheese, chocolate and so forth carefully weighed and bagged. Any surplus food, and most of the alcohol donated, was used to subsidize travel costs.

Such parsimony only worked because of the revolution in Himalayan climbing ethics. The generation that entered the Himalayan fray in the mid-1970s had new ideas based on fitness and skills gained from very hard ascents in the Alps. Our ambition was to get to the unclimbed "last great problems" before they were all climbed by siege-style expeditions.

Since most of the new generation had never been to altitude, there was now a second phase of apprenticeship to be served. Some, like Pete Boardman, learned when invited on Chris Bonington's expeditions. The rest were left to their own devices to learn for themselves. Eight-thousanders were expensive and time-consuming, and pure alpine-style tactics on very technical peaks had yet to be fully tested. So in the 1970s there was a sudden interest in the less expensive and less well-known 6000- and 7000-metre peaks. It was experience gained on these smaller challenges that provided the training and knowledge to tackle more technical challenges on the highest mountains.

The British starting point on this modern quest for alpine-style purity above 7000 metres came in 1975 with Joe Tasker and Dick Renshaw's naive but daring ascent of the southeast ridge of Dunagiri in the Garhwal Himalaya. Peaks of this altitude had been climbed by small teams from several nationalities in the past, including Alexander Kellas before the Great War and by Eric Shipton and Bill Tilman in the 1930s. But the route on Dunagiri was technical, graded "TD-" in the alpine grading system. It was achieved at practically no cost, with little preparation and almost no fuss by two climbers with no previous Himalayan experience. In just nine days, they made the ascent and returned to their base camp in wild and remote mountains.

When back in the UK, both admitted they could have easily died. They had not acclimatized properly and had not carried enough fuel to rehydrate and enough food to maintain energy. Dehydration meant that they became semi-delirious on the descent and as a result became separated. This was nearly a fatal error. Everyone who spoke with them, or read the reports, took note not to make the same mistakes, but the ascent proved that being bold and going light could bring about a stunning result.

In that same year, the British siege-style expedition led by Chris Bonington succeeded on the southwest face of Everest. A massive amount of finance was needed for expeditions of that scale, with its nine lead climbers, seven support climbers and 60 high-altitude porters. But, thereafter, most British expeditions involved just a few members.* Few climbers could attract the kind of sponsorship Bonington could. Cost, as well as ethics and aesthetics, drove the development of lightweight mountaineering.

To put Alex's achievements into context, listed below are the major British first ascents in the Himalaya during the period he was active – from 1975 until his death in 1982 –and the climbers that reached the summit:

1975 The southeast ridge of Dunagiri: Joe Tasker and Dick Renshaw
1976 Trango Tower: Mo Anthoine, Martin Boysen, Joe Brown and Malcolm Howells
1976 Changabang's west face: Pete Boardman and Joe Tasker
1977 The Ogre: Chris Bonington and Doug Scott
1978 The first alpine-style ascent of Jannu's south face: Roger Baxter-Jones, Rab Carrington, Brian Hall and Al Rouse
1979 The northwest face of Kangchenjunga: Peter Boardman, Doug Scott and Joe Tasker
1979 Nuptse's north spur: Georges Bettembourg, Brian Hall, Al Rouse and Doug Scott
1979 Gaurishankar's southwest ridge: Peter Boardman, Tim Leach, Guy Neidhardt and Pemba Lama

---

* There have been army and combined forces expeditions from the UK that sieged big peaks post-1975. Today's commercial expeditions to Everest use siege tactics, but with Sherpas doing all the preparation and rope fixing for the guides and clients who follow.

1981 Kongur first ascent: Peter Boardman, Chris Bonington, Al
      Rouse and Joe Tasker
1981 Annapurna IV, first winter ascent: Adrian Burgess, Al Burgess
      and Roger Marshall
1982 Shivling's east pillar: Bettembourg, Greg Child, Doug Scott
      and Rick White

Alex MacIntyre's Himalayan climbs during this same short period were:

1977 Northeast face of Bandaka: with Voytek Kurtyka and John
      Porter
1978 South buttress of Changabang: with Voytek Kurtyka, John
      Porter and Krzysztof Zurek
1980 Dhaulagiri east face: with Jerzy Kukuczka, Voytek Kurtyka and
      René Ghilini
1982 West ridge of Pangma Ri: with Roger Baxter-Jones and Doug
      Scott
1982 Shisha Pangma's southwest face: with Roger Baxter-Jones and
      Doug Scott
1982 East buttress of Tarke Kang: with René Ghilini and John Porter

All of Alex's ascents were made in a lightweight style developed on the
back of his remarkable ascents in the Alps at the start of this same period. These included the Bonatti Pillar on the Dru, the second ascent of
the Bonatti-Zappelli on the Grand Pilier d'Angle, the first ascent of the
Colton-MacIntyre on the Grandes Jorasses and the first alpine-style
ascent of the Eiger Direct. Alex also climbed several bold new routes
in the Andes in 1979, recorded later in this book, and made two failed
attempts on the west face of Makalu in 1981.

   Many excellent ascents from mountaineers from around the world
took place during this same period, although most continued to use
traditional expedition tactics. However, another new trend above
8000 metres was shaping how climbers thought about the future of
mountaineering. Reinhold Messner, having climbed Everest with
Peter Habeler in 1978 without using bottled oxygen, returned to

Everest in 1980 to make a solo ascent of the north ridge, again without oxygen, and during the monsoon. That had a worldwide impact. Several eight-thousanders had been climbed without oxygen by 1980, but what more could be possible? Others would soon climb much more technical routes above 8000 metres, but it was Messner who added solo without oxygen to the list of possibilities.

Most climbers agreed that going light and without oxygen brought elegance to any big mountain challenge. It was a particularly attractive proposition for a younger – and consequently poorer – generation of British climbers. Oxygen was extremely expensive. It required many more porters to get it to the mountain and Sherpa support once you got it there. For these reasons it was dismissed as an option by the younger generation.

Peak fees were not nearly as expensive then as they are today, but eight-thousanders were still costly in terms of time, which, in the Himalaya as anywhere else, means money. More time was needed to acclimatize above 7500 metres and therefore more food and fuel were needed and more porters to carry the necessary provisions for those extra weeks. Those extra porters required more porters to carry their food – and so on. For those who now travel well-stocked trekking routes, this may be hard to grasp.

By the mid-1970s, Eastern European and Japanese expeditions were consistently proving that large, well-organized teams could build on the model of Bonington's 1970 Annapurna ascent and succeed on the last great problems. For the next generation, the question was simple: Could a lightweight alpine style replace big expedition siege tactics? The race was on.

Alpine style meant self-reliance first and foremost, not being de-pendent on the support of others. But to call alpine style "lightweight" was a misnomer. Everything you needed for the climb and survival had to go into one big rucksack. The more technical the route, the more equipment was needed; and big routes could take a week or more to complete. Over time and through experience, that "every-thing" could be pared down to a minimum – but even so, leaving base camp carrying such a heavy weight was daunting.

As climbing has evolved, alpine style as conceived in the 1970s no longer applies, ironically, in the Alps. The amazing technical speed climbs being done start from well-stocked huts or are reached from the top of téléphériques or a helicopter drop at the base of the route. The helicopter then follows the progress of today's heroes who are off the mountain before lunch and don't need much in the way of equipment.

Will the same be true of the Himalaya? It seems climbing is almost there now. Until the turn of the century, most Himalayan peaks were still massive undertakings. Twice the height of the Alps, and far more remote, the logistics were daunting. The actual climbing normally didn't start until well above the height of Mont Blanc. Although the intention of an uninterrupted bottom-to-top ascent of unclimbed faces or ridges was similar to climbing in the Alps, the need to get masses of food and equipment to the base of the mountain – even for two people – was a logistical and physical struggle.

Added to that was the need for a planned acclimatization program, achieved by placing food and equipment caches on the descent route and by climbing easier objectives that, nevertheless, were often major climbs in their own right. Altitudes above 7000 metres add several dimensions to the application of alpine style. Alex knew what had to be done to achieve maximum performance. He also had the pick of partners to help him achieve his goals. Even so, the choice of climbers with the essential skills was limited. There were a handful of like-minded climbers in Britain, but there were many more elsewhere.

Of all his partners, the Polish climber Voytek Kurtyka provided Alex with his greatest source of inspiration. Voytek and Alex were very different in character. Voytek was definitely not a role model. He was simply someone with whom Alex could develop and realize a brand new style of high-altitude climbing. I was the link that connected Alex to Voytek. It started with a chance encounter in 1975 with a man called Dennis Gray.

4

A WALK ON THE WILD SIDE

Hitching back to Leeds from the Lakes, I had got as far as Ingleborough, but after an hour with my thumb out was bored with the view of Pen-y-ghent and its geometric patterns of limestone walls. My daydreaming came to a halt in a squeal of brakes as Dennis Gray's Russian-made sedan pulled up. At the time, Dennis was national officer of the British Mountaineering Council, the first to hold that post.

In those days the BMC *was* Dennis – and a secretary, the indomitable Rita Hallam, an intelligent and effective administrator, a sort of Miss Moneypenny who in her time at the BMC looked after several national officers. Dennis was a climber of huge repute, due in part to his ability to tell a good story. He was the keeper of an oral tradition of mountain lore and a member of the legendary Rock and Ice Club.* We all looked up to Dennis, if a bit askance at times, as someone with power and connections in the gathering strength of mountaineering bureaucracy.

The BMC itself was a relatively new entity and highly controversial. Most climbers could see no need for it. Anything that smacked of officialdom was to be ignored or avoided. After Dennis, Peter Boardman became national officer, followed by Alex and then Andy Fanshawe. The latter three all lost their lives in the mountains, prompting a degree of superstition around the post.

As Dennis stopped, I picked up my rucksack, ready to jump in. But when I looked again, I saw the car was packed with family and young climbing apprentices; my hope of reaching Leeds before dark faded.

---

* The club was moribund by the early 1970s, but its legendary members, Joe Brown, Don Whillans and a host of others, were still active and venerated, for the most part, by the up and coming generation.

So why had Dennis bothered? He rolled down the window and asked me a question in his nasal Yorkshire drawl that would completely change my life.

"Sorry youth, I've got no room to give you a lift, but what are you doing next week?"

"Not a lot. Climbing in Wales probably," I replied. A fortnight before, I had finished a six-month spell working for Ken Wilson at *Mountain* magazine; I had not yet found other work.

"Then come to Plas y Brenin and help us host a delegation of Polish climbers."

And that was the beginning of my connection to the Poles. I hitched from Sheffield a couple of days later to Capel Curig and the national training centre of Plas y Brenin for a week's climbing with all expenses paid.* The British climbers there included the Burgess twins, Adrian and Alan, and me, with support from Davey Jones and Dave Alcock. There were five Polish climbers, most of whom spoke surprisingly good English, and a sixth member who we decided must be the Communist Party minder. He was happy enough letting us play in the hills while he stayed in the bar and got drunk. On one occasion, he made off with a Plas y Brenin minibus to see the countryside on his own. I remember Dave Alcock, then director of the centre, being more concerned he might hurt himself in a crash than being angry about the potential loss of the minibus.

Andrzej Zawada, known as Andrez, was the one person in the Polish team we all knew by reputation. He was tall, well over six feet, with chiselled aristocratic features and a mild, well-spoken manner. The rest of the team proved to be a powerful, friendly and confident bunch, totally in tune with traditional climbing techniques, although they rarely seemed to bother placing protection at all. We had a great time, knocking off classic routes between the showers and spending the evenings talking and sharing stories in the bar at Plas y Brenin.

Zawada was not a particularly good rock climber but a great mountaineer. He was also wonderfully urbane and entertaining. He told

---

* Plas y Brenin is the National Mountain Centre funded largely by grants from government and at that time run within the framework of the BMC.

stories of suffering on winter climbs in the Tatra and the Himalaya and of his plans to climb Everest in winter, realized less than five years later when his team made the first winter ascent via the south col in early 1980. Although he rarely admitted the fact, he would have loved to lead expeditions on first winter ascents of all the eight-thousanders. In the end, he managed three successful winter expeditions: Everest, Cho Oyu and Lhotse. He also led the first ever winter success of any peak over 7000 metres – Noshaq on the border between Chitral and Badakhshan in Aghanistan – and unsuccessful winter attempts on K2 and Nanga Parbat.

By the end of the week, we were good friends, and by the end of the three-week exchange, the Burgesses and I were conspiring to be in "pole" position to make the return half of the exchange to the Tatra the following winter. So it came to pass. I quit my job as a builder's mate and in late February 1976 the three of us, joined by Mick "Jimmy" Geddes, boarded a flight to Warsaw to begin a six-week climbing trip.

In 1976, the world seemed frozen in its geopolitical shape of East against West. East meant anywhere behind the Iron Curtain under the Soviet sway. China was closed and inaccessible and not in the reckoning for the average political commentator. There were only two superpowers: the menacing, myopic, totalitarian empire of the Soviet Union and its Eastern European allies that formed the Warsaw Pact, and the United States with its xenophobic and God-fearing hinterland. The United States was allied firmly to the nations of Western Europe through NATO, although Washington looked with suspicion at the inexplicable swings between socialism and capitalism in Britain and France. I had grown up on America's more liberal coastal fringes, in Massachusetts and Oregon. In 1976, the war in Vietnam had only recently ended, brought to its humiliating conclusion, from an American perspective, by Richard Nixon in the face of mounting losses and hostility to the draft.*

In 1976, there were no major wars being fought and just a whiff of change in the air in relations between the Soviet Union and the United States. The space race had ended and joint missions were being discussed. There had been a string of treaties limiting the testing and

* The reason the author ended up in Britain.

proliferation of nuclear weapons and technology. Talks on limiting such weapons were underway. The media had to content itself with the occasional spy scandal or a fatal shooting of some poor individual trying to cross from East to West Berlin. But if there was change in the air, it was still a very tense time. Our small team of climbers was headed where few from the West were allowed – to the other side of the Iron Curtain.

It was a brilliant and eye-opening experience. We expected this walled-in society to be closed and reluctant to talk, but we discovered that the lack of open public debate had created private discussions and friendships of the highest quality. We also began to understand the devilish nature of corruption in the communist world, where black-market scams kept climbers in equipment. Those few who were well off had additional freedoms and were able to spend more time in the mountains. I noted in my diary that this "enclosed openness for the selected few was primarily a luxury of the educated and the aristo-crats. For most, life is a routine of work doing menial jobs that are mentally underwhelming. They declare there is one hundred per cent employment in the communist state but what are they making and producing? Most spare time is spent in endless queues for basic sup-plies. They are welcoming and friendly to all Westerners but I see many expressionless faces which I take as a sign of oppression."

I remember visiting a lovely girl called Eva in Krakow, introduced to me by Voytek Kurtyka's wife. Eva had given me her address after we had met at dinner in a restaurant, and when I showed this to the Burgess twins, they basically said: "What are you waiting for?" Since we were under curfew, they helped me abseil out of our window and I took a taxi to a grim six-storey apartment block, one of many, all iden-tically built on grids, new buildings on the city's outskirts that seemed half-finished but already in a state of decay. Half the occupants of the apartment block woke as news spread that a foreigner had knocked on a door to ask directions. People in shabby dressing gowns emerged on each floor as I climbed the stairs, keen to show me the correct flat. They stood packed along the bare concrete corridor as I finally knocked at the right number.

Eva opened the door and looked at me in horror. She shared a two-room apartment with her parents and brother. The pipes for the plumbing were exposed. There was a dank and musty smell and holes in the floors and the walls offered glimpses of equally squalid apartments. She almost shouted at me: "You see how we live? We have no space, no chance to move and express ourselves except when we are together with friends. I just wanted you to write to me, to give me some hope from the world outside." I had a long, dark and scary walk back to Krakow avoiding the police. Having carefully memorized the location of our hostel, I found the rope still there and pulled myself back up to our room just before dawn. Ade and Al thought my story hilarious.

Even though the overall social structure was depressing, behind that depression was an incredible resolve that things would get better, that Poland would one day be a free and independent country again. It didn't seem likely at the time, but it has, of course, come to pass. "Poland is a nation even when it is not a nation," Zawada explained to me. "We have been overrun by the Huns and Swedes, partitioned several times by the Germans and the Russians. The name of Poland has vanished from the map for many decades at a time, but we are still a great nation. In times past, we have saved Europe from the Turks and given Western culture great poets, scientists and musicians. We are like the Tibetans – eventually our nation and culture will have its own land and government again."*

For Polish climbers, having an opportunity to climb in the Himalaya offered temporary relief from the drabness of communism and a chance to have a taste of freedom and to express their individualism. Although the climbing scene in Poland was somewhat above politics, its leading lights had to play a dangerous game of balancing their status as national heroes against open confrontation with their government and the Communist Party machine. There were spies and informants everywhere, so it was not easy. But Poland was different from Russia. The government and the party were not exactly the same

---

* Recent visits to Poland have shown how true this is. It has become a vibrant nation, with many of the trappings of the West but retaining a high degree of classic good manners and culture.

thing. Some people in government appeared to be Polish nationalists above all else and paid only lip service to communist ideals.

The Polish attitude to climbing was in sharp contrast to the Soviet Russian approach. In Poland, the climbing tradition was much closer to that of Western Europe. It had been developed as a leisure activity among the middle and upper classes. Soviet communist propaganda depicted mountain climbing as a symbolic struggle of heroic men and women of the proletariat pitted against the mountains. They succeeded in overcoming all obstacles because of the strength of the state. Could a mountain really be seen as a paradigm for the workers' struggle against capitalism? It seemed so reading Soviet mountain literature. The Soviets, of course, were not the only propagandists when it came to depicting mountain conquest. The Nazis constructed similar myths.

In 1960, the Chinese were so gushing in their description of worker heroes climbing Everest with Mao Zedong in their hearts that few in the West believed they had achieved the first recorded ascent from the north. Skeptics argued that no one would take off their boots on Everest, as Chinese accounts claimed, but that is exactly what a Chinese climber had to do to climb the Second Step on the north ridge. Losing a few toes was a small price to pay for the glory of the party. This concept was far removed from the Western romantic concept of the "freedom of the hills," in which the journey of the individual is paramount. The Poles were individuals first and foremost, even when they had to wear the cloak of being part of a state-sanctioned expedition.

In Poland, climbing took a different direction to that in most other communist countries. Ironically, the new hardcore of poor but very talented climbers that emerged there had more in common with the climbing culture in Britain during Margaret Thatcher's era. Whether climbing on the dole in Britain or forced to make a dangerous living as a roped access worker in Poland, both groups developed the skills needed to face hardship and adversity – but on the climbers' own terms. The very best working-class climbers came to the fore in this way and were soon seen as part of the climbing elite. In Poland, that opened the way to state-sponsored expeditions.

Whether you started climbing from a privileged or working-class background in Poland, you still needed connections to succeed. There were a few like Zawada, who was an established and semi-independent individual from aristocratic stock and married to the famous actress Anna Milewska.*

One thing we discovered was that very few Polish climbers joined the Communist Party. Indeed, it was quite the opposite. Talking in the privacy of the homes of our hosts, or walking up to a climb in the Tatra, it was very clear that the freedom of the hills was matched in their hearts by an expression of freedom for a Poland able to make its own politics as an independent nation.

The best way to advance as a climber was to work your way up through the officially sanctioned club structure. This was a standard route for most Polish climbers and, indeed, most Eastern European countries under communism had a similar state-sanctioned climbing club structure. It was their form of a climbing apprenticeship. The end goal was to climb in the world outside. To reach the top of the ladder, you first had to become a member of the local climbing club. The first rungs would include following procedure to get an equipment allocation to climb in the Tatra. Private ownership of equipment was difficult and expensive, so most climbers relied on borrowing technical equipment from the local club pool of gear.

Once you reached a certain level of skill, you could go on club meets to the Polish Tatra and, perhaps, eventually, be given an exit permit to travel to the Czechoslovakian Tatra or even the Alps, with just enough hard currency from the local club in your pocket to manage for a month or so. But to get cash and an exit visa you needed the recognition of the elite Polski Zwiazek Alpinizmu (PZA), the Polish Mountain Association, which was sanctioned by the authorities. Becoming a member was even better. Bernadette McDonald, in her history of modern Polish mountaineering, *Freedom Climbers,* notes that climbers could be compromised when gaining permits to travel to the West.

---

* I have been fortunate to see Anna a few times in recent years. She has written a comprehensive book of her life with "Anji," which is part biography and part autobiography. Andrez was, she explained, "far too charming, and far too aware of his charm to have been a totally faithful husband."

The secret service expected information in exchange for travel permits. Some, like Wanda Rutkiewicz, were able to push back, but other well-known climbers were known to comply.

Western climbers could also be targets. I sometimes wonder what pictures might have been taken of me on a date with a very persuasive blond scientist in Warsaw. It had been arranged for me mysteriously by the PZA one evening in 1977. I was naive, but not that naive, and soon realized I was being sounded out as a potential informant. I made my excuses after dinner and returned to the hotel. When I told Zawada the next day what had happened, he just shrugged as if to say, "What did you expect?"

Despite the system and its pitfalls, if you were someone with gall and talent, you could climb your way to success and a degree of independence. Kurtyka managed to become an international climber of repute without going through the club process at all. The PZA had to admit him retrospectively so that his successes were seen as part of Poland's socialist glory. But being a recognized member of the PZA was essential if you wanted state support as an expedition climber. The ministry of sport injected hard cash and coupons for luxury items into the PZA. This often meant free expeditions for those lucky enough to be selected.

Western equipment for climbers from the East was extremely hard to come by and very expensive. It was supplemented by homemade equipment: Polish fabrics coated and turned into anoraks, ice axes and pitons forged in local blacksmiths or trainers turned into sticky rubber climbing shoes by putting on new soles. (These predated sticky rubber in the West.)

Most extraordinary of all was the trade route supplied, maintained and known only to Eastern bloc climbers from behind the Iron Curtain. It brought together climbers and gear manufacturers from across the entire communist world. You might even call it a modern-day Silk Road, since among the items traded were down jackets and duvets from China that used silk rather than nylon as the outer fabric. These Chinese jackets, along with Polish-made ropes and Russian titanium ice screws, pitons and karabiners from the aerospace factories of

Siberia, were among the goods that arrived in the Alps each summer. They were sold for dollars or bartered for Western gear on Snell's Field in Chamonix and other campsites across Europe by the few Eastern European climbers who were granted permits to climb in the Alps each year. Many of the goods traded would pass back unseen behind the Iron Curtain and find their way across the Soviet Union to climbers planning trips to the Pamirs, Tien Shan and other great Asian mountain ranges inaccessible to the West.

These corners of Asia are now popular destinations for international climbers, but before the breakup of the Soviet Union, they were accessible only to climbers from the Eastern bloc and a few Westerners taking part in official visits. As a high-altitude training ground, these ranges north of the Himalaya were the first objective for the most ambitious climbers from the East. They are serious mountains, almost on the same scale as the Himalaya. Realistically, for many climbers living behind the Iron Curtain, they were the only high mountains they were ever likely to visit because of the costs and permits required to go elsewhere. All prices were fixed at levels the workers could just about afford with club and Communist Party support. But you had to be a good climber, or very well connected, to be put forward for such a trip.

To travel outside the Soviet bloc was another huge jump. In Russia, you had to reach the level of "Master of Sport," with a record of hard ascents in both winter and summer. Few managed this, and if you were not a party member, you were walking a fine line with the authorities. I think I met only one top Polish climber who was also a member of the Communist Party. If there were more, they kept the fact well hidden. Certainly, Andrez Zawada, and as far as I can tell all those who went on his expeditions, were quite the opposite. Some were supporters or members of Solidarity, and some ended up in prison as a result.* But the Communist Party and government needed

* The most exceptional of these was Janusz Onyszkiewicz, an excellent alpinist, mathematician and, later, politician. He lectured at Leeds University when Alex and I were studying there. In the 1980s, Janusz became the spokesman for the Solidarity movement. After the introduction of martial law in December 1981, he was arrested and interned. After the fall of communism in 1989, Onyszkiewicz became a member of the Polish parliament and subsequently served twice as minister of defence. In 2004, Onyszkiewicz was elected as a vice-president of the European Parliament.

high-profile successes and Polish mountaineering brought national pride and kudos. The upper echelons in the Communist Party, those who managed the national profile in sport, recognized that the rebellious and independent nature of Polish climbers was valuable when it came to bagging summits. And there was always a deal to be made when it came to supplying items from Asia that could not easily be bought behind the Iron Curtain.

Hence, Andrez Zawada and a few others were allowed out of the country with the support of the government and with just enough hard currency in their pockets to finance the foreign part of the trip. The zloty had no value as a tradable currency outside Poland, although Polish climbers would, of course, always try to convince unsuspecting shopkeepers in far corners of the world that it did, but usually with no success. The official Polish bank rate in the mid-1970s was about ten zloty to the dollar. With hard currency, you could buy luxury goods only available in "dollar shops." Sanctioned by the Communist Party, these were supposedly open only to diplomats and foreigners visiting Poland, but there were ways for connected Polish citizens to buy from the dollar shops, especially if foreign-based Poles were sending money to their families back home.

Dollars were also hoarded in hopes of an eventual escape to the West, or a holiday if a permit was granted. Poland at the time was the most liberal of all the Soviet states, a small window on the West. The brief view I had of the black market was just the tip of a much larger and more elaborate method of laundering money. Moneychangers would approach Westerners in rail stations and market squares in nearly every Polish city. The black market rate in 1976 was around a hundred zloty to the dollar, ten times the official rate. Sterling was less sought after but would still bring 200 zloty or more to the pound, when a pound was worth a little below three dollars.

The Burgesses and I made money on this trip by exchanging hard currency for zloty, buying digital watches and top-quality vodka and then flogging them when we got home. Yet there were moments where we had to be wary and several where I intervened to stop the twins from getting into trouble. Sitting in a café in Warsaw on a snowy day, I noticed the telltale signs as they began eyeing the wait-resses and the distance to the door. They were contemplating doing a runner.

"Hey guys," I said, attempting gently to introduce some reason. "I just worked out what this three-course meal cost us in real terms – about 20 pence each!" They looked at me. They were bemused but clearly still thinking the challenge was there. "And the other thing I've worked out is that there are not too many British twins with long blonde hair wearing identical bright red down jackets in Warsaw at the moment."

They guffawed. Point taken. We paid up and left, still wondering how best to spend our pockets full of zloty. The choice seemed to be limited to digital watches, cheap runners and track suits, beautifully produced art books in Polish, sticky sweet chocolates and crystal glasses.

Official Polish expeditions could set off for South Asia with truck-loads of goods that could not be found on the shelves of the stores in Warsaw. The Poles had a well-organized import and export business, run through Polish consulates. Big expeditions had with them the equivalent of limitless diplomatic bags, the barrels emptied during ex-peditions, which were filled with goods for senior Communist Party members and others in the Polish elite circles.

When we got back to Warsaw, at the end of one trip, I happened to be at the flat of a Polish climber when some barrels that had just ar-rived back were being emptied on the living room floor. The contents included carpets, uncut industrial diamonds and other gems, silk hangings, temple relics and from one barrel emerged a foot-square block of hashish. Alex was assigned the task of making a water pipe in the kitchen while other goodies were sorted and divided up.

There was a sudden loud knocking at the door and I was sent to let whoever it was in. Expecting a familiar climber's face, I found myself confronted by two short and stocky men with crewcuts dressed in grey suits. They looked like G-men from a 1930s black and white gang-ster movie and exactly like the many government agents that had been pointed out to me during our travels around Poland. The thought of spending the rest of my days in a Polish prison flashed through my mind as I attempted to close the door in their faces.

At that moment, the climber whose flat it was peered round the corner and shouted down the corridor: "*Dobrzy moi przyjaciele są tutaj, w my jesteśmy gotowi dla.*" ("Good, my friends are here, come in.") Alex continued his bong construction to the benefit of everyone's enjoyment. This was another reason why rather aberrant political behaviour by climbers was tolerated. They went to remote places where interesting items could be found.

5

ROCKING IN THE FREE WORLD

Warsaw was grey and freezing when we landed. Soldiers with semi-automatic machine guns stood next to the aircraft as we descended to the tarmac. We had arrived in the Western cliché of the grey, crumbling communist bloc. This first impression was dispelled immediately as Suzi Quatro's "Devil's Gate Drive" blared out from the terminal's speakers.

"Hey, they've got taste in music here. That's a good start." Alan had a way of snarling and laughing at the same time. When asked how you could tell the twins apart, the answer was simple: Alan leered and Adrian blinked when they were weighing up a situation. At that moment, the Burgesses were eyeing up the women among the small delegation there to meet us, which included Wanda Rutkiewicz.* The final member of our party was the wiry Mick Geddes, a highly talented Scottish friend who had completed all the Munros by the time he was 16. Mick almost always had a fag in his mouth and we were all a bit wary of his penchant for midnight winter epics on the Ben.

It was early March 1976 and for four days we stayed at the homes of Warsaw-based climbers. Meals were offered at every house we visited and at first we assumed there was plenty of food. Slowly, it dawned on us we were eating a week's ration of eggs and meat at every sitting. We walked for miles through Warsaw and its parks, visiting the amazing palaces and museums. Best of all, we were entertained by lively discussions about the nature of freedom and comparisons between life in

---

* Wanda had yet to become the queen of Polish mountaineering. That began in October 1978, when she became the third woman, first Pole and the first European woman to reach the summit of Everest. In 1986, she became the first woman to climb K2, which she did without bottled oxygen and survived a harrowing descent in a storm. K2 was her third eight-thousander. She vanished on Kangchenjunga in 1992, which would have been her ninth.

the East and West. These took place away from public places, when we went bouldering on wartime fortifications in the woods around the city and had lunch in small dachas hidden among the trees.

Warsaw fascinated us. I noted in my diary the resilience of the Polish spirit, captured temporarily in a vacuum of booming socialism. Andrez Zawada was with us at some point every day, taking us with self-evident pride to the old city that had been completely rebuilt after it was flattened during the extended Warsaw Uprising against the Nazis in the summer of 1944. Young architectural students had sketched the buildings and captured the style of the medieval centre before it was reduced to a pile of rubble; it was from these drawings that the old city emerged in the 1950s and 1960s.*

We were itching to get to the Tatra and go climbing, but at the same time we realized we were being educated in the ways of a nation that had faith in itself and the future. There may not have been many luxuries in Poland, but the greatest was the daily diet of friendship and intelligent conversation that contrasted sharply with our own easy lifestyles in the West.

Before we could go to the Tatra, we had one big state occasion to attend. It was planned for the evening that Peter Boardman arrived. The BMC's new national officer, Pete was a formidable climber, with some excellent alpine-style ascents in the Hindu Kush. The year before he had reached the summit of Everest with Pertemba on Bonington's Everest expedition. Yet it was his official status as national officer that seemed to catch the attention of the authorities and media. While we were fortunate to be staying in the flats of climbers, Pete was immediately put up in the best hotel. It struck me that Pete's position was something the officials could understand. The rest of us were long-haired climbers with rather dodgy records of employment. While Pete was seen in Britain as one of a new breed of professional climbers,

---

* The Poles never forgave the Russians, who they hoped would quickly liberate Warsaw once the uprising began. Instead, the Red Army sat waiting on the other side of the Vistula until the brave Poles had seriously weakened the German army. When the uprising eventually collapsed, the German reprisals were horrific and the old city of Warsaw was completely flattened. The Russians came and imposed their own choices of leader, knowing the real leaders amongst the Poles were now nearly all dead.

in Poland he was immediately recognized as someone with official status. That is what mattered most to the authorities, but the climbers treated us all as equals. Although Peter Boardman and Alex MacIntyre were very much in separate camps at the time, Pete would become something of an exemplar for Alex in the years that followed.

That evening, the ambassador at the British Embassy hosted a grand reception attended by a number of high-ranking Polish government officials. There were speeches about the world coming together through sporting endeavour. We toasted the Queen, the president of Poland and international co-operation – as illustrated by our motley crew. Next morning, with sore heads, we set off by train to Krakow on the way to the Tatra mountains.

Voytek Kurtyka had been assigned to show us around Krakow and it was then that I met him for the first time. Voytek has classic Slavic good looks, as though his face had been sculpted. Asked how he had created his marble statue of David, Michelangelo replied that he had simply chipped away everything that was not David. Voytek was a Slavic equivalent to this story. He seemed to have recreated his own character, shaking off all the detritus of the repressed Polish nation under communism to leave an intelligent, spiritual and powerful individual who would become one of the climbing superstars of his era. He had a hyperactive nature that remained hidden most of the time but could suddenly flare up with intense questioning of a decision or an idea. Voytek sought new experiences and ideas wherever he went. He tried hard to learn new languages and usually picked up enough to be an effective haggler. But he never really understood British sarcasm, taking many of our jokes and comments literally.

Despite the freezing conditions, Voytek took us to climb at the local limestone crags. His strength of character and ability as a climber were immediately obvious. We threw ourselves into discussions about climbing and politics as we followed him up polished faces and cracks in the sub-zero temperatures. He was one of the few Polish climbers with an extensive record of hard new routes both in the Tatra and beyond. He was the first to establish grade VII rock routes in Poland, and had some formidable winter firsts. In 1972, he climbed two new routes on 7000-metre peaks in the Hindu Kush, including Akher Chogh's northwest face with Jacek Rusiecki, Marek Kowalczyk and Piotr Jasinski. Marek and Piotr had taken part in the Polish trip to Wales the summer before. Jacek Rusiecki and I would soon get to know each other in the weeks that followed.*

Perhaps the most revealing conversation with Voytek was about the winter expedition that Zawada led to Lhotse in late 1974. He stated frankly that he did not very much enjoy large autocratic expeditions. His last would take place that same year on an unsuccessful attempt on the east ridge of K2 that failed just 200 metres below the summit.

Voytek could not spare any time from work, so I did a few routes with the Burgesses while Pete climbed with Mick. Then the five of us decided to attempt a winter traverse of the main peaks of the Polish Tatra. Conditions on the faces were unstable. It snowed continuously for a week after we arrived in Morskie Oko. Six young Poles were killed in avalanches while we were there, but the ridge itself was relatively safe, if very exposed. Once the snow stopped, we waited two days. It seemed to me much like a hard winter in New England, with lots of deep unconsolidated snow, and very different from Scotland, where regular thaws leads to better ice conditions.

The five of us set out at two in the morning and had reached the main ridge by dawn up steep and unstable snow. For the first hour or two, we all climbed unroped with Pete leading much of the way. As we entered more complex and technical ground, the Burgesses roped up. I set off after Pete, half-thinking I would soon catch him and get a rope on as well. Mick carried on soloing after me.

After another hour, I stopped at the bottom of a tower with a big drop down both sides. There was no sign of Pete, but small hand and

---

* During five days of bad weather, Jacek (known as Jack) asked me if I played poker. I was introduced to a game with two other guys I did not know and the four of us spent a day and night in the classic smoke-filled room during which time I won a small fortune in zloty. We stopped at 5 a.m. and agreed to reconvene at 8 a.m. Though exhausted, I couldn't sleep knowing I had to somehow lose it all back, as I assumed I was taking money from poor Polish climbers and I was a guest in their county. When we reconvened, I purposely lost almost all of my previous winnings. Afterwards, when the two other guys left with their wads restored, Jack rounded on me and asked what the hell I was doing. "I thought they were your friends? I couldn't take their money." "You idiot – those swine are party bosses and they print the stuff. You could have bought a chalet in the Tatra with what you won!"

footholds had been cleared of snow on a wall that led across the right side of the tower. Peter clearly had continued on alone. I attempted to follow, but gravity immediately tried to suck me off the tiny edges where my 12-point crampons barely found any purchase. A thousand-foot fall seemed a likely outcome if I continued, so I heaved myself back up, removed my sack, got out a rope and waited for Mick. He arrived a couple of minutes later, long hair matted with Rastafarian-like beads of snow, a woeful expression on his pale, thoughtful face.

"Where's Pete?"

"Somewhere ahead. He was out of sight well before I got here. He's really travelling."

We looked down into the beckoning void and then along the white towers shining ahead of us in the morning sunlight. With no sign of Pete, Mick took off his sack and lit a cigarette.

"What's got into him?"

This came from one of the leading mixed climbers on the Scottish scene. If Mick wasn't happy soloing ground like this, then no one should be. His question required a careful and diplomatic response. Adrian appeared behind and climbed over to join us.

"I've been wondering that myself Mick. You know, I think maybe he's still coming down from the summit of Everest."

I was referring to Pete and Pertemba's near miss descending to the top of the fixed ropes on the southwest face in the previous post-monsoon season. Having reached the summit late in deteriorating weather, they just managed to find their way back to the top of the ropes in a blizzard at dusk. It had been a seminal experience for Pete, something all high-altitude climbers dread but inevitably almost all experience, the feeling of being a zombie, the walking dead, caught in an inescapable situation. Even when you think all is lost, you draw on an inner strength, a life force that wakens strength and skill that lie so deep they only emerge in the most desperate circumstances. Afterwards, the experience can create a false sense of immortality and invincibility. Pete had survived that descent from Everest and it seemed to me he was still motoring on that experience. He was, after all, the foremost young star in Britain, national officer of the British

Mountaineering Council and a member of the professional climbers' front rank.

Mick finished his fag and tied on to a proffered end of rope I had dug from my rucksack.

"That's it, you're right. He's still a mad bastard in his head. He's climbing like a demon." With that, I set off on the traverse. We remained roped for the next two hours and finally caught Pete at the base of another vertical tower, stopped at last and looking a bit cold after his long wait.

"You mad bastard," Mick grinned at him. The three of us continued roped together, enjoying the exhilarating mixed climbing on snow-plastered gendarmes and knife-edged crests. The camaraderie and climbing were some of the best any of us had experienced, sharing leads and stories. Al and Ade caught us as dusk dimmed the sky and ominous snow clouds gathered on the highest summits. Neither Al nor Mick fancied a bivouac in a storm and scurried off down toward Morskie Oko from the highest peak, Rysy, via the easy summer route. Ade, Pete and I decided to take our chances with the weather, two privateers and one professional working together.

The storm blew past and the next day was another fine day of climbing in a mixture of sunshine and cloud. We stopped for a comfortable bivouac just on the Czech side of the ridge looking down less steep ground toward the ski areas near Poprad. Ade and I cleared snow and made a luxurious flat surface while Pete got the stove on and cooked. I walked a few paces from the bivvy to relieve myself over the other side. The lake of Morskie Oko was a black eye in the rapidly darkening valley beneath.* The bite of winter night was wrapping itself around the spires of the ridge. I involuntarily shuddered before slipping back into the comfort of my sleeping bag. Rocks plastered with snow probed my right side while the reassuring hulk of Adrian Burgess brought some warmth to my left. His deep steady breathing spoke of a man of the mountains at home and nearly asleep.

---

* "Morskie Oko" translates to "Eye of the Sea." According to legend, the lake was connected to the sea via an underground passage. In the legend, a princess comes to find her lost lover, who went to sea never to return, by gazing into the lake.

A full moon shouldered its way above the mountains of the Czecho-slovakian Tatra. On the other side of Ade, Peter Boardman's voice greeted it with the poetry of T.S. Eliot:

"Let us go then, you and I/When the evening is spread out against the sky/Like a patient etherised upon a table."

I carried on: "Let us go, through certain half-deserted streets,/The muttering retreats/Of restless nights in one-night cheap hotels."

"And sawdust restaurants filled with oyster shells..."

"Can't get any hotels cheaper than this, aye Pete? Wouldn't mind a sawdust restaurant though."

We lay silent for a moment looking up, wrapped in darkness but floating among stars. A near absolute silence was broken only by the tinkle of cascading ice as it snapped from rock spires in the plummeting temperature. The marrow of our bones sensed the absolute zero of space. A sudden breeze whipped ice particles around our bivouac. I switched to A.A. Milne:

"And nobody knows, (Tiddely-pom)/how cold my toes (Tiddely-pom) /how cold my toes (Tiddely-pom)/are growing."

Pete responded with Robert Frost: "Whose woods these are I think I know./His house is in the village though;/He will not see me stopping here/To watch his woods fill up with snow ... The woods are lovely, dark and deep/But I have promises to keep /And miles to go before I sleep, / And miles to go before I sleep."

That was enough for Ade. The rugged blond kraken that lay between us suddenly sat bolt upright, his arms emerged from the cocoon of his sleeping bag and flayed about threateningly in the moonlight.

"And if you two bastards don't shut up and go to sleep, I'll bloody thump you until you're bloody dark and deep. I mean it. I've never heard so much crap. Let's get some sleep so we can get off this bloody ridge tomorrow!"

Peter and I lay in our sleeping bags stifling laughter. I shut my eyes and let the words scroll through my mind: "Because I do not hope to turn again /Because I do not hope/Because I do not hope to turn/ Desiring this man's gift and that man's scope/I no longer strive to strive towards such things." Then sleep came, and with it overnight snow.

At dawn, we were woken by a patrol of armed Czech mountain troops who had been sent up in the night to investigate lights on the ridge. They spoke no English. We smiled and offered them tea, explaining as best we could that we were the guests of the Polish government and were heading back down to Poland. We packed up and scurried off along the ridge before the sergeant had made up his mind whether these dangerous foreigners who had camped illegally in the Czechoslovak Socialist Republic should be escorted down to the police station on the Czech side of the mountains. A long and dangerous day eventually saw us safely off the ridge and back to warm bunks in Morskie Oko. The Poles said we could have been in trouble if the Czechs had followed their laws and regaled us with stories of Polish climbers' encounters with authorities. Solidarity and Lech Walesa were still four years in the future.

6

LET IT BE

"One, two, three, four, Alex at the cottage door,
Five, six, seven, eight, picking cherries off a plate."
Alex's favourite nursery rhyme

"When was this picture taken?" I asked Jean MacIntyre, Alex's mother. I wanted to hear the story behind it. We sat at Jean's polished pine kitchen table on a cold December day a couple of years after Alex was killed. I had come to pay my respects, as I did now and again. Since the last time we'd met, Jean had made a pilgrimage to Annapurna base camp with Alex's girlfriend, Sarah Richard, and his friend, Terry Mooney. I wanted to know more about how she felt and about Alex's early days and I told her as much. I thought maybe one day I'd write a book about Alex.

The picture she was holding showed her as a younger woman kneeling with Alex's proud and slightly overweight father, Hamish. She was smiling. Alex's sister, Libby, kneels between them, her expression coy but happy, her dark hair in a perfect ponytail. They are in the garden of the family home, tucked away in a leafy corner of Letchmore Heath in Hertfordshire. The garden is lovely and, like the house, has an individuality that separates it from the more modern, suburban houses nearby. At their feet is a small mound of ropes, ice axes, pitons, ice screws, stuff sacks and all the other paraphernalia of an impending climbing trip.

"Now, looking at Libby, I would say 1978?" She hesitated. "No, that can't be right. Alex's father died in 1976 so I'd say 1975. That's it. He was sorting all his gear to go out to Chamonix for the summer. He ran into the house and called us out, so we followed him. 'Stand there and I'll take a photograph,' he told us, so we did."

His family and his climbing gear: the two things most precious to Alex. It made perfect sense to me.

Jean covered the table with memorabilia and filled the room with laughter, recalling the delight she felt bringing up Alex. There was a stack of scrapbooks and photo albums of Alex's early years and we went through the lot.

Jean was a compact, but not a tiny, woman. She was always neat and tidy, not necessarily someone you would immediately notice in a crowd unless, of course, you said something she did not like. Then she would tell you why she didn't like it in a clear, penetrating and forceful southern Scottish lilt. It was one of those voices you had to listen to and not interrupt until she had had her say, but then she would expect you to defend yourself. She demanded an intelligent response, or she would soon lose interest.

Jean was also brave, something she displayed in her long fight against cancer, continuing to travel extensively to satisfy her insatiable love of art history. She was knowledgeable on most subjects, believed that politics and poor behaviour came in the same package and yet was generous to most faults. She balanced her criticisms with witty comments as though we couldn't expect any better "from that lot," as if it was no fault of theirs. Most of all, she loved her children, Alex and Libby, with a passion until her own death in 2012.

"Look at all these wonderful photos of his childhood," she said. "Most of these seem to be of Alex. We certainly took far more photos of Alex than Libby."

I was and always had been in awe of Jean. I met Alex's father only once, just months before he died, but during the decade that I climbed with Alex, I got to know Jean MacIntyre very well. It didn't take long to understand where Alex had developed his debating skills. Alex would never let "loose thoughts" go unchallenged. And it was from his mother that he also inherited his quick, inquisitive mind, his spontaneity and his wicked sense of humour.

She showed me a photo of a smiling, cherubic infant.

"You can see even as a baby why the girls were going to love Alex. He had crushes on a number of girls, but there were only two girls that he really loved, Gwyneth and Sarah, and they were both super girls. Hamish was very fond of Gwyneth. They were both strong. They had to be to live with Alex. I remember taking him to the airport when he was flying down to Peru just after Gwyneth had broken it off. He was really very upset and said: 'I don't think I can take it Mum.' But he soon found solace, didn't he John, being Alex."

Alex was born in Cottingham near Hull in Yorkshire in March 1954, their first child. Both parents were Scottish and devout Catholics, from Campbeltown near the Mull of Kintyre.

"We'd moved down from Scotland when Hamish got a job as an agricultural rep with ICI not long before Alex was born. Everyone adored him. His great aunt Joan on his father's side terrified the whole family, but not Alex. He was such a bonny baby and he knew how to use his charm."

It was true. Alex was incredibly charming when he wanted to be. But, sometimes, he used his charm as a front from which to launch his acerbic wit. Being on the receiving end could be a real test. But it was the gentler side of his personality that captured most of us and made his friends protective. I picked up another photo of Alex with his father.

"I can see a lot of Alex in this shot, Jean – those inquisitive dark eyes." He always seemed to be detecting something outside the frame and beyond the photographer, some idea he was working on in his head. "He talked a lot about his father."

Alex's father Hamish was a hard-working and dedicated man, but not someone interested in outdoor pursuits. Golf was his game and he encouraged Alex to take it up. On bivvys, when we talked the night away about everything under the sun – or a frozen moon – Alex had told me many times how well he got on with his father and how much he respected him, just as much as his mother for sure. And he took up golf to please his dad. He was on his grammar-school team before climbing took hold.

There are a lot of closet golfers in the climbing community. The quote sometimes attributed to Mark Twain that golf is "a good walk spoilt" works well as a description of climbing when things go wrong.

The one time I played a round with Alex was in a threesome with Tim Lewis, then editor of *Mountain* magazine, on the Silecroft links course on the West Cumbrian coast. It was mid-winter, five degrees below freezing with a bitter wind blowing down from snow-covered Black Combe. Alex had an excellent swing and hit some long but occasionally wayward drives – not surprisingly since we were all wearing down suits and double boots. No one came close to par that day.

"You know John, I think Alex developed his tenacity and loyalty from his father. Hamish was like that. Once you were his friend he stuck by you." Jean paused for a moment. "But we can never know what will happen next. I remember sending Alex off in one of those awful vans with Nick Colton on the way to climb the Eiger. I wondered if I would see him again. And then two weeks later, his father keeled over and died of a massive stroke, totally unexpected. By the time we got word to Alex, it was too late for him to get back for the funeral. When he phoned, he was terribly shocked and couldn't really accept what had happened. Even when I explained how his father had died, he just said, 'I know, Mum, but what's wrong, what's wrong?'"

When Nick Colton and Alex were stormed off the Eiger, they escaped into the railway tunnel where some railway workers stopped them: "Is one of you Alex MacIntyre?" Thinking this might have something to do with an unpaid bill, they replied in the negative and having reached the valley, loaded the van and headed back to Chamonix. Arriving at Le Brasserie National – the Bar Nash – they joined the usual crowd of half-inebriated climbers when Alex spotted Alan Rouse looking at him with an unusually solemn expression. Alan came over and quietly said: "You don't know the news about your dad, do you?" It was then that Alex rushed out and phoned his mother.

"Alex did come home once he found out. His father's company left him a ticket at Geneva airport. He was home for a while and then went back up to Manchester. Then, two weeks later, I collapsed and went into hospital to have a hysterectomy. I was about to turn 50 while I was in hospital and on my birthday Alex arrived unexpectedly with a big bunch of flowers, a bottle of champagne and a bottle of whisky. 'We have to celebrate, Mum, it's your birthday.' Well, we sat with all the nurses drinking champagne, and I had a small whisky even though I felt like death. That was Alex for you, he could be so generous and spontaneous."

There was one thing in Alex's life that Jean did not understand. She remained highly critical of Alex's climbing all the time I knew her. It scared her, but she also disdained all the generally bad behaviour that was part of climbing in the 1970s. I suggested to Jean that our entire generation behaved badly in the eyes of their parents and the authorities. The world seemed a mess, swinging radically in one direction and then back again. The three-day week led to the "winter of discontent" and then the election of Margaret Thatcher with her clean broom to sweep away the unions. We might have behaved badly, but so did the punk and rock bands we listened to, and the football team we followed – Leeds United.

"You know John, when we walked in to Annapurna, I understood even less about why Alex would want to go climbing. It became harder and harder as we approached the mountain, it looked so terrifying, cold and steep. Why would he not rather be in Hayfield with Sarah?"

"Alex was incredibly good at what he did, and he loved mountains and climbing." I tried to tackle an unspoken question. "If he thought he was going to die, he wouldn't have gone I'm sure." But I only half-believed what I was saying. We all knew the risks. In truth, Jean was very proud of Alex's climbing successes and all the media attention he got. And if spending a bit of extra time with Alex meant offering a shoulder to cry on when he needed it for emotional support, or giving him a few quid when he was short, or a ride to the airport, then Jean would make sure she was there.

The MacIntyres were reasonably well off but not wealthy. They rented a large, draughty farmhouse in West Newton in the East Riding of Yorkshire. The house was filled with an assortment of cats and a family dog. "Between the cats and Alex, the dog had a pretty miserable life," said Jean. "Alex was always trying to ride him like a horse."

I remembered Alex's disdain for cats. He tormented them, not in any cruel way, but simply by ignoring them, not letting them get what they wanted. When he came to stay with Rose and I, our cat soon learned there would be no sign of interest or affection and just left Alex alone. It was a tactic he could use as effectively with people.

Alex's sister Libby was born when he was five. "He adored his sister, but not her constant pestering. When she was two and always wanting to play, Alex would take a book and climb into Libby's cot and sit there reading in the middle where she couldn't reach him. But as they grew up, Alex became incredibly fond and protective of his sister."

Libby was a bright, good-looking teenager during Alex's climbing years. Very few of Alex's climbing friends were introduced to her. I remember meeting Libby only once and he tracked our conversation, watching me with knife-like eyes. Neither Jean nor Alex wanted Libby falling for a climber. They both knew too much about us. Mostly, Libby was never there when we passed through. She'd be staying with friends, and that may also have been Jean's doing.

The family used to spend three weeks each summer back in Campbeltown, visiting relatives and taking long walks on the open sandy beaches that extended along the coast or up into the wooded hills. One of Jean MacIntyre's mother's brothers – Uncle Andrew – owned a herring drifter, a single-masted, broad-beam fishing boat.

"Ever after, Alex asked us for a boat, but we never lived near enough to water to justify the investment. Maybe that was a mistake, perhaps if we had bought him a boat, he never would have taken up climbing and he'd still be with us."

When Alex had passed his eleven-plus exams, his parents decided he should attend a good Roman Catholic school. They felt he needed some stability since his father's work was moving him around a good deal. He was enrolled at the Jesuit Mount Saint Mary's College on the outskirts of Sheffield as a boarder. (Old boys are known as "mountaineers," which is apposite in Alex's case.)

"Being a Catholic, I wanted him to go to a Catholic school, but it was a waste of money because he never went to church afterwards. Well, only occasionally just to please his mother. He said to me after he left Saint Mary's: 'Prison would be a doddle compared to that school.'"

Alex's first experience of climbing came after his parents moved to Letchmore Heath. Hamish had once again changed jobs and it was now a long way for Alex to go home for weekend visits. He said he wanted to go home to be with them and Hamish agreed – but only if his "O" Level results were good enough to gain him entry to Watford Grammar School for the sixth form. Set a goal he wanted to achieve, Alex would make sure he delivered. His exam results were good enough.

"Watford Grammar was a superb school and Alex excelled there. He really settled in and got very good results in sixth form. I remember meeting one of his teachers on the main street in Watford when I was with Alex. I said that he must have his hands full with this one. He'd replied: 'On the contrary, Alex is one of our most gifted pupils.' It just showed he could work when he wanted to."

Almost as soon as he entered Watford Grammar School, he joined the London Mountaineering Club and frequently went on weekend meets to Snowdonia in Wales. "There was one very nice couple who were kind and sympathetic toward a penniless teenager. I used to drop him off somewhere near the motorway on a Friday night, and pick him up again at God-knows-what hour on Sunday evening. It set the pattern of things to come. He always expected me to be there when needed. He was a selfish devil that way."

Jean paused, looking at the black coffee she was holding. Then she looked up at me sitting across the dark living room. "Well, you all were, weren't you? You boys always expected everything to happen for you."

I sat swirling my own coffee, admitting it was true. The tension was immediately broken by laughter as Jean launched into a new story. "I remember one time when we were at home with some old friends who had just driven down from Scotland. The phone rang, and it was Alex: 'Please Mum can you organize some cars and come down and pick us up at Liverpool Street Station.'

"Well, we quickly finished dinner and I asked one of our guests if he would take his car as well. I knew there were four climbers with bags to pick up. It was an awful journey in – our friend got lost. When we all eventually arrived at Liverpool Street Station, there was no sign of Alex. Hamish spotted a pub across the road and there they all were.

"Hamish asked him: 'Why weren't you at the station looking out for us?' Alex said: 'Because I knew you'd know we'd be in the pub.' And then the next day we had to go back to get you."

I had forgotten. Returning from Afghanistan, Alex, Terry King, Howard Lancashire and I set off together from Poland by train on the last leg home. During the farewells in Warsaw, we'd forgotten to eat and had had far too many Vodkas. We reached Poznan, a scheduled 20-minute stop, so I jumped off to get some bread. I arrived back on the platform to see the train vanishing down the line. The boys were left to get home via East Germany without passports. I had them all in my back pocket. But it was going to be equally difficult for me since my train ticket and money were all on the train with my bags. Twenty-four hours later, I managed to talk my way onto the next train and I arrived at Liverpool Street a day after everyone else. I phoned Alex from the station: "Do you want this bread or what?" And, of course, Jean drove Alex into town to get me.

Alex loved his mother's company. "He used to take me places occasionally, like the winter in 1979 when he insisted that I come out to Chamonix for Christmas. Sarah was there along with a big bunch of his mates. I remember Alex introducing me to Alan Rouse. 'Alan, this is my mother,' he said. Alan looked quite shocked and then with a big grin said: 'Bloody hell Alex, it's bad enough that you've brought your girlfriend, but your mother?' Alan was like that; it was very funny."

Alex phoned Jean to cadge another lift to do a lecture for his old school, Watford Grammar. "I sat at the back to watch. I was expecting shots of beautiful mountains but most of the slides were of his horrible awful digs in Leeds and dirty washing. Everyone thought it terribly funny, except me. Afterwards, someone came up and said: 'Wasn't it nice of Alex to bring you to his talk?' I had to say, it was me who brought him to this talk or else you wouldn't have had one."

In the era of Johnny Rotten and the Sex Pistols, many young climbers thrived on punk's anarchic, anti-establishment message. "At one black-tie dinner, where he'd been invited to give the after-dinner speech, he came wearing a black tie as required, but with a t-shirt." Jean paused to reflect. "I think that was just him attention-seeking."

Jean thought Alex could be a "right toad" at times. "I remember after

Hamish had died, I had a large dinner party for our close friends. Alex was home for the weekend from Leeds. One of Hamish's oldest friends was there, a well-known barrister in London. He knew Alex had changed his course to law. He came over to congratulate Alex and to ask why he had chosen to be a lawyer. Alex thought for a moment and said: 'Well, it was the only thing I could think of where you can make an awful lot of money without having to do much work.' Alex thought that sort of talk funny. I just thought he was rude."

In 1972, Alex took his "A" Levels and got stunning results: four grade As. He then had a choice to make, Cambridge University or Leeds. "I've no doubt Alex chose Leeds because of the reputation of the Leeds University Climbing Club," Jean said. "He had his heart set on that." That autumn, almost exactly ten years before he died on Annapurna, his mother and father drove him up to Leeds and deposited him at his new digs. "I decided to go have a look and followed Alex upstairs to his room. I was so shocked by how dirty and untidy the whole place was that I rushed back down to warn Hamish not to come in. It would have been too much for him. We'd both wanted Alex to go to Cambridge."

My afternoon with Jean passed and darkness crept under the kitchen door. With it, sadness replaced the laughter and glasses of Scotch replaced the coffee. Jean reminded me of the conversation we always had before Alex and I set off for the Alps or further afield. "Look after my little boy won't you John? He can do stupid things I know, and take too many chances, but you'll do your best won't you? Bring him back to me."

Now our sense of loss was complete. I could only imagine how much deeper it was for Jean. I found myself trying to define where responsibility for the actions of other people ends and where individual responsibility begins. I didn't know then and do not know now. I broke away to a new subject.

"Would Alex be a barrister today, do you think? Wearing a proper black tie and white shirts to dinner parties?"

"I'm not sure really. Maybe he would have stuck with the law. Sarah told me she thought he would be a great TV presenter, with his personality and gift of the gab. One thing's for sure, he'd have a bit of a laugh at the idea that you'd be writing a book about him. Or as John Barry said, have a climbing hut named after him."

I suggested another career, having mentally reconstructed the list of routes and pieces of equipment that he designed and which might have borne his name. "Don't you think he might have been a climbing equipment designer?"

"You know John, I would have enjoyed whatever he would have been. We all knew he would be a success, that's what we wanted to share."

I accepted a strong coffee and prepared myself for the six-hour journey back up the motorway to the Lakes, a journey I'd made many times with Alex. Jean reminded me of one poignant moment as we stood at the door saying goodbye. "That last morning we saw you at the airport, John, it was so strange. We were late and you were there waiting outside the terminal with a pile of bags. The reason we were late was we'd gone ten miles when Alex said: 'Turn round Mum, I've forgotten my passport.' By the time we arrived at the airport, there was no time for the usual goodbyes. He had to dash, but he did something he had never done before. He ran back and put his head through the window and said: 'Look after Sarah and Libby for me.' It was quite strange. It was not like him to come back and say anything. I have wondered sometimes if he had a premonition."

I suddenly recalled that moment, me shouting: "Come on, Alex! We're going to miss the plane." And Jean and I had failed to say goodbye. We had missed our parting ritual, that little conversation to one side when Jean would tell me to look after Alex and bring him back safe. I felt the waves of guilt and sadness sweep over me as I drove up the motorway toward the hills of home.

7

DON'T FEAR THE REAPER

In 1972, the Leeds University Climbing Club (LUCC) was going through a period of change. A new irreverent group was taking charge and I was one of them. We were mostly disorganized, dishevelled and disrespectful, and sometimes dishonest. Climbing was our shared passion. We couldn't understand why everyone didn't climb but were glad they didn't. *Mountain* magazine was our bible. One copy would pass around the entire club. Apart from *Mountain* and climbing, lunch in the salad bar on the first floor of the student union and a string of pubs – the Pack Horse, the Eldon, the Swan with Two Necks and the Fenton – gave structure to our lives.

Mainly, we went climbing, managing to fit in just enough university work to keep our tutors satisfied. There were nearly daily sessions on the Leeds indoor climbing wall and many impromptu outings to the nearby gritstone crags. There were regular club meets every Wednesday afternoon, since there were no classes that day and most weekends we climbed regardless of the weather. The weekends away occasionally turned into a week, and weeks occasionally into an entire month. Doing course work was a low priority compared with climbing.

None of us who came together at Leeds University in the early 1970s could have foreseen the impact we would have on the climbing scene or the tragedies that fate had in store for us. The majority of us weren't even serious climbers when we first met. A host of factors – group dynamics, adventures born from frustrations, nihilism, sexual and spiritual immaturity, mass hysteria, drug and drink-stimulated delusion, anarchy – coalesced to inspire something exceptional.

Yorkshire gritstone offered the nearest climbing and Almscliff was our favourite. It became a place of worship for the one world-class rock-climbing star in the club – John Syrett. There were others in the club nearly as good: Rob Wood, Alan Manson and Pete Kitson. And when I say "club," some "members" were just part of the scene and not studying at the university.

In the next year or two, more extremely talented rock climbers arrived as Leeds students, including Mike Hammill, John Allen, Steve Bancroft and Chris Addy. Between them they climbed lots of new routes, although Syrett, until he severed a tendon in his hand trying to open a tin of lobster with a knife, remained the best in the club. Another talented rock climber and habitual student, Bernard Newman, was at Leeds throughout this period, from 1969 to 1975. He edited the famous *Leeds Journal* of 1973 and eventually became editor of both *Mountain* and *Climber* magazines.*

When Alex arrived at the university, some excellent alpinists were also emerging at Leeds. Brian Hall, Roger Baxter-Jones and John Stainforth had many hard routes reported in *Mountain* magazine, like the Bonatti Pillar on the Dru and many first British ascents. John Powell and Tim Rhodes arrived about the same time as Alex.

The notoriety and success of the Leeds University club resulted in an extended family of climbers from both Britain and the United States coming to visit, or to meet us in the mountains. In Britain, our closest club association was with the University of Cambridge, whose leading lights were Alan Rouse and Mick Geddes. The Americans were mainly New Englanders from my original home. When I went to Leeds to do post-graduate work in 1972, many friends came over to climb. Among them were Roger Martin, John Bouchard, Henry Barber, Steve Arsenault, Chuck Ziakowski and, later, Ed Webster, Andy Tuthill and Chris Elms.

Many of them had a real impact on both the British and European climbing scenes. In 1974, Roger Martin made the second solo ascents of *Point Five* and *Zero Gullies*, a feat Alex repeated the same year. John Bouchard did a number of new routes in the Alps. Henry Barber was sent to the UK by ex-pat Paul Ross to wind up local climbers with his exceptional skills and clean ethics. The year before he came, he had

* In 2013, Bernard was appointed honorary editor of the *Alpine Journal.*

been nicknamed "Hot Henry" for his phenomenal solo ascents and on-sight leads in Yosemite.* He discovered a like-minded companion in John Syrett. John's approach – climbing ground up and on sight – was a mirror image of his own. Some other excellent climbers of the day, Pete Livesey and Ron Fawcett among them, would occasionally inspect a new route from above and there were whispers of preplaced slings to make routes easier to protect and even chipped holds.

None of us could match Syrett, Alan Manson or Pete Kitson on rock, but we adopted our ethical stance from them. Any route done with a rest, or with a fall, was not considered an ascent. Some credit could be gained by being lowered to the ground, then pulling the ropes through before trying again. But it was still considered a flawed ascent and duly noted as such in our handwritten journal. This arrived at the salad bar under Bernard's arm at lunchtime for members to record their ascents and other antics.

There is no doubt that a clean and free style of climbing influenced Alex's approach, first in the Alps and then in the Himalaya. We were not the first to practise this clean tradition, merely the keepers of the purist flame. The influence of the group was perhaps best recorded in the pages of *Mountain* magazine throughout the 1970s, but individual tributes still appear, in the writing of Jim Perrin and others.

A formal structure and published program of activities was required to get grants from the student union, but such things were anathema to most members of the LUCC. Still, we had to make the effort. Elected officers were often appointed because they were absent from the pub on the evening of the annual general meeting. Executive officers had the habit of never actually joining and paying their dues, but there were plenty of new arrivals, not yet disillusioned, keen to join the club for fifty pence, or about $1.50.

New victims enrolled during the freshers' fair at the student union building each year. The benefit of membership was dubious to say the

---

* Just as Henry left to go back to the States, in 1974, there was a gathering at the Padarn Lake Hotel for a couple of farewell drinks. Don Whillans was heard to comment, loud enough for Henry to hear: "Henry's just a flash in the pan, and anyway he can't drink." After a season of training, Henry returned the following year not to climb but to drink all the British hard men under the table, which he pretty well succeeded in doing.

least. First of all, having paid over your money, unless you were part of the inner circle, you were not invited to join the club officials later that afternoon in the pub to drink away the club's subscriptions for the year. Next day, the list of new and existing members was taken to union officials as proof of a vibrant and growing club.* A grant was then awarded on a per capita basis, which usually amounted to several hundred pounds.

This money was used in a variety of ways. On the first Saturday in the first term of each year we held an official meet and rented a bus to take us to Stanage or some other more distant crag. This gave the club some credibility among the paid-up new members. It was also evidence that we were doing what we said we were doing to impress the student union. The credentials of new members were carefully weighed: Could they climb, did they have any money, did they have a car and were they female? That was more or less the order of priority. There were not many female "stayers" in the club. A few became the anchor of sanity for some of the more dissolute and disillusioned members of the club – Syrett in particular. Some of the girls joined in with antics that on several occasions made national press headlines: "Vicar's Daughter Arrested in Pub Theft" was one; others included "Skylight Collapse Near Death Fall For Leeds Uni Fresher."

On the whole, the male club members were men without women. We were basically too interested in climbing and short-term kicks – in other words, too immature. There were some excellent women climbers in the club at the time: Cynthia Heap and Angela Faller to name but two. Although they joined in on many trips, they found the conversation and pub antics of the leading lights in the club pretty inane. Angela Fowler once famously said of the climbers in the club: "I can't really tell the difference between the drug addicts and queers." It is

---

* The Leeds club was definitely trumped by the clever approach taken by Rouse and Geddes at Cambridge. They didn't bother with sitting around enrolling people. They put up a large flip-chart-like poster with these words at the top: "Anyone wanting to come to a party with free beer and drink on Saturday put your name, college and contact details below." At the end of the day, they then collected the sheets and carefully peeled off the stuck-on "free drinks" announcement to reveal the wording actually written on the sheets: "The following are paid-up members of the Cambridge University Climbing Club." The proceeds from the Student Union Grant funded Rouse and Geddes's travels and alpine trips for an entire year.

difficult to know these many years on if that is really how she saw us all – as far as I know the club had neither.

Alex joined the club during fresher enrolment. John Powell recalls seeing him in some of the classes they shared together. "He always sat on his own, but he had a Joe Brown rucksack, a leather jacket and, of course, his hair was out all over the place, so he didn't quite fit. He was not quite the picture of your normal student at the time. So I thought he might be a climber and I went over to talk to him. But he was pretty stand-offish, wanted to play it cool."

Alex was quite taciturn when he first arrived at Leeds. It was his nature to stand back and weigh things up, particularly with new people, before he opened up. For the first couple of months, he did not attend a club meet, or join in at the evening sessions at the Leeds Climbing Wall.* But that would change soon enough, mainly through his growing friendship with John Powell, who was reading the same course. Alex joined the fast track to develop his climbing and gain access to the inner clique.

"Once I got hold of a van," John said, "the regular crew of John Syrett, Andy Wild, Alex and I were getting out every weekend, climbing and then gate-crashing parties in the evenings. Climbing and partying were joint-top in our list of priorities. In fact, we combined them the very first time I climbed with Alex, shimmying up a drainpipe behind the student union building to get into the freshers' ball. We never paid for entrance to anything if there was another way in."

* The Leeds Climbing Wall was built in 1964, the brainchild of a sports trainer and climber called Don Robinson. It was the first indoor climbing wall in the world. It ran along two sides of the outside of a squash court and the sounds of squeaking court shoes and the "ka-twack-kathump" of the ball accompanied sessions on the wall. Given the standards of today's climbing walls, the Leeds wall was primitive. It consisted of natural rocks of various sizes cemented into a normal brick wall of about 15 feet in height. Mortar had been dug out between some of the bricks to provide small edges. There were also short, vertical jamming-cracks placed one above the other, cut out of the bricks and then lined with cement. It was a great place to work out, although shredded fingers and twisted ankles were commonplace. There were no mats on the cement floor and a drop from the top was guaranteed to leave the feet stinging. The wall explains a lot about the success the club had on the crags – we had a secret training regime, which was unheard of at the time. Everyone tended to go at least twice a week – Tuesday and Thursday evenings and, occasionally, classes were skipped for an extra session during the day. I remember one day in 1969, during my final undergraduate year at Leeds, having a dark-haired Adonis-like figure pointed out to me by Bernard with the phrase: "Watch this kid, it's his first day on the wall." To our astonishment, he jammed up the notorious sequence of cracks almost with grace. This was John Syrett.

Blue Ford vans were popular among climbers; they were cheap to run and easy to repair. There were at least three owned by club members: John Powell, Bernard Newman and Alex himself. I doubt if any of them would be legal today. Tax, insurance and MOTs were all seen as unnecessary and expensive accessories. Tires were worn down until the metal cores showed through. All the vans were constantly in scrapes and prangs, but no one ever had a serious crash. A new dent happened almost on a weekly basis. If another car was involved, it meant cash had to exchange hands pretty quickly, especially if the car was also without insurance. John Powell recalled having to swallow his panic when stopped by the police during a late night drive up to the Lake District after the pub.

"You seem to have been driving all over the road, sir," the officer said, shining his flashlight on each of the faces of the occupants of the van.

"Sorry, officer just a bit tired you know."

"Come far then?"

"Oh yes, from Leeds." The officer was silent for a moment. Leeds was less than an hour's drive away.

"All students are we?" he said, shining the light on Alex's face and wild hair, and then around the rest of us sprawled in the back. "Best be on your way then. Mind how you go."

Had he checked, as he would now, the officer could have got him for bald tires, no tax and no insurance, as well as being over the limit, but society was more tolerant of these things in the early 1970s.

Although the vans ultimately belonged to individuals, they were treated as communal property by the club and we all drove them. The fleet was occasionally augmented with a few cars borrowed from parents or those rented by visiting Americans. Rarely did these go back to their owners without a new dent or two.

When the moon was full, driving back from the crags without headlights seemed a normal thing to do. On a single-lane humpbacked bridge near Malham, Alex and John Powell met a car also without headlights at the crest of the bridge. Fortunately, they were in Powell's father's solid Morris Oxford and there was little damage to it. The other car was a near write-off. The other driver was a farmer on his way back from the pub, already banned for drunk driving. He had been driving without lights to avoid the attention of any police car in the area. They cleared the farmer's wrecked car from the bridge and then took him home where enough cash to repair the Powell family vehicle was proffered.

Alex's van became so badly dented that only the rear doors opened. Stopped by the police, the officer had a shock when he asked Alex to step out of the car. As he stood by the driver's door, the back doors suddenly flew open and five scruffy lads jumped out before Alex himself climbed out the back. Having recovered from this shock and ascertained that we were all students, we got the usual "mind how you go" speech and set off again.

In his first years in the club, Alex was not a particularly strong rock climber. He often drew irreverent comments when his name appeared in the Leeds "Book" – the journal recording the climbs and the antics of the club, illustrated with pictures of particularly spectacular falls and car crashes. Exactly when Alex gained the nickname "Dirty Alex" is not recorded in the Book, but it does appear halfway through his first year. Like most students, Alex was not often seen at the laundromat. His face was usually unshaven and his unruly hair reached his shoulders. Alex was doing grunge well before anyone tried to build a fashion around not washing.

John Powell recalls that despite this, Alex drew attention. "There were a lot of really smart girls on our course and Alex was always in demand, but he never made any effort with any of them. I remember going on a weeklong fieldtrip to the Isle of Man and Alex had the same trousers and shirt on all week. And, of course, he had a leather jacket that lasted him through Leeds that was rarely off his back. He even climbed in it."

It went with the motorbike he had brought to Leeds. Not many people dared climb on the back with Alex. Although he was naturally someone who tried to be safe, he was also very inconsistent. That also was true of his climbing.

Luck smiled on most of the Leeds club during those years. Long falls were commonplace and most of our equipment was basic. Few had more than half a dozen runners. Equipment had to be pooled for serious routes. Many of us still had a selection of real nuts with the threads filed out and threaded with slings. Equipment was now improving and we snapped up new gear as we could afford it. MOACs were the most prized, a two-size-only range of British nuts that were a precursor to Yvon Chouinard's Stoppers.* Clog hexes and a few slings to thread chockstones or to hang over flakes made up the rest of our climbing rack. The placement of pegs was completely taboo except for Scottish winter climbing and the Alps. In the USA, the early 1970s was the transition period between the use of any pegs for protection and the widespread availability of a range of small wires. The arrival of a more sophisticated approach to protection was something American visitors like Steve Wunsch and Henry Barber brought to Leeds.

The club rarely missed a chance to go climbing; even after late night parties and through the damp and dull winter months, climbing was happening. Many cold wet days were spent on the gritstone and the high crags of Wales and the Lake District, excellent experience for the future in persevering.

Under the tutelage of John Syrett, Alex learned a lot about perseverance and determination. Syrett was a master of spotting unlikely routes and always approached them on sight, which almost inevitably meant falls and failures before success. Alex was a reliable and long-suffering "rope boy," willing to put in many idle hours belaying Syrett to watch a master at work. What Alex lacked in skill, he repaid in interest with his unflappable manner. Whatever was going on inside, Alex rarely revealed his feelings, even in extremis. Mostly, he came to the crag with a wisecracking and competitive spirit, which spurred the rest of us on.

During his first year at Leeds, Alex worked hard at all aspects of his climbing and improved dramatically. He progressed from climbing Severe (5.5) on rock to leading E1 (5.9 or 510a/b) in his second year. He never pretended he was a great leader and would always hand the

---

* When 12 sizes of Stoppers, based on the original MOAC design, were manufactured by Chouinard in 1972 as part of his "clean climbing" revolution, not only did the folk at MOAC realize the missed opportunity but there was some mild outrage that the Yanks were claiming the invention of "clean climbing" when for the Brits it was their rock-climbing tradition.

lead to his partner if he was not feeling confident. He did have moments of inspiration. I remember him romping up a number of mid-grade Extremes in the Lakes in miserable conditions. As with many aspiring rock climbers, his first Extreme was *Brant Direct* in the Llanberis Pass. Although not terribly difficult, it was a cold and wet November day. Alex knew what routes he wanted and needed to do and worked his way through them. Some were more painful than others. When abseiling down after an ascent of *Cenotaph Corner* on Dinas Cromlech, on his way to do *Cemetery Gates*, Alex got his hair caught in his figure of 8 abseil device 40 feet off the ground. After cursing and swearing for a bit, there was nothing else he could do to free himself but pull all the offending hair from his head. He completed the descent and went on to the next climb. It was a mistake he made only once.

The club had drawn Alex to Leeds. His reasons for choosing geography and economics were less obvious. By the end of 1972, he had decided to switch and went to his tutor to ask if he could change to law. He applied and was accepted, but wouldn't start until the following year. That gave him the chance to take a few months off, some of which he spent in Leeds climbing. The rest he spent on the beaches of North Africa not doing very much of anything, before returning to Leeds for the autumn term in 1973.

Only Bernard Newman and John Syrett had live-in girlfriends. The rest of us just got on with climbing. But when Alex returned to Leeds in 1973, he met the first love of his life – Gwyneth Rule. She had joined the club during freshers' week and Alex just happened to be manning the club's information point at the time. Gwyneth was a trim redhead from South Wales and a perfect foil for Alex. His taciturnity was matched by her extrovert manner and sense of fun. If the boys could do it, she would have a go. They shared a one-room bedsit just off Hyde Park Corner in Leeds for the next three years. The room was never tidy; the floor, the broken-down sofa and the few chairs were always strewn with dirty clothes, empty bottles and dirty mugs. It seemed a challenge between the two of them: Who would crack first and clean up the mess? It rarely happened, but Alex did seem to shave more often and take more care generally in his appearance. In Gwyneth, Alex had been lucky to find someone who would draw out his own sense of fun and, to a degree, a greater self-awareness and confidence.

Perhaps he needed a better image in the law department, but he also changed from grunge to a more glam-rock look, essentially just showering a bit more often, washing his hair and buying a new leather jacket. His climbing improved enough for him to gain more deference in the Book. Entries about him changed from Dirty Alex or just Dirty to D.A. or even just Alex. There was certainly only one Alex in the club.

I first met him on my return to Leeds to work on an M.Phil. Running a climbing school in New Hampshire was good fun, but taking money for something I enjoyed as a sport was uncomfortable. The school was reasonably successful. In the summer there were as many as four instructors. On many days, I gave them the work and I climbed for fun or played golf. But the Alps and the raw hills of Britain were calling. I began to respond to letters from my professor encouraging me to return to academia. I had saved up enough while working in the States and crossed the pond once again. I was eight years Alex's senior. He was 19 and I was 27, but I now had a lot of alpine experience from time spent in the Rockies and winter climbing in New England to add to my earlier seasons in the Alps.

For the first year of my post-graduate work, I lived in Leeds, sharing a house with some nonclimbing mature students near Hyde Park. The majority of the climbing fraternity was within easy walking distance and I soon fell in with them. When we weren't out climbing or in the pub talking about climbing, we spent a lot of time poring over guidebooks and reading magazines in one house or another.

In early March 1973, Alex had his first experience of ice climbing; it was almost a disaster. A strong team from the LUCC travelled up to Craig Meagaidh in the central Highlands and took along two beginners – John Powell and Alex. For whatever reason, these two were left to their own devices while the rest of us charged off to do other routes. They decided to try *Centre Post*, a grade III low down on the main face.

As it turned out, the route was too low down; it was a mild day and the ice was soft and collapsing.

It was Alex's first time wearing crampons and, plodding up the snow slope toward the bottom of the climb, he managed to shred his brand new over-trousers. He took them off and threw them down the face from the bottom of the first ice pitch. With only one ice axe each, they failed to make any impression on the ice above despite several attempts. The rest of us made a number of ascents of much harder routes and this annoyed Alex further. The next day could have been much worse. It snowed heavily overnight and was still snowing hard in the morning. Most of the club headed home, but Alex persuaded John Eames and John Powell to return to Craig Meagaidh. Despite the fact it was still snowing after the two-hour walk-in, they started up *South Post* – at grade v, a much harder proposition.

John Powell traversed across *Centre Post* toward the bottom of their intended route but had only just clipped into a peg when a massive avalanche roared down the gully, nearly plucking him from his stance. When it stopped, the rope was running straight down the gully. With visibility at zero in the white-out around him, John immediately assumed that Alex and John Eames had been swept away. But his shouts were answered and he realized they were still attached to the crag on the other side of the gully. The rope had been cut by falling ice. They beat a hasty retreat.

In the summer of 1973, we headed out to the Alps. Well supplied with tinned food from Leeds, there was so much weight that the vans kept overheating and as a consequence the journey took three days.* This was an annual club event and although we habitually based ourselves in Snell's Field outside Chamonix, members would travel to many other areas over the summer, usually in search of better weather and better conditions. Despite this, the Mont Blanc range drew us

---

* Many club members had part-time jobs to help pay their way through university; some were in positions that helped support their climbing. This included a petrol station attendant where the odd gallon of fuel was pumped for free, and overnight supermarket shelf stackers who placed tins stamped with new low prices at the back of rows to be collected and paid for the next morning by accomplices.

back year after year and it was there that we did most of our most notable ascents and suffered our many epics.*

That year was my third season in the Alps. I had climbed in Chamonix
in 1967, doing a hard rock route with the rising Scottish star, Jim
McArtney, on the Pointe Albert and some moderate snow climbs on
higher peaks. (McArtney, who Tom Patey described "as large as life
and radiating enthusiasm like an open furnace," was tragically killed in
an avalanche on *Italian Climb* on the Ben in 1970.) I returned to
Chamonix in 1969, completing a number of routes with various partners I met at the old Biolay campsite up in the woods above the
Montenvers railway station. I suffered several forced bivouacs, including one very serious one in the Peigne couloir after climbing the north
ridge. Getting back to camp, I discovered the gendarmes had finally
cleared the Brits off the unlicensed and unhealthy but free Biolay site.
With unexpected compassion, the well-known owner of Snell's
Sports – the climbing shop in town – acted swiftly to allow the Brits
and the Eastern Europeans to move to a field he owned a mile or so up
the road at Les Praz. That's where my tent had been taken. It was the
start of the era that made Snell's Field a legendary hive of British
Alpine activity for decades.

Climbing conditions in 1973 were not good. After a first week of
good weather in early July, it began to rain, with snow reaching right
down to the valley bottom. We doggedly stuck it out, walking several
times up to the Plan de l'Aiguille to stay in a woodcutter's hut in hopes
of improving weather. We also climbed on the valley crags, practised
ice-climbing technique on the Bossons glacier and spent afternoons
in the Bar Nash or the hotel in Les Praz, drinking wine and playing
cards. We were typical, easy-to-please students with few cares in the
world and a penchant for jokes in bad taste.

In late July, a morning visit to the météo office revealed a period of

---

* Over the many years that the Leeds club climbed in Chamonix and the Alps, there were very few
serious accidents or deaths. The most notable was Roger Baxter-Jones, who died when seracs on
the north face of the Triolet collapsed when he was guiding a client in 1985. RBJ was arguably the
fittest of all the UK's Himalayan climbers at the time and his death was pure bad luck. Georges
Bettembourg, a member of the extended circle of friends, was killed in a rockfall while crystal
hunting in the Chamonix Aiguilles.

beau temps lasting at least three days. I was in the Alps with John Bouchard and at the beginning of the season, in the short periods of good weather, we had managed a couple of ED rock climbs. But he had promised to do a route with Steve Arsenault, another old friend on a flying visit, and everyone else was fixed up. That left Alex and I to make arrangements.

I had climbed with Alex a few times in the UK and we got on fine, although I knew both his limitations on rock and his lack of experience on ice, although the heavy new snow meant ice faces were not in the equation anyway. I fancied the south face of the Fou, a route that Al Rouse had soloed earlier in the summer, but the couloir approach could be dangerous. We opted instead for the continuous and classic line of the adjacent east face of the Pointe Lépiney. Alex had arrived halfway through the season and said he was happy with anything since it would be his first route in the Alps.

Before we packed up, he went into town to rent some boots. He had somehow managed to lose one boot in transit. And so we boarded a train for Montenvers that afternoon with Alex wearing boots of two sizes; on his right foot, one of his original boots, on his left, the nearest fit he could rent. Fortunately, he remained blister-free on the two-hour walk up to the Envers Hut. It was a beautiful evening and our planned route looked appealing.

8

ALADDIN SANE

Alex is not used to early starts. In fact, this will be his first ever early-morning start. I wake him at two, shaking him when he rolls over and tells me to go away. Everyone else is still asleep.

"What the hell? Why do we need to go this early?"

"Because we have miles to go before we sleep."

Alex crawls out from beneath his blankets, fully dressed apart from his breeches and boots. He thrashes around looking for an extra sock he'd brought to pad out his badly fitting left boot.

"Come on kid. It's miles back to Chamonix and we've got some mountains to get over, the Fou as well as the Lépiney."* I realize I am nagging like an old man – and I am. He tells me to stop hassling, that he is doing his best and calls me "an old woman." That I am not.

We drink coffee from a flask left by the warden. Alex has what seems to me a disgusting habit of consuming condensed milk straight from the tube. Its gooey sweetness does seem to fire him up. His first big peak awaits. Switching on headlamps, we tramp across the wooden porch, no doubt waking everyone else, before the soft thump of our boots is swallowed by the icy mountain night.

The walk up onto the glacier to the base of the peak is confusing. The heavens are pierced by the jagged black outlines of the Aiguilles. They eat up the stars as we approach, rearing up above us as we put on crampons and rope up. There is harmony in our progress, measured by the reassuring squeal of crampons biting into snow as we work our

---

* Nowadays, the normal descent is back to the Envers via an adjoining route, but the recommended way in our guide was up the southwest ridge of the Fou and then a descent via the Fontaine Ledges on the Blaitière to the Nantillons. Having done the west face of the Blaitière earlier in the year, I was confident of finding the way.

way into the Fou couloir. The first red light of dawn stretches across the Aiguilles as the stars fade.

"Shit. It's too dark to be absolutely sure, but I think it must be about over here the route starts. Let's get the gear out and by then we will probably see enough to tell."

It is the right place. I can now see the line of the chimney that splits the face. But the glacier has drawn back from the base; the first pitch up an exposed slab is desperate and without protection. Alex follows with freezing fingers. I hand him the rack to continue up the first true pitch of the route, which looks straightforward. He climbs up to the first bulge.

"I'm too cold and this is too hard."

"Go on, you'll be fine."

"No I'm not. I'm in trouble here. I can't lead this in a boot that's the wrong size."

I take over the lead. It is cold, steep and loose. I decide for the sake of speed to lead for the rest of the day. I remind Alex never to climb again with boots of two sizes – he looks very unsure of his footing.

The pitches drift by, the sun comes up and the glacier falls away. It is pleasant. We are on our first Alpine route together and love climbing. Where are John Powell and Bouchard and the rest our team? Somewhere on peaks nearby, moving upwards as we are, sharing the same time and space but unseen. We are up with the clouds in no time. Or is it that the clouds come to greet us? On the summit, a mist envelops us and the wind picks up as I begin to rig an abseil. And then it gets worse. The mist seems to be buzzing. Then the ice axes start humming.

"Bugger. We've got to move quickly. Forget the Fou. We'll find our way along the Fou traverse."

A cold rain begins to fall and the cloud thickens. I put on my anorak before clipping in my figure of 8. Almost immediately, I am dropping over an overhang. I spin round as I abseil and realize something is not right. The wind whips the clouds away beneath me. The ropes are hanging into a void. I am abseiling the wrong way and nearly panic when I see there is no knot where the ropes end. A sudden and unknown strength takes hold. With one hand I hold my weight and with the other manage to get two prusik slings onto the rope. The strength stays with me back up the ropes. When I get back over the overhang, it drains from me like water from a sink. I lean against the rock in the lashing sleet until I recover. When I reach the stance, it is getting decidedly dark.

"What a fucking shambles," Alex shouts. "Are you trying to kill us?"

"This is great fun, kid, isn't it?"

FLASH – CRASH

A bolt of lightning X-rays our immediate surroundings; the pink granite spires seem to shake in the second the flash illuminates the col. The shape of the Fou appears projected against the swirling clouds by lightning. Then there is only murk and sleet sheeting across the ridge.

FLASH – CRASH

The Fou appears again. I see the direction we need to go, but the wind is so fierce, to abseil in that direction will be tricky. I am still un-sure of the exact line. I make a decision and shout it into Alex's ear.

"Back down to the top of our route. It will be safer there."

FLASH – CRASH

"Yeah, if we don't die first."

"Don't worry about that. If it comes, it comes, this isn't as bad as it can get. Let's get down there."

The wind is lashing the ropes horizontally. We are both already soaked. The wind makes even face-to-face conversation hard. Finally, I manage to get on the ropes and force them down against the elements. Chamonix and safety are now a long way away.

FLASH – CRASH

FLASH – CRASH

"Oh boy, this is going to be one long cold night."

One rope length down, we clear a ledge of rocks, get the mats out of the back of our Joe Brown rucksacks, sit down and pull the extendable sleeves over our legs. The storm slowly dies and the darkness becomes complete, except for the eerie light seemingly emitted from the falling snow. We sit with our shoulders against each other and the rest of our bodies pressed together. I wish for a sleeping bag, but what use would it be in this wet snow. As the snow settles, the cold in my bones settles deeper. I have had tough bivvies before, but each one seems worse than the last. We forget so easily. I know the night will pass, but Alex is clearly alarmed.

"You know, I thought I'd had it up there," I say to Alex. "There was nothing at the end of the rope from the top but a big drop. The guide-book must be wrong. There was no knot at the end of the rope. That was dumb. I was pretty glad to get back over the overhang and see you again."

"All I could hear was you shouting through the wind," Alex says through chattering teeth. "I had no idea what was happening, but at least I had the ropes if you did drop off."

"Oh thanks."

Alex slowly sucks at the end of his tube of condensed milk. I dig out a soggy bar of chocolate from a pocket to share. I slowly melt a piece in my mouth, making it last as long as possible. Then a second piece, then a third and then it is gone and half an hour has passed. The other half of the bar goes into an inner pocket. Then we just talk and shiver and try to keep ourselves amused with stories.

Each time we drift off to sleep, we are soon awoken by convulsions of shivering and beat our arms and legs to warm up. The snow stops and we stand up to warm ourselves, shaking off the snow and jumping up and down on our tiny cloud-bound eerie. Maybe our efforts have an effect on the weather. The clouds slowly fall away from the Aiguilles like veils. The stars appear in multitudes along with a new intense cold. We return to shivering back-to-back and talk about meals we'll have when we get down. The lights in the valley shine with the promise of comfort. That helps but does not remove the deathly cold. Alex's shivering is now uncontrollable.

"I think I'm going to die here."

"Don't worry about it kid, just stay awake and enjoy the view. You'll get used to this after a few times."

The night seems to last a week, but, finally, the blackness turns a dim grey. Looking up, we see the snow-covered route back up to the top. Then the mist returns thicker than ever. I dig out the other half of the chocolate and break it in two.

"Here take this," I say, passing half the chocolate to Alex. "As much as I don't like it, I think we have to go down the way we came up. The cloud and snow will make the descent from the Fou too difficult to find."

After a couple of abseils, we begin to warm up. We enter the routine of retreat. When the nuts to abseil from begin to run out, I cut a length from the rope to make slings. Alex watches everything I do as a dog watches when you are preparing food. I work as efficiently as possible, hiding my desperation – make no mistakes, try to be safe. Each abseil anchor is checked three times; sometimes there's just a thin tape around a tiny nubbin. Then the rising suns breaks through, easing the deep chill in our bones. With each abseil, the glacier ascends to greet us.

"Back in time for a late lunch with any luck."

"At this point, I don't know whether to think you are a complete idiot or some sort of hero. But if we do get down, I'm buying the meal."

The ropes jam on a V+ pitch and I solo back up to free them. The final abseil down to the glacier requires acrobatics to clear the bergschrund. A yellow mental haze accompanies us back to Montenvers and then a black haze of tiredness all the way back to Chamonix. I remind myself to bring money for a return train ticket in the future. We go straight to the Bar Nash. Rouse and a team are already there as rain begins to fall from a dark afternoon sky. He laughs at Alex as he comes through the door.

"Bloody hell. It's Dirty Alex. We thought you were goners when you didn't get back last night. First climbs can be the last around here."

"Maybe that will be my last climb, the last with Porter anyway."

A couple of weeks later, on a pitching ferry back to Dover, John Powell has purloined some cold, half-eaten chicken and chips left on a nearby table.

"Here, have some of this." Alex nearly throws up.

"I just want to be home and in my bed, then I'll think again about climbing, maybe."

9

PICTURE BOOK

There were some parallels between Alex's approach to climbing and his approach to the study of law. He rarely rushed to conclusions; instead he tried to find the rationale for any particular point of view or course of action. If he could not settle his own mind on a subject, he would either drop the debate or select some dialectical opposite to pursue.* That could be trying and annoying. Most of the time, he focused on what he was doing. For Alex, thinking was a process to inform decisive action. Speculative or abstract thought he considered a waste of time and a mug's game.

The flaw in this pragmatic approach is that it can box you in, a flaw shared with any thinking based solely on logic. To make a decision to follow a course of action meant you had to accept the consequences. It is perhaps one of the underlying reasons people climb big mountains. It extends the period of action during which there is no need to consider anything else but the climb. The dangers intensify the experience of the decision made. Alex was not a man to avoid a tough call. Not backing away from a decision was part of Alex's character. To do so would have been seen as weak.

After our season in the Alps, Alex decided not to quit climbing but rather to turn it into a way of life. That meant much more than climbing being a lifestyle. We had plenty of friends who had one of those; it usually implied more time in the pub and in bed than out on the crag. Alex realized if he was to overcome his fears about climbing, then he needed to get a lot better at it. That didn't mean entirely giving up

---

* Doug Scott points out that Alex's ability to argue both sides of a subject was due to his education by Jesuits at Mount Saint Mary's and being required to make an argument one day and the counterargument the next. See *Shisha Pangma*, published by Bâton Wicks, page 27.

everything else and organizing his life around climbing. And it didn't happen immediately, as with most climbers who aim to be professional. It developed over a few years.

To achieve his aims, Alex decided to do three things: first, climb as much as possible; next, find ways to keep doing it – meaning money; and finally, avoid going crazy or killing himself, as some climbers were beginning to do. Despite a later reputation to the contrary, Alex lived a much more organized and restrained lifestyle than many other climbers. Unless someone else was buying, two pints was about right for an evening.

During my second year of post-grad work, I moved up to the Lakes to live in an isolated farmhouse above the Duddon Estuary, ostensibly to finish my M.Phil. I worked hard initially. Every fortnight British Rail transported me over to Leeds to hand in a stack of writing to my tutor and then I'd go climbing with the club. By the end of the second year, I became disillusioned with my thinking and the whole academic construct. When climbing teams arrived at the house to stay, sometimes for extended periods, I would do no work at all. This was especially so when Americans friends came over on extended climbing trips. When Ken Wilson asked me to join *Mountain* magazine as deputy editor in early 1975, I accepted and so ended my investment in formal education. Although London was not my favourite place and far from the hills, under Ken's tutelage I learned a great deal about the wider world of climbing and the industry that was growing up around it.

So I did not climb much with Alex in 1974 and 1975, but this was when he made his breakthrough. He was greatly improved on rock and with winter conditions in Scotland more or less guaranteed in those days, Alex was also getting a feel for ice. The summer of 1974 was a revelation. It started in the Bregaglia. While John Powell was doing field studies for his geography course, Alex teamed up with Tim Jepson and did three very respectable rock routes from the Sciora hut: the west ridge of the Torre Innominata, then the *Piodakante* on the Punta Pioda di Sciora and, finally, the *Fuorikante* on the Sciora di Fuori.

They moved on to the northwest ridge on the Punta Albigna and then crossed the Passo di Zocca to the Rifugio Allievi, sleeping in the toilet because the hut was closed. They had two famous routes on their list, the south ridge of the Punta Allievi and the southeast ridge of the Pizzo di Zocca. But they failed to find the start of the first and left their technical gear behind in the toilet on the second.

"It was a successful trip," Tim said, "thoroughly educative and enjoyable. Alex and I got on very, very well on the hill; Alex gave me most of the harder leads, but otherwise we experienced the mountains as equals. However, for some reason I can't put my finger on, we didn't hit it off when we were in the valley and we hardly spoke to each other until it was time to ready ourselves for the next climb. I also recall that Alex had the habit of rubbing lemon juice onto his skin, believing it would stop it from wrinkling in the sun."

Alex parted company with Tim after the Bregaglia and with John Powell drove their van to Chamonix to join the encampment of Brits and Yanks at Snell's Field. They went immediately to do the north face of the Col du Plan and then the west face of the Blatière, with Alex leading the notorious *Fissure Brown* free, an indication of his improving ability on rock. After that, they did the Bonatti Pillar on the Dru. The route still had a considerable reputation, in part because of the dangers of rockfall reaching the start. The pair opted for the longer "top-down" approach from the Flammes de Pierre.

"It was a long hike up," John recalled, "and we bivvied just as it was getting dark. In those days we used to cook food in the valley and take it up in bags.* I remember we had liver and onions that night, a fact I could not forget all the next day. The descent before dawn was

---

* This practice was normal and meant a saving on fuel. On the whole, our knowledge of good mountain food was nominal. The value of slow-burn, high-energy food was not as well understood in those days. To save weight, we sometimes took freeze-dried food despite its high cost, but more often it was cheap dehydrated stuff. This was almost inedible and took too much water from the body during digestion, sometimes causing stomach cramps. When it comes to the most extreme examples of poor food choices, the award must go to Cambridge University. Alan Rouse went through a period believing dextrose tablets were all that was needed for most alpine routes. Most of us tried this approach until we realized that short bursts of energy from eating the tablets were followed by enervation. The award for the worst ever mountain meal also goes to Rouse. Having forgotten to buy food for a stay in the CIC Hut on Ben Nevis, extra portions of fish and chips were purchased at a Dumbarton chippy and carried up for the meal the following evening, by which time they were a frozen, congealed mass.

terrifying. We abseiled into the darkness in hopes we were on the right line to find the next station. The gear was sketchy. I remember one hanging stance with just a single rusty peg. We'd only brought five pegs for the route itself so we couldn't waste any getting there. We got to the start of the route and fortunately most of the gear on the big aid pitches was in place, just as Roger Baxter-Jones and Brian Hall had said. The only other aid Alex and I had done was *Cave Route* at Gordale. We failed on that in the dark after the first pitch."

John and Alex were well matched and keen to get as much climbing in as possible. As the summer weather deteriorated, they finished the year with a very rapid ascent of the west face of the Petites Jorasses. Alex took a 40-foot fall near the top when a ledge on which he was standing collapsed. He was badly shaken but recovered his composure. They completed the route in a faster time than their more accomplished LUCC friends Roger and Brian, who had climbed the route earlier that year. In the dark and with a storm raging, they only just managed to find the refuge on the Italian side. The weather had closed down for the season.

Returning to university, Alex continued his routine of climbing and studying. He now owned his blue Ford van. This secured his position as a full member of LUCC, perhaps even more than his growing reputation as an alpinist. He was not often boastful, but he was known to tell people how great he was after too much to drink.

Alex was also the club treasurer in 1974, a bad year because the club had got itself into extreme financial difficulty. The reason deserves a short explanation. In 1973, Bernard Newman decided to produce a commercial version of the annual journal. The idea was to produce a high-quality and entertaining magazine that reflected the modern British climbing scene. The result was snapped up by all the climbing shops and even some bookstores and sold well. Proceeds were used to purchase gear and fund the club's annual journey to the Alps that summer. The cover set the tone. Chris Bonington's first book, *I Chose to Climb* (1966), had the great man on the cover hanging one-handed from a boulder problem at Ilkley, apparently many feet off the ground. Our cover had many of the leading lights from the club hanging in exactly the same pose. But the final photo of nine frames on the cover was the punchline. The ground is revealed to be just a few feet below the holds, while Tim Jepson, on crutches and with his leg in a cast after a recent ground fall, stares up hopefully. The caption read: "They also chose to climb."

The magazine was Bernard Newman's first in his long career as an editor, and running the *Leeds Journal* seemed to become a prerequisite for a job at *Mountain* magazine. I followed Bernard's first spell at *Mountain* for eight months in 1975. The following year, Bernard and I collaborated on a sequel. This time it was more ambitious, with a colour cover and some rather risqué articles and photos that inevitably got us into trouble. It turned out to be hugely popular with the UK climbing fraternity, with contributions from a by now extended LUCC that included the likes of Jim Perrin and Rick Sylvester. Publishing even at the highest standards can be fraught with unexpected disasters. In hindsight, ours was all too predictable.

We finally got the journal to print only days before heading out to the Alps, far too late to organize distribution and invoicing. This would have to wait until the following term. We left the journals piled in their boxes in our digs with strict instructions to leave them there until our return in the autumn. But the temptation was too great for some conniving club members who stayed behind to climb in Britain. They loaded their vans with journals for excursions to Scotland, Wales and Cornwall. Most of the stock – around 2,000 copies – was sold in climbing shops and other outlets. The proceeds were rapidly pissed away into the tills of various hostelries around the country or used to finance gear. Bernard and I returned from the Alps to find a large printer's bill waiting and no magazines to sell to pay it.

As treasurer that year, Alex bore the brunt of criticism. The most telling shot came from the main culprit, who suggested Alex had been "unable to fiddle the books competently." The club was now not only in serious debt, it was also in danger of losing its status on the university's list of recognized organizations, with the dire consequence of no further grants or the right to run "fresher" days to sign up new members. Alex would have to explain what he intended to do at the annual club dinner, held that year at the Rose and Crown Hotel in Bainbridge, one on a long list of hostelries that would eventually ban us.

Leeds dinners were rowdy events even by our standards. By the time the various club officials were called to give their "official reports," Alex had consumed more alcohol than normal. When Bernard, as club president, called for the treasurer to speak, Alex staggered to his feet at the top table and pronounced: "Sa finanshul hituation issht bad. In fact issht very bad. No, issht wurst. Issht booggared."

Pausing for a moment, Alex managed to focus long enough to spot me sitting near the end of the main table. "And sa reashun it issht booggared isht because of shhat bashtard saht there," he shouted, pointing at me.

Alex then grabbed his table knife in one hand and staggered toward me. Supporting himself with his other hand on the table, he began spilling people's drinks and flattening plates of gateaux as he passed. No one knew what to do except laugh. Fortunately, when halfway, Alex stumbled. He keeled over, fell beneath the table and passed out. There was a gasp from the hundred or so onlookers. Bernard, not one to miss the moment, got to his feet: "And that concludes the treasurer's report for 1974."

It was not quite the end, however. We still had to find a way to pay our printer, Werner Trimmel, who was not only excellent at his job but also part of our climbing scene and a superb skier. He was also known for occasionally violent outbursts and as a hard puncher, perhaps the result of a childhood on the streets of Allied-occupied Vienna. A week after the dinner, Alex arranged for us to meet Werner at a Leeds wine bar to talk over the unpaid bill. He hoped that a bottle of whisky would help smooth the situation, but it had the opposite effect. Things started off chummy enough as the drink took effect.

"I've a great idea," I said to Werner confidently. "Let's produce a journal next year and you can take all the income to pay for the last two journals."

"But you will pay for the last one now?" he asked.

"Sorry Werner," said Alex, "we've got no money."

The truth dawned on Werner's face. We owed him a substantial sum in the middle of a recession that was threatening his business. Having decided he had heard enough nonsense, he reached over the table, grabbed me by the throat and swore he would kill me. In a flash, Alex pulled Werner's glasses off and flung them across the room. In the ensuing mayhem of what was now literally "blind rage," Alex yanked me out of Werner's grasp and shouted: "Run!" We didn't stop until we were a mile away.

The bill was finally paid through a piece of creative accounting of Alex's invention. Centre Sport in Leeds was one of the country's best specialist climbing shops, owned by a climbing friend, Dave Clark. It was where the club bought all its communal equipment, like tents, on account each year. The bill was submitted to the university and paid directly. Dave was a good friend of Werner; they went skiing together each winter. When told the sorry tale of the *Leeds Journal*, Dave agreed to provide us with a false invoice to pass on to the student union. Dave then paid Werner's outstanding bill.* Problem solved. With all bills settled, we obtained an additional annual grant from the university. I recall arriving at the salad bar one day to discover the half-dozen tables usually occupied by the club were empty. Realizing the cheque for this new grant would have been banked that day, I headed off down the road to the pub for a lunchtime session.

In the winter months following the dinner, Alex's climbing reputation advanced in a new direction, one that astonished some of us.** He had been working his way through the classic ice climbs on the Ben

---

* Dave went to Nepal soon after to act as Chris Bonington's base camp manager on the successful southwest face of Everest expedition.

** Ice-climbing equipment was changing fast at this stage. When Alex moved in with Gwyneth, John Powell took a university room on campus. Al Rouse and Mick Geddes arrived one night on their way up to Scotland. After a long evening in the pub, a few of the team went back to Powell's room, where Al took out his new ice tool, a curved Charlet Moser 65-centimetre ice hammer. At the time, most people climbed with one longish axe – 70 centimetres or so – and a short ice hammer, Chouinard's design being preferred. The new idea was simple: two long ice tools were better than one. By putting a hammerhead rather than an adze on an axe, you created a multipurpose tool. Al ably demonstrated this point by going up the wall and across the ceiling, using his ice tools and new 12-point Grivel crampons to good effect. Of course, everyone else then wanted a go. The revolutionary new system was a hit. There wasn't much plaster left anywhere on the walls or ceiling by midnight, but the slumbering ice heroes were too far gone to feel the lumps of plaster in their sleeping bags. The university caretaker arrived the next morning and threw them all out.

but had yet to do a grade V, the hardest grade back then. Having completed a grade IV route with another Leeds team member, he was descending when he spotted some familiar faces beneath one of the best-known grade Vs – *The Curtain*. The Burgess twins and Tut Braithwaite had just done the route, and Tut had then done it again, this time without a rope. He had just returned to fetch his rucksack when he spotted Alex.

"Hey man, if you think you're an ice climber, go solo this – it's in perfect nick."

The Burgesses looked at each other in disbelief at this wind-up from Tut, one of those rare all-rounders whose skill was matched by his composure on just about any ground. He was as good as any alpinist in the country. Alex couldn't resist and set off on the first pitch. The Burgesses looked on, fearful of what might happen next as Alex wobbled his way up. Luckily, there were a few buckets for his feet and placements from earlier ascents for his ice tools, but the route was not in good shape as Tut had suggested. The ice was shattering. According to Ade, it was a close-run thing. After the story got back to Leeds, we assumed Alex would now calm down for good.

That winter, my New England-based friend Roger Martin had set up a base in Fort William, a beat-up trailer that officially slept two but could accommodate up to four uncomfortably. Alex moved in for a fortnight, skipped classes and climbed daily. Two weekends after his precarious ascent of *The Curtain*, Alex soloed two of the great test-pieces on Ben Nevis – *Zero Gully* and *Point Five* – during the afternoon of 14 March 1975. This feat had only been done three times before: by "Big Ian" Nicholson, then Dave Knowles and, a month before Alex, Roger Martin. In one bold afternoon, Alex proved that his climbing had come of age. He could be considered among the leading ice climbers in the country, or at least the boldest. It was the platform from which he began to perfect his technique and created a reputation that he would have to work hard to sustain. It was also the precursor to many far more serious routes he was planning in the Alps.

10

NEW ORDER

The first ascent of Mont Blanc, the highest mountain in the Alps, took place on 8 August 1786. It was an amazing achievement by just two men, Jacques Balmat and Dr. Michel-Gabriel Paccard. Larger, better-equipped parties had previously failed. Both men were from the Chamonix valley, born in the shadow of the mountain, so they knew the environment and were drawn to the heights, albeit for different reasons. Their climb was burdened by the amount of scientific equipment they carried and by the necessities for survival: food, firewood and blankets. They carried long staves to slam into the snow and haul themselves up. It was a slow and exhausting process, long before the invention of ice axes or modern crampons. Balmat's fellow "guides," who learned their mountaincraft hunting chamois and/or exploring for crystals, deemed the route chosen by Dr. Paccard impossible. So it's not surprising they didn't reach the summit until early evening.

After the ascent, Balmat collected a large reward offered to the first to reach the summit by Horace-Bénédict de Saussure 25 years earlier. De Saussure was an accomplished scientist. Originally drawn to the mountains as a botanist, he began to appreciate the complexities of geology as seen in the strata of rocks and the slow process of erosion by ice and water. He became convinced that mountains held the secret of the earth's creation and that the world was much older than people had been led to believe.

Balmat was also given the honorary title of "Le Mont Blanc" by Victor Amadeus III, king of Sardinia and sovereign of Piedmont and Savoy. He became a notable guide and next year took de Saussure himself to the summit, making the third ascent. But Balmat, in the words of Eric Shipton, later became "boastful and conceited." His fame went to his head. Nevertheless, he lived a full and successful life until falling while hunting gold at the age of 72. Dr. Paccard settled down, married Balmat's sister and continued his medical practice, later becoming Chamonix's justice of the peace and a solicitor. He also had a successful life and died naturally at the age of 71.

Over the two and a quarter centuries since the ascent of Mont Blanc, climbing mountains has became not only a popular pastime in the Alps, it has spread worldwide. Members of the Alpine Club, founded in London in 1857, invented the word "alpinism" to distinguish between those who climbed for the sake of it and those who went to the mountains for spiritual pilgrimage or scientific study – or to gather crystals or gold, like Balmat. Latterly, "mountaineering" has become the more commonly used term, but the spirit of that first ascent of Mont Blanc has been continued in the concept of "alpine style": facing an unknown challenge and climbing it from bottom to top and back in one push, with only what you carry to keep you alive.

The high-risk activity of mountaineering today is often described as "a pastime" and mountains as "playgrounds." It does seem that is what they have become, at least in the popular imagination. In an average season, over 20,000 people a year climb Mont Blanc. Mountains have become places to set records and gain personal fame. A plane landed on the summit of Mont Blanc in 1960, and a helicopter on the summit of Everest in 2005. On 11 July 2013, the fastest overall time for ascent and descent from Chamonix was set at a fraction under five hours. We pay less attention to the climbing fatalities in this "playground" of Mont Blanc, but the death toll has exceeded 30 in a single month (July 2007) and, if all adventure sports including skiing, parapenting, BASE jumping and wingsuit flying are taken into account, over a hundred die each year in the Chamonix valley. The mountains remain a dangerous place to play.

During the course of the 20th century, the so-called Greater Ranges, the Himalaya and Andes, became the new Alps. As with early Alpine ascents, those of the world's highest mountains were described as "conquests." Nations competed to be first in placing their flags on notable summits.* But the mountains are also a place for individual exhilaration, adventure and self-discovery. The best mountaineering literature testifies to the fact that most climbers see "conquest" as a word that applies only to managing your own fears and limitations. That attitude comes through in the wonderful understatement of Alex's two articles published later in this book.

In the summer of 1975, Alex carried on in the Alps, where he had left off in the previous winter, perfecting his new ice-climbing skills and working hard and determinedly on rock.

By any standards, he had a truly exceptional Alpine season. Even getting to the Alps showed Alex was in luck that year. We had only one roadworthy van between us. Straws were drawn to see who would have to travel out by other means. Alex was one of those who failed to win a place in the van. On the morning we left, we crammed Alex and his bulging rucksack into the van and took him as far as the beginning of the M1 south of Leeds to begin his long hitchhike to Chamonix. We wished him good luck. It was a slow journey out that year with a number of essential roadside repairs on the van and we reached Chamonix 24 hours after leaving Leeds.** We pitched our tents in Snell's Field, cooked a meal and then headed into town to see who was around. Alex sat at a table in the Bar Nash drinking with some friends.

"What took you? I've been here for hours," he smiled. We were astounded. Within a couple of minutes of being dropped on the

---

* For me, there is a strong case to be made that the conquest of the 8000-metre peaks between 1950 and 1964 was an extension of the so-called Great Game played by the British and Russian empires in the 19th century. Tensions arose from the expansion of the Russian Empire eastwards toward Khiva and Persia, and a fear of continued British rule in India and hegemony over Nepal and Tibet. It led to the ill-conceived first Afghan War in 1829 that set the stage for geopolitical issues that dominate to the present day.

** Experiences in the blue vans were sometimes more dangerous than climbing. One game was to open the back doors, and then two or three of us would stand up and, holding onto the rain gutters, complete the remainder of the journey with whoops and shouts. One snowy night in Chamonix, John Powell fell off the back and no one noticed. On the next bend, Alex lost control and the car spun wildly a few times before coming to a halt unscratched. He set off cautiously again with the snow now falling heavily. An apparition suddenly appeared to them, a figure staggering down the middle of the road blinded by the headlights and covered in snow. It was John Powell. The car had come to a stop facing the wrong way after its spin. On another occasion in Leeds, with Powell driving, Henry Barber saved my life by grabbing my knees and hauling me in the back when Powell decided it would be fun to accelerate and keep swinging the wheel "until we get that bugger Porter off the back."

motorway, a wagon on its way to Milan had picked him up and dropped him in Chamonix. He had slept most of the way, unlike the four of us crammed into a packed van.

His circle of climbing companions had expanded beyond the Leeds club during the Scottish winter season. Among them were Terry King, Gordon Smith, Nick Colton and the Burgess twins, all formidable climbers and all sharing a vision of perfecting alpine style. In rapid succession, Alex did the north face direct on the Grands Charmoz, followed by *The Shroud* on the Grandes Jorasses in very bad weather with Terry and Gordon. They followed this with an unroped ascent of the Brêche de Triolet, this time joined by Nick Colton.

Alex then did the *Cornuau-Davaille* on the north face of the Droites with Tim Rhodes. It was Tim's first Alpine route, during which he dropped one of Colton's borrowed ice tools. Alex also soloed the *Swiss Route* on the north face of the Courtes and did the *American Direct* on the Dru with Chris Handley, leading all the pitches. After that he tried the Dru Couloir with Tim Rhodes. Having done the difficult first section, Alex got off route on the connecting aid pitches between the upper and lower couloirs, fell off and lost his axes. After their earlier success, Rhodes, on only his second Alpine route, remembers being annoyed with Alex for getting so high and then getting lost. Alex's only other failure of the year was on the *French Direct* on the Aiguille Sans Nom, where he was stormed off from high on the face.

The most exceptional climb of his summer was the first British ascent of the *Bonatti-Zappelli* on the Grand Pilier d'Angle with the Burgesses and Tut Braithwaite. The tale of this ascent is the subject of one of Alex's very few pieces of writing, "The Big, the Bald and the Beautiful," published in *Crags* magazine. The twins and Tut had been planning the ascent in secret for some time. Secrecy was often part of the game. New routes and important repeats carried kudos in the climbing scene. If a team's objective became known, a race might ensue, leading to too many people on a route and bad feelings. It was better to remain silent, even if it meant snubbing friends.

In some cases, it was impossible to find out what people were doing until the end of the season. Perhaps the most secretive British team in the early 1970s was Joe Tasker and Dick Renshaw. They worked their way systematically through a list of major Alpine routes, but it was only when we read *Mountain* after the season was over and saw their centrefold colour photos of the Eiger's north face that we learned what they had been doing. More historically significant than the Eiger was their second ascent of the east face of the Grandes Jorasses. Their secretive approach ensured that they were held in awe by the more extrovert scene at Snell's Field.

Needing a fourth person for the *Bonatti-Zappelli*, Braithwaite considered his options. John Bouchard, a friend from New England, who had already done a new route on the north face of the Grands Charmoz that year, made it clear that he was also seeking a partner to attempt the *Bonatti-Zappelli*, but as yet had no takers. For reasons never clear, the British trio opted to invite Alex to join them rather than Bouchard. One possible explanation is that Braithwaite and Bouchard were seeing the same girlfriend, and John at least didn't know this. (Neither of them knew that Alex was also spending time with her.) More likely the dynamics of the team would not have worked so well if the incredibly fit, competitive, hyperactive American had been asked to join. In his article, Alex described him merely as the "obnoxious Yank," but the two young stars always enjoyed their verbal jousts over a beer.

Braithwaite and the Burgesses decided to keep their true objective from Alex, telling him they were going to do an ascent of the easier, safer and more direct *Cecchinel-Nominè,* which had a number of steep rock pitches. The *Bonatti-Zappelli* was mixed with some hard ice pitches. Looking at the gear put together for the climb, Alex puzzled over the lack of rock pegs for what he thought would be a rock climb. Tut, relishing the wind-up, simply said: "You're right Alex, put in a couple more ice screws."

In the end, the team made a rapid and well-executed ascent. Alex was told the true goal only when they reached the hut. Although a passenger on much of the rock, Alex was, in the Burgesses' estimation, "way good" when it came to the crucial ice pitches, leading the twins through this section, while the exceptional Braithwaite rope-soloed the pitches above. In the meantime, Bouchard, "smelling a rat," had raced off after them, intending to solo up the *Cecchinel-Nominè* and surprise the other four. He got lost in the dark and ended up soloing a new route. To the amazement of the twins, Alex and Tut, Bouchard appeared at dawn 200 metres below their bivvy on the crest of the Peuterey Ridge.

"Hey you guys," he called up to them, "I just soloed a new route on the Grand Pilier. Can you do that?"

Al Burgess drily shouted back: "You're not finished yet. Better get up here."

When Bouchard arrived, he climbed straight through, telling the others: "See you guys in Chamonix." A race ensued to reach the top of the ridge, Bouchard and Braithwaite vying for the lead, while the other three trailed behind. The twins were the last to leave the bivvy and caught Alex slumped over his axe and clearly struggling, breathing hard and not enjoying the altitude. According to Alex's article, he was suffering the consequences of a bad tin of mackerel acquired from Braithwaite. There were two lessons that Alex took away with him for future climbs: avoid taking tins of anything that might be off, or hard to digest, and, at altitude, competition is a killer. Know yourself and know your pace. He accepted that he had fallen behind in this contest, forced on him by Bouchard, and in future he never again worried about falling behind others as long as he was comfortable with his own progress.

Now Alex was at the point of exhaustion and something had to be done. Adrian Burgess rummaged through his rucksack and found some amphetamine pills, as recommended by Hermann Buhl on Nanga Parbat. The pill slowly brought Alex back into action, but it took him awhile to get going, so Adrian stayed with him all the way. Once he felt better, they made rapid progress up the last of the ridge and all five joined together where the Peuterey Ridge ends before the final summit dome.

By now, Bouchard had forgiven the deception and was in a euphoric state brought on by his solo of a new route. All the team were in high spirits as they were about to make the final traverse of Mont Blanc when, to their amazement, they were suddenly joined by a solo

German climber who smiled and asked if they would take a photo of him. Everything is relative. They had been overhauled by one of the great alpinists of the time, Helmut Kiene, who had just completed the first solo ascent of the Peuterey Ridge, a worthy parallel to their efforts on the Pilier d'Angle.

The season ended with a road trip to Italy with the Burgesses, Colton, Rhodes and various girlfriends. The old blue Ford vans had been replaced by a single big white Transit, which could carry the entire team. Weather in the Dolomites was not perfect, but MacIntyre and Rhodes did the south face of the Marmolada and the *Aste-Susatti* on the Punta Civetta. The holiday ended with a trip to Venice where the van broke down and the team more or less ran out of money. While the girls managed to secure free meals, the Burgesses got the van going by acquiring the necessary parts from other vehicles in the parking lot. They nursed the van halfway back to the Channel before it broke down again and was sold for just enough to buy train tickets home.

11

THE BOYS ARE BACK

The summer of 1976 found Alex working on a number of projects on his Alpine hit list. The cherry he most wished to pick was a "last great problem" on the Grandes Jorasses – the vertical ice couloir that splits the wall to the right of the Walker Spur. It was an iconic problem on a face that had attracted the great stars of alpinism for decades, as Alex points out in his introduction. Chris Bonington, Dougal Haston, Mick Burke and Bev Clark had tried to climb this route in the winter of 1972 using the kind of siege-style tactics then employed in the Himalaya. In his article "Cold Enough for Comfort" in *Mountain* magazine, Alex showed respect for his predecessors. But, for Alex, the greatest way to display that respect was to learn from them, then to succeed where they had failed.

Cold Enough for Comfort

If by chance you had been looking for Anderl Heckmair on the afternoon of 1 July 1931, you could not have done better than to be somewhere on the great sweep of glacier that flows down from the north wall of the Grandes Jorasses. At that time the face was unclimbed, but Heckmair and his companion, Gustav Kroner, were intent on changing all that. They made their bid in the Central Couloir, but turned back after three hundred feet so you should have met them on their retreat.

Their friends, Hans Brehm and Leo Rittler, were less fortunate. They adopted much the same approach to the problems presented by the wall, except that they started on the right-hand side of the initial ice slope, under the Pointe Whymper. They were wiped out. Their bodies were found shortly afterwards by Heckmair and Kroner, who had returned for another attempt – which they promptly abandoned, along with their general designs on the couloir.

The same year also saw Franz and Toni Schmid on the scene, fresh from their Matterhorn climb. The phenomenal Willo Welzenbach, and his equally talented partner, Ludwig Steinauer, put in an appearance as well. To men of this calibre, the initial ice slope must have seemed a tempting way on to the face, whilst the easily visible ribbons of ice above must have tickled the imagination with hopes of success.

All were very experienced ice-climbers. Welzenbach's remarkable achievements in the Oberland and elsewhere are well documented and the *Heckmair-Kroner* finish to his route on the Charmoz north face has impressed at least three modern ice-climbers I know.

However, none of these attempts met with much success. The spurs on either side of the Central Couloir were eventually climbed, but the couloir itself came to be regarded as a deathtrap. In view of the time-consuming nature of ice climbing at that time, a successful outcome would have been a tenuous affair in all but the most favourable conditions.

A dramatic indication of what one might experience on this part of the face came during the first ascent of the Pointe Whymper by Walter Bonatti and Michel Vaucher in July 1964. Initially, the pair followed the line taken by Brehm and Rittler, but then they moved up on to the rocks of the Pointe Whymper, where they made their first bivouac. During the night they were bombarded by stone-fall, which cut their ropes. Nevertheless they continued the following day and eventually found an old piton, which probably marked the line of the 1931 attempt. That evening they bivouacked again, under the shelter of an enormous bulge. It was just as well, because during the night there was an enormous rock avalanche.

Bonatti wrote: "I woke with a jump: the rock was shuddering as though in an earthquake. I had a terrifying sensation of falling … no, it was the mountain collapsing around us. As I stared up through the blackness I saw the slope beginning to give off fire as though a volcanic eruption were taking place. The air was full of a deafening, terrifying, continuous roar. In a moment the fire was pouring towards us, was upon us, incredibly passing over us. By its light I saw dark blocks the size of railway carriages thudding into the face.

"Each blow struck another fountain of sparks, while all around everything was pulverized and disintegrated. I heard myself yelling as I flattened myself against the rock, trying to retract my head into my shoulders, to disappear completely; then I stopped thinking at all and simply waited. A blast of air squeezed me against the wall, taking my breath away. The rumbling became less intense, the showers of boulders and sparks continued on their way towards the glacier. I was completely buried in stone and ice rubble, a freezing shower, which was almost pleasant as being a sign that I was still alive. But what had become of Vaucher?

"Before the thought was complete I was calling out his name just as his voice rose up from below calling mine. The mountainside was now still again as though nothing had happened, but I was seized with uncontrollable fits of trembling that only gradually faded out into sleep.

"As daylight came, the mountainside revealed itself transformed, almost planed. Projections and ledges had been shoved off by the thousands of tons of falling rock that we could now see spread out below us on the glacier, which was blackened and ironed flat for hundreds of metres.

"The first three huge crevasses and seracs had entirely disappeared."

Such incidents did little to attract climbers to this part of the world.

It was equipment development and the growth of winter alpinism that put the Central Couloir back on the map. 1972 was a bumper year. First on the scene were British climbers Chris Bonington and Dougal Haston, supported by Mick Burke and Bev Clark. They chose a line of ice fields and narrow gullies running up the northwest flank of the Walker Spur.

"By dawn our sleeping bags were damp, and there was no sign of a let up in the weather. After twelve days of effort on the face we were near the end [of] our drive. We had only eight hundred feet to go – probably two days' work in good conditions – but we were in no condition to sit out a storm. It was impossible to dig out a good ledge in hard ice, and the whole face seemed a raging torrent of spindrift."

Meanwhile a Japanese team, led by Yasuo Kato, had arrived with the intention of making a new route directly up the Pointe Whymper. This proved too difficult, however, so the group turned their attention to the main Central Couloir and, after thirty-seven days of effort, succeeded in forcing an exit at the col between Pointe Walker and Pointe Whymper. The following year, a French party consisting of Yannick Seigneur, Louis Audoubert, Marc Galy and Michel Feuillarade made the first ascent of the direct route up to Pointe Whymper. Having prepared the route in advance, they made their final push in mid January, taking sixteen days to complete the climb. They made use of a helicopter in stocking up with supplies and in getting off the summit.

Thus the only line that remained was the one that had been attempted by Bonington and Haston. It had been described as a line too cold for ethics. But it was a good line, one to be followed rather than constructed, taking the easier way rather than avoiding it; a classical sort of line, but in the modern idiom. And, above all, it was a line without end, a plum line.

Which is why, one night when 1976 was slipping into July, Gordon Smith and I were sniffing around in the moat beneath the 'schrund system that fronts this line. Haston had found a way on screws on the overhangs above, but it was now French summer time and we were most interested in beginning this affair with some momentum, rather than in indulging in a vertical takeoff. That meant a low-level girdle; a cluttered, magical mystery tour, up hill and down dale, inspecting the winter debris. ("Is this a foot I see before me?" You can tell he studied classics!) Fishing for Jason the Argonaut down a mean little waterhole, stepping daintily over the bottomless blue monsters, but boldly over the tottering white towers, all the while craning our necks, searching for the all-elusive easy way, for a button, a rune (so to speak) that would lower the magic bridge from the slopes above. But the slopes lowered an avalanche instead, so we scampered back to our happy home, *crêperie extraordinaire*, Frenchman fantastic.

Next evening, wined and dined once again on those amazing rum omelettes, we meandered off, budding Captain Cooks on a rolling white sea, away to stake our claim for England's Glory, for Queen, country and the SNP. Astonishingly, we had a plan. We would begin just before nightfall, and we would pincer, fooling this nasty bergschrund with an outflanking manoeuvre over near the Croz and, through this subtlety, this monstrous right hook, we would arrive miraculously, *à la* Brehm and Rittler, and move up and under, yet essentially across, sneaking past the mouth of the Japanese Couloir to the base of the insidious little gullet which is the key to this issue.

So we ambled up the ice slope to the right of the broken rock buttress that runs up into the Whymper, just beside a stone-chute that hails from behind the first tower of the Croz.

All's quiet … when to go?

"Now's as good a time as any, lads."

But now was not as good a time as any.

They did not seem to be in any great hurry at first, lingering on ledges to pick up friends, laughing and chattering, making merry little leaps, having a sort of jovial frolic, and all in slow motion. We slammed the gear in, hung on tight and waited. Then came general commotion: a din, whines and whirrs, a thud, a cry, and there he was, hanging slumped over his terror, LBWed on the knee-cap by a fair sized brick. ("I think I've broken my leg!") Then convalescing, clipped to a convenient peg in a handy rock island, while I hid elsewhere and mourned the impending loss of that ice-screw I had so foolishly lent him.

Nothing else came down and, when the appendage was sufficiently numb, we three-legged it along and carried on, in a curious canter up and across, but essentially under and close. Bonatti has been up there. You can tell:

"The spell this route cast over me stemmed from the fact that it had all the qualities that lend fascination to a route. The difficulties and dangers were very great, yet of a traditional kind, proper to the character and atmosphere of the north face in general … This time it yielded to my insistence, allowing me to make my way up its treacherous armour of steep, brittle ice, though truly I was like the prey in the jaws of a monster."

We felt a little like that, too. Mind you, the stones were not as big as railway carriages. About the size of an average dustbin, I'd say, but it

was a veritable avalanche of rubbish that bounced and leaped, rico-
cheted and crashed, and all so close, oh so close. How close? Nine
inches in 3,000 feet close. Thoughts of Brehm and Rittler. We snug-
gled in below those walls but Gordon took a little one on the other leg.
(By little I mean only that it didn't actually take his leg off – more dam-
aging to a Scot than losing his head!) We limped to a halt.

In the meantime, the weather had deteriorated alarmingly. Despite
the twilight, the temperature was going through the roof. An enormous block, a veritable Pullman special, screamed out of the Japanese
Gully and raked the flanks of the Walker. The effect of the rum omelettes was beginning to wear off. It began to hail.

So we aborted the mission and reversed the basic rhythm, diving
down and submerging, scuttling from one imaginary hiding hole to
another, until at last we reached the shattered pillar. But here we had
to push the boat out and run the gauntlet, rappelling, tumbling down
in the dark, the slopes on either side awash with white slurry. Finally,
we hung in harnesses suspended above the moat, with me craftily arranged so as to hang under Gordon, just in case. Then, with an ear-
splitting bang, night turned to day, and the whole spur was raked,
strafed and peppered from end to end – flashing, sparking, reeking of
the devil, granite on granite at terminal velocity.

Unbelievably, we slid into the moat and away, heat-seeking blood-
hounds, craving blankets and brews, heading back to our genial
Frenchman who honestly believes that "they" let us out of the loony
bin each summer just to come and see him. And, when the storm had
passed, and the day stayed that way, there was more rum crêpe; then it
was back to Chamonix, haunted by every passing Aschenbrenner or
lobster-clawed Grivel.

Three weeks of bad weather passed, and ideas changed. Terry King
turned up, and Gordon came back from Leysin. They directed their
considerable charms towards the *Croz Direct*. I wanted to do the Dru
Couloir and teamed up with Nick Colton, an "aristocrat" from
Longsight and one of the scruffiest people on God's earth. Once, having just had a vision in which he had cleaned the Fissure Nominé, he
threw away all our hardware except for an ice screw and a couple of

Bugaboos. (Ever lost eighteen krabs and twelve pegs at one go?) That night, two "enlightened" persons perched themselves on top of the Petit Dru, to freeze in the teeth of a northeasterly and study a starlit and by then plastered Jorasses north wall. Visions of Armageddon faded, and around midnight we cracked. We decided to go back for another try.

Which indeed we did, though we nearly didn't because I left my headtorch behind and so dedicate this affair to the congenial Froggy who lent me his, and to the half roll of Sellotape with which I repaired it. Ten-thirty on the night of 6 August 1976 found two little lads at the foot of the Walker Spur. This time we had decided to beat the 'schrund with a short left cross. Water was still running, but the face was quiet and the night clear. To start the spur, we took the left-hand rock alternative – the initial ice slope did not exist – and followed this as far as the main ice slope that cuts into the buttress on the right. Then it was softly, softly rightwards, to slip between the upper bergschrund and the rocks above, out on to the ice field for a tense tip-toe affair, like ants going the wrong way up a bowling alley, with not a sound uttered lest we bring the house down. We hung left to avoid being anywhere below the mouth of the Japanese Gully – vulnerable, so vulnerable. A roar: hearts in boots, we froze in fear, but it was only a plane passing low from the south.

At two-thirty in the morning we hung back on our ice screws, sorting the gear, roping up, peering and wondering, because it looked steep up there. At least, it looked steep as far as we could see, which was as far as you can throw a headtorch. There was no moon and it was dark in the couloir.

There followed five pitches in a grand Scottish illusion: steep, bulging, demanding, all engrossing, totally rewarding. Up through a spindrift flow, in the teeth of a biting wind. Belays for sitting, but not for falling. Few runners – no time – fantastic stuff. We emerged with the daylight on to the ice field separating the two rock bands. Around us, ropes darted in and out of the ice like frozen umbilical cords. I counted footage, but thought in cash. We rescued a couple of shiny krabs and took a hefty swing at a little blue sack, but its coffin was hard and rubbery and it would have taken an hour to release, so we left it with parting tears. It was no place to linger: a sensational, exposed, vulnerable, fifty-degree platform in a vertical sea, a mean place to quit in trouble.

Above, fixed ropes ran up a broad shallow gully of compact looking rock, but we were hungry for ice and, a little to the left, there seemed to be a connection with the runnel above. It looked a little like *The Curtain* on Ben Nevis, but the first fifty feet or so turned out to be unconsolidated powder, so we took to the steep and deceptive pile of rubble on the right. It was loose, a fact to which Nick swore blind as he sailed past for a sixty-footer on to a hapless second.

"Just hold tight and I'll monkey up the rope."

He did, and reached the top of the pitch for a belay. There followed a full and interesting run-out, on the border between ice and rock and, finally, we were through the second barrier, with one thousand feet of sensational climbing behind us. Then it was away up the cold blue runnel that broadens out into the second ice field. We front-pointed. Audoubert understands:

"Now begins that very special ice dance, a rhythmic ballet in four movements, a mixture of barbaric and primitive gestures and classical movement. The character before his mirror of ice makes precise steps with his front points, like a lead dancer rehearsing. In this special ballet pirouettes are forbidden. The emphasis on the curve of his calves and the strength of his ankles equals the fierce, attacking look on his face. The best dancer, like the best toreador, strikes only once."

It was a long haul. Away to our right we could pick out more ropes, relics of the mammoth Japanese siege. Somewhere round here Lachenal and Terray passed by, but I think it must have been in pretty bad visibility. We heard voices but saw no one.

The ice was hard and, after three years' wear, my poor Chouinards (God bless him!) let my toes know there was no more curve left. What had appeared to be three pitches up the ice extended to five, and we regained the rocks with creaking calves.

The final headwall is about eight hundred feet. In it, a well-defined gully system curls up and left in behind the Red Tower, to join the

Walker Spur about two pitches below the summit. For about four hundred feet it is backed by a thin ice weep. But this wouldn't take the gear, so we kept to the right wall. It was mean stuff: deceptive, awkward, and inevitably loose. And this was no time for mistakes, for we were tired now. It seemed a long way from that nine o'clock rise the morning before. In the northerly wind, the rock was bitterly cold. Above, sunlit walls beckoned, but progress was slow and any thoughts we had dared to entertain of reaching the heat receded to the summit. Incredibly, we had seen no stones all day, but Nick made up for that by burrowing away through the rocks above. In places the second is nastily exposed. I took a slate on the leg, with much wailing and gnashing of teeth. Nick solved the problems of getting back into the gully bed by falling off.

"What's happening?"

"Nowt. Just fallen off."

… and finally we arrived at the summit of a dream, a couple of pitches down and desperate for a brew.

We charged on up but then there were these two little ledges just asking to be sat upon, so much more comfortable than the cold wet snow on the other side and so much more convenient. So we sat down, just five minutes short, to dine on cheese and ham butties, with coffee by the gallon. Rare moments: we were asleep before the night came.

Next morning we woke late. The weather had closed in and it was doubly bitter. The stove worked, but the theory didn't. Twenty minutes could only provide water on the rocks. We dozed over this cold brew until shouts from below drew us out of our lethargy. Two Japs appeared, fresh as daisies, despite their fourth bivvy. They were the first party up the *Walker* for weeks. We chewed hurriedly at laces and gloves and raced them to the summit. They had come thousands of miles to climb this hill. It was like Christmas on top of the Walker.

Oh yes, I nearly forgot:

"And they all lived happily ever after."

"Cold Enough for Comfort" was Alex's first significant climbing article. It was a talking point for everyone who read it. Its blend of history, camaraderie, community, humour and understatement made it an instant classic. A year later, he and I were on our way to Afghanistan. Alex had served his Alpine apprenticeship and passed with distinction.

12

SHOULD I STAY OR SHOULD I GO?

At the end of our exchange trip to Poland, Mick Geddes, the Burgess boys and I returned to Warsaw from Morskie Oko. Andrez Zawada invited us to dinner at the large comfortable house he shared with his gracious and accomplished wife, Anna. It was the night before we were due to return to England and the first time we talked seriously about a joint expedition for the following year.

"We can provide the equipment and transport, you can bring the dollars we will need once we are in Afghanistan," Andrez said.

It was simple, so it seemed. Everything was in our favour; the cost was incredibly low compared to organizing everything from the UK, and the Poles knew the Hindu Kush well, had good relations with the authorities in Kabul and a list of possible objectives. We had become friends in our weeks together. I liked Zawada. He was from a breed of climbing warlord that existed only in Eastern Europe, in command of his troops and able to get anything he needed from the state to make his expeditions happen. Some said he was too cozy with the communists, but he refuted this. He was Poland's equivalent of Chris Bonington, except that the rules of the game were very different in Eastern Europe.

"What is the difference between me seeking sponsorship from a corrupt political corporation, and Bonington getting money for his expeditions from big powerful capitalists?"

What the Poles lacked in freedom, they made up with a luxury not well known in the West: that of an intense friendship born in adversity to the repressive politics and economics in their own country. I understood instinctively that this degree of friendship among the Polish climbers was the secret of their successes in the Greater Ranges. I left

Poland with a plan to return the following year with the same team and head east.

It was not that simple in the end. None of the team who came to Poland that winter was available for the summer of 1977. The idea of a joint expedition seemed too uncertain for the others. Instead, the Burgesses and Mick joined a legendary year-long trip to South America with Alan Rouse, Brian Hall, Rab Carrington and an extended cast of climbers. Part of this story is told in *The Burgess Book of Lies*. Pete Boardman was going elsewhere in the Himalaya. I had to start from scratch.

Things became really complicated when I phoned the BMC to see what help they could give. Dennis Gray phoned me back the next day to say it was the BMC's job to organize the trip and select the members since the discussion of a joint expedition had come during an official exchange. The bureaucracy that Mike Thompson had predicted would emanate from the 17th floor of Dennis Gray Tower suddenly rang true. I seemed to be left high and dry, without a team and without the likelihood of official support, despite the ongoing agreement and conversation I was having with Zawada and he, in turn, was having with the PZA.

Having left *Mountain* magazine, I had returned to the 17th-century farmhouse above the Duddon estuary in the Lake District where I had worked abortively on my thesis. My uncle and aunt rented the place, but while they visited occasionally from London, I was on my own most of the time, working as project manager for the county council. I had a little money saved. To lose a chance to go to the Hindu Kush was unacceptable, so I continued to argue with Dennis. I didn't care who organized it, as long as I was part of the team, but I needed Zawada to write to the BMC.

Communications between Poland and a Lakeland farmhouse were complicated in those days. Calls to Poland had to be booked at least a day in advance. The local operator, invariably a helpful woman with a BBC voice, would put you through to an international operator, invariably a man enunciating like he was on the World Service, saying: "This is London calling."

"Hello Andrez. What news? Have we got support from the PZA for the trip? Did you write to Dennis Gray?"

"Yes, yes, the PZA will support an expedition for ten climbers: five from your country, five from Poland. But I need all the details of your team. Have you received all the forms to take to the Polish Embassy?"

I had, but I needed to find a team and get the BMC to agree. I procrastinated.

"Give me a month. It will all be arranged."

Zawada was still keen to make it happen and wanted me as the contact. But in the meantime, the BMC advertised for expeditions to bid for the opportunity to go. To me, this seemed a totally unacceptable bureaucratic intrusion, something more expected in Poland than the UK. Nearly 40 years on, I can understand the BMC's approach. I was known for Alpine routes but had never been to altitude. The Leeds club, from which I intended to draw my team, had a terrible reputation as organizers. This would be the first joint expedition with an Eastern European country to try an objective outside of the Soviet bloc. The BMC did not want such a potentially high-profile enterprise to fail.

In the end, the trip came together with a certain logic, but it was not the way any of us would have organized it. Another team did apply, but there were only four of them and the intention was for five climbers from each country. Howard Lancaster, Peter Holden and Malcolm Howells had been to the Hindu Kush the previous year and were keen to return to the big walls they had spotted in the Mandaras Valley. As it happened, this was the location Zawada also favoured. The final member was Terry King, an excellent alpinist and Scottish winter expert who had climbed with Alex. In the summer of 1975, they had done *The Shroud* on the Grandes Jorasses and the north face of the Grands Charmoz together. At last, since the plan was originally mine, Dennis agreed that I become the fifth member. Since Zawada and I were by now talking dates, finance and logistics, I met Peter Holden, the leader of the British contingent.

It was a good team, even if only three had high-altitude experience, but it was April by the time it was finalized. I got on with the paperwork, the long-distance planning with Zawada and the writing of begging letters. We all had full-time jobs, but I worked flexi-hours and some weekends so could find time during the week. Lord Chorley agreed to be our patron and we also had Chris Bonington's endorsement. Boxes of useful food and accessories began to arrive at my Lakeland home throughout the spring of 1977. Malcolm Howells had a good contact at White Horse and also at Harrods, and soon cases of whisky and a huge hamper of specialist food arrived.

Zawada led the Polish team, as impressive as it was strong. Every one of their members had experience above 7000 metres on more than one trip. Marek Kowalczyk had been part of the exchange that came to Britain in 1975, as had Piotr Jasinski. They had climbed in the Pamirs and Hindu Kush, as had Jan Wolf, who was also known for some audacious Alpine ascents. The fifth member was Voytek Kurtyka, who I had climbed with on the rocks around Krakow the previous year. I remembered his aquiline and intense face. Behind this was a calculating but caring mind. Even then, he was seen in Poland as one of their finest, and most philosophical, climbers. Over all the years and expeditions that followed, Voytek was one of the few who could say he never lost a climbing companion on a trip.

LUCC members began to arrive in droves. John Syrett, John Powell, Adrian Garlick and a host of others made the journey ostensibly to climb in the Lakes, but the timing just happened to coincide with the arrival of loads of free "swag" for the expedition. I had to hide the whisky and food. Some of them, unknown to me, found my uncle's store of rare wines to supplement evening meals of fish and chips. They also had a great time taking the piss out of me for my high altitude pretentions.

The phone rang one evening near the end of June, a few weeks before departure. It was Malcolm Howells. "I've got some news you aren't going to like. I'm going to have to back out. My wife has taken ill and it's impossible for me to go."

Malcolm was the most experienced member on our small team. He had been my major support and help with planning. Departure was imminent and Polish visas had been issued, not a simple matter in those days. I immediately phoned Doug Holden, who I had worked with at the Eskdale Outward Bound during the endless hot summer of 1976. He declined since he had a trip back to Antarctica planned for the following autumn and it didn't fit his schedule.

Next day, Alex's blue Ford van arrived in the yard. We had planned a couple of days climbing. I cooked a huge spaghetti dinner and the following day Alex was climbing as well as I had seen him and talked about his ideas for the Alps.

"I've got a plan with Nick Colton and the boys. We'll finish our big three – the *Desmaison* and the *Whymper* on the Grandes Jorasses, and the *Harlin Direct* on the Eiger. Oh, and a few other things on the list."

In the summer of 1975, Alex, with Nick Colton, Terry King and Gordon Smith, had drawn up a list of routes in the Alps that they intended to climb completely free, applying the clean ethics and passion of young climbers of that era, especially from the UK and America. There would be no so-called French free, pulling on in situ pegs. They planned completely unaided ascents. One worry for them was that this clean ethic was no longer just an Anglo-Saxon obsession. Many French and European climbers like René Ghilini and Jean-Marc Boivin were drawing up similar lists and applying the new ethics. There was a race to be the first to do these routes.

When we stopped at a pub on the way back from Esk Buttress, I decided to try to persuade Alex to change his plans. We still needed that extra member and the Alps would always be there and there would always be new lists.

"Are you sure you want to go back to the Alps this summer?"

Alex sat at the table, pint in hand, giving me a quizzical look from beneath his curly mop of hair.

"What else would I do?"

"Fancy the Hindu Kush instead?"

His face became a picture puzzle as a range of emotions and thoughts went through his head. There was a slight pause and then he said: "When do we leave?"

"Good on ya – it's about time a Leeds team headed east. We've got three weeks. You'd better go home and get some gear sorted."

I was surprised how much work the often-indolent Alex managed to do for the expedition in the time remaining to us. His Scottish winter and Alpine reputation stood him in good stead with equipment manufacturers like Rohan. I had been totally unaware of his work with them testing and developing gear. Alex arranged for the British contingent to have their latest salopettes and jackets, which he had helped them develop as part of their specialist clothing. These were of a tough yet warm stretch material and proved to be perfect for the dry mountains of Afghanistan, with its relatively stable weather.*

Alex also had friends among retailers, most notably Brian Cropper, who ran the YHA shop in Manchester. So, when I phoned Zawada to explain the last-minute changes of personnel, I was also able to report that we would be bringing a selection of the latest ice screws and pegs, compliments of Brian, and a selection of high-altitude, freeze-dried meals from Mountain House, compliments of Eastern Mountain Sports in New Hampshire.**

It was a rush, and a time of uncertainty. A few days before we left, Alex arrived with John Syrett to help with the final packing. We then piled everything into his van and drove down to his family home in Letchmore Heath. On the last call to Poland, Zawada told me that he had managed to change dozens of bits of paper in triplicate to get visas sorted in Eastern Europe and Afghanistan. One question he asked several times was: "How many dollars are you bringing?"

"Plenty, Andrez – around $5,000."

"Can you bring more? That is not enough for so many people. We have difficult plans to achieve and the trip may last many months."

---

* Rohan provided shiny-gold, water-repellent salopettes and outer jackets for us all on Changabang in 1978, which proved ideal for the climb with sudden changes in weather from scorching sun to blustery snowstorms.

** EMS manager Rick Wilcox sent a huge box, including freeze-dried ice cream, which was unique. Rick expected a wholesale payment, but we had no money to spare so it was some months after our return before I could go halfway to settling the bill. I made up with him by purchasing large quantities of food for Everest in winter a few years later. Freeze-dried worked at lower altitudes, but above 7000 metres, it played havoc with digestion. It had the advantage of miniscule weight. Bivvys with the Poles in 1977 and 1978 became a ritual of tea or Tang, followed by borscht mixed with noodles or instant potatoes, then one freeze-dried meal passed between us, spoon in-situ, a quota of two spoonfuls before passing it on until it was gone. The meal always finished with hot chocolate. Coffee was saved for the morning.

"I'll try Andrez, but we're just climbers."

What Zawada didn't tell me was that he had been denied permission by the Russians to travel by train across the Soviet Union. He was desperate to get more money together to pay for flights or else the whole expedition might have to shift at the last minute to the less expensive Pamirs or Caucasus. I approached Barclays out of the blue, knowing that Chris Bonington had been successful with them in the past. When they found out we were seeking more money with only a few days to go, both our patron and Dennis Gray rang me to express their displeasure. What was I thinking? It was totally naive to think that a bank would, at such short notice, bail out a group of relatively unknown climbers, even if it was one of the few East-West expeditions during the Cold War.

I rang the members of the team to say we had to dig deep and beg or borrow as much as we could to contribute personally to the trip. In the end, we managed to scrape together another £1,000.

It would have to do.

13

SOMETHING BETTER CHANGE

Alex was never without music. His favourite ghetto blaster that came with us to the crags was now on its way to Afghanistan. He kept hold of it most of the time, but it didn't matter: we all shared the same taste in music. 1977 was a great year for punk, but we were also immersed in other new sounds: Fleetwood Mac, Brian Ferry and ELO; it seemed impossible not to like them all. Alex and I were about to get our first taste of high altitude, fuelled by the music. I can still see him at base camp, with the ghetto blaster nestled in his lap so everyone could hear.

Howard Lancashire and I spent the last night before leaving Britain at Alex's family home outside London. Jean fussed over us all evening and in the morning drove us to Liverpool Street while a neighbour towed their horse trailer full of our personal equipment and the gear and food we had organized, including the two all-important cases of White Horse Scotch we had been gifted for the trip.

We knew Howard only by reputation. He was an exceptionally strong rock climber and had already made a couple of first ascents in the Hindu Kush. We joined the lineup for baggage amidst many Poles returning home from work in the UK and watched as they haggled with the train officials about their baggage.* The last thing we needed was a hefty excess baggage fee. Howard, as an old hand, took the initiative and whisked most of the bags on two trolleys around the line,

---

* This was another anomaly of the era. Polish workers have always found a way to come to England, where they are well respected for their skills and willingness to work very long hours. There was a joke going around before the 2012 London Olympics that went something like: How will you Poles be able to prepare for the 2012 European Football Championships when all your construction workers are in London? Answer: They'll fly home in the evening and come back to London the next morning.

avoiding the excess baggage lineup. His plan worked. We helped him jump on a train that left 20 minutes before ours.

"See you in Harwich."

Terry King joined us at the station with a lithe, bare-footed, blonde Dutch girl who seemed very pleased with all the commotion. Terry had climbed with Alex in Scotland and the Alps. The fifth member of the team, Peter Holden, would join us in Kabul due to his work commitments. We were still overweight with the remaining bags, but we managed to argue away the time with the British Rail baggage controller until our train was due to leave.

He finally waved us through. "Get going; bloody students."

Jean and Terry's girlfriend waved sadly after the train as we hung out the windows and watched the platform slide away behind us. We stumbled to our seats through a corridor half-blocked with climbing gear, a feature of the rest of our train journey to Poland. Howard had prepared the porters on the dock with a tale of our planned adventure and they willingly helped us get all our bags onto the boat. It seemed sharing just a small part of our adventure was tip enough. We travelled through West Germany and then in Berlin we entered East Germany. It was the first taste of being behind the Iron Curtain. It felt far more like a front line than the relatively open society of Poland. All passports were checked and rechecked in the presence of soldiers with submachine guns. Fierce Alsatian dogs straining at their leads sniffed the undercarriages of the train.

In Warsaw, Zawada came to meet us with members of the Polski Zwiazek Alpinizmu, and we were quartered in people's homes for a few days as the rest of the Polish team assembled. Alex and I stayed with Andrez and Anna and were treated royally. The Zawada flat was far more luxurious than others I stayed in on my earlier trip to Poland. Both Andrez and Anna took to Alex immediately and he responded with great courtesy. The Polish shared with the British middle class a sense of social decorum and politeness, which Alex understood.

There was little time for sightseeing. The huge amount of equipment and food assembled at the PZA storerooms in Warsaw had to be checked, itemized on a central record sheet and then packed carefully

into the yellow hardboard barrels commonly used on many Polish expeditions of that era. Luckily, it doesn't rain much in Afghanistan since
these barrels disintegrate when they get sodden. Apart from Zawada
and Voytek Kurtyka, the three other Polish members of the team were
Jan Wolf, Piotr Jasinski and Marek Kowalczyk. We also had a climbing
doctor, Robert Janik.

I had climbed with Piotr and Marek in Wales during the exchange in
1975 and we all got on well as we settled down to the tasks of the expedition. As the total number of barrels was now more than a hundred,
we began to feel there was far more stuff than a team of 11 might need.
Then we discovered there was also an associated trekking party of
around ten, and that other climbers would be travelling with us. Two
of these turned out to be Alex Lwow and Krzysztof Wielicki, on their
way to make a few illicit ascents, but it was years before I realized the
extent expeditions were used as cover for black-market trading.

The big issue was finance. We did not have enough money to fly us
all to Kabul as the Poles had hoped. The plan now was to cross the
Soviet Union by train. We handed over half of our available dollars to
the treasurer of the PZA. I suspect this was traded on the black market,
and that greatly increased the zlotys available for last-minute acquisi-
tions of food and to purchase our train tickets.

The problem was this: we had no permits to travel across the
Soviet Union. The route was closed to Westerners at the best of
times but now was forbidden for security reasons. In advance of the
invasion of Afghanistan, huge amounts of military hardware were
being sent by train and stockpiled where we planned to cross into
Afghanistan. Poles would have to smuggle us, not in yellow barrels,
but by using a bit of guile. Zawada decided to take a big chance and
book the train journey. Who would notice five Western Europeans
among so many Polish climbers and trekkers? No doubt Zawada
had to pull strings and pay a few bribes when eyebrows were raised
at names like Alex MacIntyreovich and Terry Kingski entered on
the travel documents.

The six-day journey from Moscow would take us across the Volga at
Kuybyshev, now called Samara, then down between the Aral and

Caspian seas to Bokhara, and finally to Termez in Uzbekistan, which is where we would cross the Amu Darya – the Oxus.

Moscow was an eye-opener for all of us. It seemed a city occupied by its own army, like many Chinese cities today. We had a couple of days to wander around free of the restraints normally put on Westerners. Terry, Howard, Alex and I walked for miles while Zawada and the others haggled and bribed their way to securing our onward journey.

Although a beautiful city, the signs of oppression were obvious. I noted in my diary that it had "all the bad aspects of a big city but none of the good … dirty, sweaty, expensive, fast and turbulent. People push and barge about without any consideration for those in their way." Motorcades of Zils with Soviet flags on the four corners raced past, escorted by motorcycles. Unmarked trucks with darkened windows cruised the back streets. We saw armed soldiers jump from one of these and break down the door of a house, but we didn't stand around to watch. Like all the other pedestrians on the street, we hurried on as if nothing was happening. The number of drunks in the parks stunned us; these men seemed more ragged than the drunks in London parks.

Warsaw seemed positively attractive compared to Moscow. I understood why the Poles spoke so scornfully of the Russians. Zawada took me to Red Square. He told me how he had once been arrested and questioned about some anti-Russian comments he had made in public.

"They kept asking the same questions until three in the morning. I kept telling them that my father had fought alongside the Russians in the war and my grandfather had fought for Russia during the revolution. I just didn't tell them he fought for the White Russians!"

We stood in the centre of Red Square. The main attraction was the impressive changing of the guard at Lenin's Tomb, the soldiers moving slowly with their exaggerated stride. Zawada asked me: "What do you see missing here?"

I looked around. Huge hammer and sickle flags waved from the Kremlin's intimidating walls. Tourist guides were herding a line of

Western sightseers toward Saint Basil's Cathedral. I guessed some silly things: Harrods, hot-dog vendors, advertising?

"No, no, no – they don't matter." He was agitated. "Do you see here any beautiful girls like in Poland? There are none, the Russian communists have killed them all or use them for their own purposes." I looked at him, thinking he was joking. Zawada was both angry and serious, and the volume of his mini-tirade increased. We were attracting a few stares from men in fake leather jackets. I suggested we go back to join the others.

The most amusing moment occurred in the Moscow Metro. We had gone to see the famous socialist art deco interiors that seemed both magnificent and overblown. Standing on the platform, a man and a woman offered to exchange their jeans for our Western jeans and ten dollars. The second-most amusing moment was another tirade from Zawada when he realized we were going to have to offer two bottles of our precious Scotch to the master of the goods yards to secure a freight wagon for all the equipment.

"Polish vodka is far too good for these Russians. To give them Scotch is a crime." But it had to be done.

With the goods wagon, plus 30 carriages, our passenger train headed east. We were still totally in the dark about the risk we took travelling a route not sanctioned for Westerners. The Poles simply warned us not to speak to any Russians and answer all questions with "нормально" meaning "I agree" and "it's all okay" in the same word.

There were six days and five nights ahead of us to practise this one word before we reached Termez. The massive train was large and comfortable. Four of us shared each compartment and beds were made up at night. A large samovar at the end of each carriage dispensed free black tea to anyone travelling.

As we pulled out of the endless goods yards of Moscow, a continuous stream of marshal music from the Red Army Choir blared from speakers in every compartment and in the corridor. A couple of hours after we had cleared the suburbs of Moscow, Zawada paid Terry, Howard, Alex and I a visit as we sat playing cards around the expedition cassette player, blasting out Led Zep to counter the Red Army Choir.

"Alex, where is this new ice tool you showed me, this Terrordactyl hammer that you have?"

Alex got up and rummaged in his sack, pulling out the radically designed (and knuckle-breaking) tool that was one of his prize possessions. He passed it to Andrez, who hefted the tool appreciatively.

"Ah, yes, thank you, this will do the job."

With that, Zawada stood under the speaker above our heads and swung the pick into it. He then proceeded down the corridor into each of the other compartments in our carriage knocking each speaker to bits. We sat stunned as Robert Plant gained further ascendancy over the Red Army Choir with each blow.* Andrez returned from his work and handed Alex back his ice tool.

"Thank you," he said, offering an urbane and wry smile. "In Poland we do not allow this militarism and bad taste."

We fell into a routine of playing cards, drinking tea, talking, reading and sleeping over the next six days. Only on one day did we succumb to temptation and dig out a bottle of vodka, which we shared around. We crossed the Volga at Kuybyshev, and the train snaked on through low wooded hills. Some scenes were repeated at most of the stations where we stopped. Apart from the vendors, who moved down the platform with their trays selling food and drink through the open windows, there always seemed to be a camp of gypsies at one end of the platform. I was never certain if they lived there or were just waiting for another train. They would send their children to beg for sugar and cigarettes and other luxuries that might be found on a train from Moscow.**

---

* On my 40th birthday I had an unexpected pint with Robert Plant at the Blacksmith's Arms in Broughton Mills, one of Alex's favourite pubs. The now independent rock star had been to see Barrow AFC play at home that Saturday and arrived with a small entourage to sit at our table. He apologized for interrupting the game of crib I was playing with Rose. Had I not been in awe, I might have remembered to tell him about this battle of the bands.

** On the return journey, we found caviar on the menu in the dining car on one of the rare occasions it was open. I asked the attendant if it was possible to buy some caviar. "Только за доллары" came the reply and I understood "dollar." I returned with a large empty honey jar, which he promptly filled to the brim with black caviar for $5. I gave it as a present to my aunt and uncle, whose ambassadorial home in Geneva was a useful watering hole when the weather turned foul in the Alps. My aunt is Russian and was overwhelmed. She told me later it was worth at least $500 and of the finest quality. This in a small way repaid some of the losses incurred by my aunt and uncle when some of the Leeds team discovered the secret stash of wine and luxuries like the tinned lobster that cost John Syrett his climbing career.

Two days later, we awoke at dawn in the middle of the white and arid landscape of Kazakhstan, extending with pure consistency in all directions, perfectly flat. Once south of the Caspian, there was a gradual transition onto the more fertile plains of Uzbekistan. Every hour or so, we pulled onto a siding to let trains pass, headed toward distant Moscow loaded with wheat and other produce. They reminded me of the great freight trains of Canada, but these were even longer and the larger gauge of Russian trains made them more massive. As many as eight engines roared past us before the wagons began; there were engines in the middle and another pack at the end rattling the windows of our carriage as they passed. Many were adorned with images of Lenin and the ubiquitous hammer and sickle. At times we passed freight trains on sidings letting us pass. You could always tell which direction they were headed – produce was travelling west, trucks and tractors were heading east and, once or twice, trains loaded with tanks and artillery passed us, going who knew where.

At Bokhara, Zawada left us to fly straight to Kabul to deal with paperwork and permissions. Jan Wolf was left in charge with "Doc" Robert. At some time during the last day of the journey in Uzbekistan, Voytek appeared in our compartment, smiling and licking his lips.

"Alex," he said, "would you like maybe to try Bandaka?"

"Sure," Alex replied. "Do you eat it hot or cold?"

"No, no, Alex, is not something you eat, it is mountain. When you see it you will want big sheet. Here, look at these." He passed us each a black-and-white photograph of a great triangular face bearing some resemblance to the north face of the Eiger, except it was much bigger. And that was the opening gambit of Voytek's plan, harboured from before we left Poland, to organize a breakaway group within the expedition.

Although he respected Zawada, Voytek did not enjoy the big expedition mentality. Zawada's plan, and the one we had followed up until now, was to travel halfway up the Wakhan Corridor to the Mandaras Valley and climb a number of mountains from there. That is what the Afghanis had tentatively agreed to in our correspondence with Kabul, pending the essential bribes, of course. But there was only one clear plum in the valley: the north face of Mandaras itself, a technically difficult, 1500-metre face on a 6400-metre peak.

Voytek had a different objective in mind, the 2300-metre unclimbed northeast face of Koh-i-Bandaka (6850 metres), the highest peak in the central Hindu Kush. We would have to leave the main party and head southwest toward Kafiristan before entering the Wakhan Corridor. I recalled Doug Scott had made an early ascent of this peak. An experienced Polish team had tried and failed to climb the face the year before. It seemed a perfect idea, to divide the group to avoid any competition on the main objective in the Mandaras. Ten of us vying for the same north face might have forced us into a siege-style approach, which I suspect may have been what Zawada hoped.*

"Good, that's settled. Jan Wolf wants to go as well so we will be two ropes. Now we must say nothing until I have seen Andrez and agreed it with him."

The train trundled to the end of its journey at Termez, a small city in southern Uzbekistan on 14 July. The climate and rich agriculture resembled the San Fernando Valley. Well-kept orchards and fields of wheat were juxtaposed with rows of melons that seemed to have multiplied in numbers too great for the size of their vines. There were even occasional vineyards. It seemed idyllic as we unloaded the bags and stacked them on the platform, but not for long.

A Red Army captain and four submachine gun-slinging soldiers were working their way down the platform checking everyone's papers. As soon as he reached us, things became complicated and rather unfriendly. How could it be that four Brits were suddenly in their midst?

Doc and Jan tried to convince the Russians that the unexpected English contingent were not spies. Voytek joined in the discussion with his remarkably calm and persistent way that seemed to ease the tension.

"We need stay here only a few days. We go to climb in Afghanistan, international expedition, important for Polish People's Republic." He

---

* The Mandaras team had a hugely successful time. Terry King climbing with Zawada, and Piotr with Marek, made the first ascent of the north face of Mandaras. It was a technically difficult climb throughout. Terry led Zawada the entire way. The rest of the team got up major routes on mountains nearby.

paused. "Sorry, you should know from Moscow of this. All must be in order because we had no trouble getting here." In the Soviet Union, having the right papers was always paramount, but when they were not possible to obtain, having no papers was the next best thing.

From the Russians' perspective, any Westerner in Termez must have seemed a threat. It was impossible not to be aware that preparations for the invasion of Afghanistan were well underway. We saw more military equipment in just a few minutes than we had seen all the way across the Soviet Union. Lines of T-72 tanks rumbling past the station headed for big sheds on the river. Armed soldiers were all over the city and there was tension in the air.*

To our amazement, the captain relaxed after his conversation with Voytek and told him to come back every day to see if our goods wagon had arrived. He would tell us then what would happen.

We were put under a sort of house arrest in a small hotel. It was on a pleasant, sunny, palm-lined street opposite a large leafy park with statues of Lenin and Stalin. We walked unhindered. The only harsh words directed at us were the result of a lack of domestic decorum. We had draped our washed undies over the balcony facing the main street. Within minutes, a delegation of large Uzbek ladies appeared, wearing almost identical skirts and colourful headscarves to cover their hair. They berated us from the street below. We soon got the message and removed the offending clothing.

It was an uncertain time, however. Terry and Howard were in a state of demented despair, expecting the worst possible result. Even Voytek was not optimistic. I shared some of the gloom, a sense of imminent failure. We would probably not even get as far as Afghanistan. Only Alex remained stoically cool. For two days, we Brits contented

* The Soviets invaded Afghanistan from the north on 27 December 1979. The initial force comprised 1,800 tanks, 80,000 soldiers and 2,000 armoured personnel carriers. As in all previous wars in Afghanistan, resistance from united tribes was fierce despite the official Soviet story that the Afghan government had invited the Red Army in for security reasons. The war against the mujahedeen, supported by US military aid to a host of "freedom fighters" including Osama Bin Laden, dragged on until the final troop withdrawal in February 1989. When I got back to the UK, I contacted the UK foreign office with details of everything we had seen in Termez. It was very appreciative, but I was told: "You've got nothing that we don't already know." The good news for the West was that most of the tanks and eight divisions had been withdrawn from Eastern Europe to wage the Afghan war.

ourselves as best we could with bottles of fermented yogurt and playing cards, while the Poles tried to sort out the mess with the Russian officer assigned to this embarrassing case.

We gave him the nickname Captain Bollocksoff. For Captain B, it had to be a case of damage limitation. To send us back home or throw us in jail would have created a small international incident. We were, after all, the first joint expedition in this period of détente. Zawada had reflected on this conundrum in advance and knew the Russians would have only one choice: hustle us across the Amu Darya into Afghanistan as soon as possible.

Early on the second morning, we were told we would be leaving for Afghanistan in an hour. We packed up and piled into the truck to take us to the boat. The big problem now was that the train wagon with all the equipment and the Polish goods for barter had not yet arrived in Termez. Had the whisky bribe for the goods yardmaster in Moscow been enough? With heads bowed and cameras hidden, we Brits were sent across the Oxus with Voytek and Doc to Mazar-i-Sharif while the remainder of the Poles stayed behind to await the equipment.

Crossing the river on a barge-like motor vessel, we could see the huge scale of the docks, clearly not intended for normal river traffic. Machine gun turrets marked every few hundred metres on the Soviet side above well-irrigated fields, but to protect the population from what? I realized they were there to keep people in. Foolishly, I tried to take a photograph. In the same instant there was a shout and an armed soldier grabbed my camera. "фотографии запрещаются! Вы потеряли Вас камера! Pictures are forbidden. Your camera is forfeit."

Voytek appeared and had a protracted and calm conversation with the soldier some way off. I sat on the deck feeling a thorough idiot. I feared I was going to get into deeper trouble having broken an explicit order not to take photographs. To my amazement, after about ten minutes Voytek strode over and handed me my camera.

"Bury it deep in your sack. You know, we have a saying about these encounters with Russian soldiers: funny but frightening, like fucking a tigress."

The endless deserts of northern Afghanistan drew closer as we manoeuvred upstream. Customs consisted of a table with a rather corpulent Afghan officer and a couple of shabbily uniformed privates who tried to sell us large blocks of hash before stamping our passports. We trucked to Mazar-i-Sharif, meaning "tomb of the exalted," named for its famous blue mosque – the Shrine of Ali – with its exterior faced with the holy stone lapis lazuli. All the women wore a full burka, every man a turban of a colour befitting his status.

We settled into a hotel configured like a traditional caravanserai, the motels of the medieval trade along the Silk Road from China and India westwards. One large internal quadrangle provided parking for the ubiquitous Tata trucks. Three floors of rooms faced each other around the quadrant. Long caravans of camels moved through the streets to the edge of town and beyond. These were nomadic people from many tribes travelling in long lines of ambling beasts laden with goods. Women in jet-black *chadori* clutched infants atop the loads as they plied the timeless deserts between Rajasthan, Iran and Central Asia.* In the days to come, as we headed east on the back of trucks, we passed many black tents that looked like bats clinging to the ground, always pitched just out of reach from the road.

We were in Mazar for nearly a week. During the day, we played cards and walked the dusty streets, stopping every half-hour for a melon or diving into a chai house to escape the intense heat. I stood outside the mosque, transfixed by its interlacing design of spheres and the opulent facing of lapis. Some believe it is the tomb of the cousin and son-in-law of the prophet Mohammed, Ali ibn Abi Talib. Not far away were the ruins of one of Alexander's great cities, the ancient Bactrian settlement of Balkh, once the centre of Zoroastrianism. We could not explore it; the bags and the team might have arrived from Termez at any hour.

After a few days, the heat and the anxiety began to wear us down. Terry concluded that Afghanistan was a country "with only two meals, kebab or kebab with rice, and one song." But the kebabs were delicious and the pilaf rich and subtle with spices. The songs may have

* The Russian invasion, the years of the Taliban, new countries with "borders" and the rush of modernity has almost completely wiped these nomadic people from the face of the planet.

sounded all the same, but there were at least two themes, love for a beautiful girl and prayers for the love of Allah. At night, we pulled our mattresses up onto the roof into the cool night air. Horse-drawn buggies trotted past with bells chiming in unison on secret liaisons well into the early hours.

After a week, the bags from Termez had still not arrived. Zawada summoned Terry and me to Kabul to complete new paperwork. Voytek had argued our case for Bandaka with Zawada over the phone, and I was now able to add my voice.

"It is the best plan Anji. It will mean more peaks are climbed by your expedition."

Andrez agreed after some hesitation. Peter Holden had arrived from the UK and absorbed news of our current situation and the tale of our journey over beers and food at a hippy restaurant on Chicken Street. Walking back to the hotel, we spotted a British-registered truck with the words "Carlisle Kishtwar Expedition" emblazoned in bold but very dusty letters on its panels. I scrawled "Barrow Boot Boys Rule OK" in the dust-encrusted back windows.* It would be years before I met one of the expedition members and, until then, the Carlisle lads could not solve the mystery of who played the prank.

We haggled with Afghani officials for two days over our permits. Bandaka, they said, was impossible. We settled on the necessary bribe for the Mandaras Valley. It was settled, but it seemed our plan for Bandaka was now ruined: "It's perfectly normal," Andrez said, almost relieved that we had just one destination.

News came from Mazar that the bags had finally arrived and the team was about to move east to Faizabad. We headed north to Kunduz, travelling by bus to save money. Zawada wanted to hire a jeep. It was Polish National Day, so perhaps we should have been more generous, but we were dangerously low on hard currency.

From Kunduz, we reached Faizabad after a 20-hour journey in the

---

* Football hooliganism was a major problem in the UK in the 1970s amongst violent followers of some football teams. Gangs came just to fight rather than watch the football. There was also intense rivalry between the talented groups of climbers based in Barrow and Carlisle at the time. Nearly every weekend saw the addition of high-standard, high-quality routes by rival teams on the high crags of the Lake District.

back of a truck shared with local families, monks, mullahs, salesmen and military men on leave.* They seemed to come from all the clans of Afghanistan: Uzbek, Turkmen, Pashtun, Hazara. Most were strikingly good-looking. The children, especially the adolescent girls, were dressed in bright colours – too many to take in, like the languages and the rapid telling of stories shouted above the grinding roar of the truck. We shared food and laughed off the frightening moments, ca-reering on a single-lane road hundreds of feet above the river. Hashish smoke billowed from the driver's cab.

At a caravanserai in Faizabad the entire team assembled for the first time. All the bags were unpacked, re-inventoried and allocated to the different climbing and trekking teams. Voytek was determined to pro-ceed with his plan for Koh-i-Bandaka and we were amazed at how easy it was to create a false permit with the help of our Afghani liaison of-ficer Anwar. There was a shop with a large wooden box camera. We had a photo taken of the permit issued in Kabul, the word Mandaras covered with a piece of paper. On the newly printed permit taken from the photo, Anwar wrote in Koh-i-Bandaka as the objective au-thorized in Kabul. It looked surprisingly genuine.

Some of the yellow barrels had goods for sale to the Afghanis and more local currency was acquired. But at the last minute we were ex-pected to pay a large bribe to the local governor before proceeding. He was a large man and seemed pleasant and accommodating, but Anwar told us he was known to be cunning and avaricious. He held all the cards. We had enough dollars for the Mandaras bribe but not enough to add Koh-i-Bandaka. It was not looking good for our break-away group. Zawada again seemed almost relieved that the four Bandaka boys would have to rejoin the main party. Negotiations were at a stalemate when Voytek unexpectedly appeared in the doorway.

"Quick – we have one hour. I have negotiated for the four of us to travel with a Spanish team going to the same range." The governor did not quite understand what was happening as I hastily paid my

---

* At the height of the Taliban expansion in the 1990s, Faizabad remained one of the few cities unscathed and was the stronghold from where Massud and the Northern Alliance began their fightback.

respects and left. Zawada continued to negotiate the Mandaras bribe. Voytek and I scurried back through the dusty streets to the caravanserai and joined Alex and Jan to complete the loading of our gear onto the Spanish truck.* We were off.

---

* The Spanish had already paid their bribe and had hired two trucks, each of which, we later discovered, cost three times what Zawada negotiated for their two trucks. The Spaniards were happy for us to contribute a quarter of the cost for one of their trucks.

14

KISS THAT FROG

We trundled off toward the Wakhan, along rough hill roads, dropping periodically into fertile valleys. We spent the night on the roof of a farmer's house and set off at dawn the next day. After a couple of hours bumping along, the first majestic snow-clad peaks emerged from the shoulders of foothills and billowing clouds. In the late afternoon we forded the braids of a major river system flowing out of the mountains, heading to the Tajik village of Zebak.

By splitting the expedition, some of the Mandaras team members felt a trust was being broken; it meant some might succeed while others failed. Who had the best objective? To me it didn't matter, but our parting had been fairly emotional and tense as the rest of the group motored off on the rough road into the Wakhan. The four of us were now on our own. I recorded in my notebook some thoughts I shared with the others that evening.

"The real reason for coming all this way begins. I am sure we will succeed. Doubt has passed in the same way that happiness and loneliness are no longer relevant here. In the mountains, emotions should only respond and relate to our surroundings, and the few things we need to survive. 'We will make,' said Jan. Alex smiled. Voytek seemed distant but said: 'We are good group.'"

Fortunately for us, the Spanish expedition whose trucks we shared was on its way to a peak not far from Koh-i-Bandaka. We had become friends, especially with their liaison officer, Mr. Daoud Zebak; this was his home village and he cleared things with the headman enabling, us to go to Koh-i-Bandaka with our "permission from Kabul." I could see they weren't fooled by our piece of paper.

With donkeys laden, we set out on an ancient trading route

connecting Badakhshan and the Wakhan with Kafiristan and the Dorah Pass into Pakistan. We were in great spirits. To save money, and to train, we each carried loads of around 25 kilos. After eight hours walking each day in the dry desert heat, conversation was limited and our shoulders sagged.

During the walk-in, Mr. Daoud spent most of the time with us rather than the Spaniards. He explained that he was a Soviet sympathizer and wanted to learn more about life in socialist Poland. He knew the Russians were coming and talked of a future with roads, hospitals and schools for all children – and the end of corruption. Nearly 40 years of war later, Afghanistan has still to realize almost all his aspirations. Mr. Daoud was also a chess grandmaster. We all played a bit, but Jan and Voytek were both excellent and at least held their own in a few games. Over the chess board, they gave him warnings about the Russians, but he remained hopeful, believing communism would save Afghanistan.

The higher up the valley we climbed, the poorer the villages became. We camped in places designated by the headman each night and became the evening entertainment for the villagers. They came to watch these strange men who left their homes to seek riches in the mountains. The children especially gathered around Alex to dance and shout with joy at the sound of unfamiliar rock music, the Rolling Stones, the Who, Led Zep. After the third day, the Pamirs fell away across the distant Soviet regions and we became more enclosed in our own valley.

At the end of the fifth day, we reached a high mountain pasture and pass called Bandikhan. The goats and animals from lower pastures had yet to arrive. If we carried on, we would be in the fabled land of Kafiristan, the land of the infidels. But, to our right, a massive glacier with a mighty torrent racing from its snout led west. Rearing above the surrounding hills, a plume from the summit of Bandaka gracefully drifted across the sky. "We have finally seen our mountain," I wrote in my notebook, "a day's march away, disrobing from a sultry covering of cloud, like a woman before a mirror. It looks equally inviting and fearsome. I understand why the locals have called it the knuckle of Allah. If we are hit, it will be the wrath of God. The face will not resist, but it may not relent. The main concerns come from within us. Fear of death is not the issue, that is just the passing of days, the unveiling of clouds, the end of resistance."

Early next morning, we climbed loose moraine onto the glacier and set up our base camp at around 14,000 feet. We had 25 days to climb the mountain and return to Zebak to meet the team for the journey home. The massive northeast face rose straight off the glacier a mile or so away. For three days we acclimatized, climbing a steep line left of the main face up to a col at 20,000 feet, part of our intended descent route. We left food and gas and descended the other side of the mountain into Kafiristan, then back around the mountain in another day.

A week was gone and so was Jan Wolf, banished by Voytek. The bad cough he developed on our acclimatization climb got worse, not better. Jan did not want to go and Voytek had to be ruthless. Alex and I sat some way off, pretending to be noncommittal, but we knew Voytek was right. Jan left in tears to trek all the way to one of the Polish camps further up the Wakhan. We told him we hoped he would be better by the time he arrived; it would take him at least a fortnight to walk.*

We sat and watched the wall for three days. The mountain was real now, not just the photo Voytek had obsessed over. We all struggled to come to terms with what we saw. The 8,000-foot face was a battlefield between the force of gravity and the reach of altitude. During the day, even at a distance, we heard the crash of falling rock. The wall itself was complex: first a 3,000-foot section of couloirs and bands of rotten multicoloured rock, then 1,000 feet of vertical rock rearing up at half-height, followed by another 2,000 feet of mixed ground leading to a steep entrance to the final 2,000 feet of summit snowfields that were guarded by two huge cornices directly above our proposed line. I nicknamed them "the frog's eyes."

"And what if the frog blinks?" asked Voytek.

---

* Jan Wolf did indeed recover. He had an exciting solo trek first to the Mandaras base camp but, realizing that everyone there was already on climbs, he continued on and made a solo ascent of Noshaq. I saw Jan off and on over the next few years until he was killed in the Tatra in 1992. His wife, Mrufka, was tragically caught up in the 1986 disaster on K2. She set off for the summit and got quite high, but Al Rouse convinced her to turn around when he came down from the summit as she was going too slowly. They were among those who later died during the descent that only Kurt Diemberger and Willi Bauer survived. Jim Curran's K2: Triumph and Tragedy tells that story.

It was not an easy place to sleep. Alex's usual calm became interwoven with ambiguous emotions. Voytek tried to read the landscape as though it were a book within himself. I worried that at any moment we would all agree it was hopelessly dangerous and abandon the project.

The day before the climb, it nearly did unravel. Voytek had a serious moment of doubt. Given the serious undertaking, we were not well enough known to him, or to each other for that matter. Without trust, the risks would be unmanageable. Alex seemed to both of us to be in a state of near panic. He sat in the tent much of the day listening to music, rocking back and forth. He described his fear of falling stones to me several times. I tried to laugh it off.

"Don't worry kid, we'll just have to duck more than usual."

That did not impress him; I overheard him expressing his concerns about the state of my mind to Voytek, but by then I had purged all doubt. Doing the climb was the only thing of any substance left. There was nothing in my past I wanted to hold onto, nothing in the future I wished to aspire to, except the here and now; all there was in front of me was the opportunity to engage with the mountain and share something remarkable.

I spoke to Voytek outside the tent. We reassured each other and renewed our commitment to the face. Then together we joined Alex inside. With no further words, we dispelled our worries and got down to the basic practicalities. We packed our rucksacks for the next day, making a few final adjustments – four batteries exchanged for an extra ice screw, two Mars bars for one Kendal Mint Cake. We checked the number of tea bags, the cocoa, milk, and gas cylinders, then the stove and, finally, passed around handfuls of reassuring pitons to pack between us.

The sound of stone fall diminished almost in proportion to the amount of sunlight left in the day. I squeezed in an hour of complete peace sitting just above our camp, treasuring the moment, the panoply of stars above, the brightly lit tents with their human cargo beneath and the dark expanse of silent mountains.

Day one: In mid-afternoon, we work our way into the wall. I say "into" because the opening couloir is a gateway to a hellish world, one of darkness, fear and continuous threat. A mile above our heads, the wall leans out and throws down a continuous bombardment of rocks and ice. The constant explosions on the blackened snowfields to our left miss us by a hundred feet, suggesting perhaps this is just a game, the mountain just trying to frighten us off. On this multilane highway from hell, we are the only travellers on the road, tucked in beneath the right-hand bounding wall for protection. We stop to watch several car-sized blocks excavate huge craters in the snow, then, almost comically, like an oversized acrobat, they tumble end over end down the couloir and out onto the glacier a thousand feet below.

We reach the narrows at the top of the entry couloir at dusk; the mountain is sleeping now and we move quickly up safer snow slopes on the left. With headlamps on, we climb until nine then bivouac on a broad ledge, the best bivvy of the climb. With a meal of freeze-dried stew and endless cups of borscht and tea in our bellies, we are satisfied with our day.

Day two: The rock is like crumbly old marble cake, without doubt the most dangerous climbing any of us has ever done. I force myself to be doubly careful and yet some of the huge blocks we tell each other not to touch suddenly collapse into the void. Every pitch of the ten we climb today is another bridge burned. Near the top of one, an entire 20-foot rib suddenly dissolves beneath Alex's feet and the crumbs fan out across the wall beneath. Fortunately, Voytek has him on a tight belay and Alex gets back on what remains and continues. I lead the final two pitches with ice gear, kicking in my front points and placing axes in a trifle of yellow and red sponge even worse than the marble cake below.

Finally, we are below the central overhanging wall. We leave Alex to clear a stance and move left to fix ropes on two further pitches while it is still light. In the cold afternoon air, the face is silent again. Voytek climbs a ramp leading to the big chimney we have studied from camp. It is one of several that split this pillared overhanging wall, the one that appears most direct and safe. I lead the next pitch. An initial tight slot widens until I reach the bed of what is best described as a vertical canyon. At its back is a V-shaped chimney where the canyon meets the mountain. It looks hard but climbable. We leave the two ropes hanging so we can start quickly in the morning and rejoin Alex, encouraged that we can escape upwards. We settle into our three-man bivvy bag and spend an uncomfortable night on the gravel-covered sloping ledge. It is like lying on some impossibly steep beach with the towel repeatedly sliding out from under us. We are at around 19,000 feet, a third of the way up. At least there is a promise of sounder rock for the following day.

Day three: We awake at dawn to the pattering of stones from above. The sun is already at work on the frost, releasing this confetti of pebbles. The patter soon becomes a torrent, like road stone flowing into a truck, only there's nothing to catch it, just three fragile humans looking on. I suggest to Voytek that we need to get moving before it gets worse, but he has been watching the mountain more closely than I.

"No, we will wait until afternoon."

I argue, and even become quite angry. "We cannot afford to sit half a day with most of the face still to climb! This is stupid." Alex remains silent, noncommittal. Voytek remains firm in his decision and settles in for a long wait knowing what is coming. Then it really starts.

Just a few hundred feet from our bivvy, the central amphitheatre once again becomes a galactic highway; we're caught in an asteroid belt, watching transfixed as tons of stone falls past us each minute. The largest blocks have their signature sound, like a Stuka bomber howling toward its target, like angels thrown from heaven. We move hastily to a safer but much narrower ledge further away and await developments. Alex says he would rather be on Blackpool beach with the tide out. Voytek counts our pitons and realizes that even if it were an option, we do not have enough to retreat.

Our chosen line where the ropes are hanging gets its share of cosmic debris. Our chimney is like a cyclotron. Particles of all sizes accelerate before being fired into the abyss. All morning we pray that the sun will remember that this is a northeast face. Once the sun moves past the east bit, we should return to north face conditions. And so it comes to pass, at around one o'clock in the afternoon.

I have the worst possible job to start my day, jumaring the ropes left hanging the evening before.* I think of John Harlin.** The first rope holds and seems unscathed. Protective angels must have passed this way. I am halfway up the second rope when a part of the wall I touch falls apart, just seems to evaporate. Except it doesn't, and a hail of book-sized blocks, a full library shelf's worth, tumbles toward Voytek just as he is starting up the first rope. They pass over his head and angry Polish phrases float up toward me.

"Sorry, sorry, sorry!" I promise to be careful. Alex tells me later he expected to see my body amongst the rubble.

Miraculously, both ropes are intact. They are our lead ropes and much depends on them. Apart from them, we only have a static line – no good for leading – that Alex jumars. He seems happy to leave the climbing to us. In the canyon, Voytek takes off his sack and starts up the chimney, bridging most of it. The climbing looks awkward in double boots, and spectacular. We agree later it is technical – around English 5b (5.10a) – but we aren't really counting. One hundred and twenty feet up, Voytek is climbing smoothly and calmly up the overhanging chimney. My nerves are beginning to settle as the difficulty and danger seem manageable again with a master at work. He stops below a large overhang, which is really a massive chockstone the size of a car, wedged in the chimney. After a short pause and a warning to take care, he pirouettes up and over the hanging block far above our heads. There is a sudden shout of panic and then half the block comes crashing down, just missing us. Miraculously, Voytek has somehow

* Jumars are mechanical ascenders that slide up the rope but lock when weight is put on them. By attaching one to the waist harness and one to etriers, long slings with multiple loops for feet, it is possible to use a frog-like action to move upwards on the rope – step up, slide up the harness jumar, sit and lock, slide up the etrier jumar, step up, slide up the harness, sit and lock, etc. – yes, it's that tedious.

** John Harlin was an iconic American climber whose vision was to make a new route directly up the centre of the north face of the Eiger. The completed route is much harder than the original 1938 route. They sieged the face in 1966 and Harlin was killed falling from high on the face when the rope he was jumaring snapped. Alex made the first alpine-style ascent just after Bandaka.

managed to jump onto the remaining solid half of the block. Alex and I look at each other with sparks in our eyes and the smell of cordite in our noses. I follow the pitch, also without a sack. The mountain is now completely still; all the angels have fallen. Once on top of the big chockstone, I haul the two heavy sacks up hand-over-hand. Voytek shouts down to leave them for Alex. I explain this will save time rather than Alex needing to jumar three times with each one. He understands and takes the sacks up to his stance 20 feet higher.

It is getting dark when I reach the stance and lead through. A bulging, narrow chimney ends in a hand-jamming crack filled with ice. I nearly fall off the final overhang, but don't, because I am 40 feet up and there is no protection. Now a 45-degree rocky ramp leads right. A couple of hundred feet above, like looking through a gun sight, I can see the last of the evening light.

We scramble and climb our way up the exit ramp, with headlamps spraying light left and right, to escape the muzzle of the cyclotron. At the top, we emerge into a planetarium – the stars are spread above us. We have cracked the main difficulties of the wall. We take renewed care, as we do each night, dig into our sacks, drop nothing, put sleeping bags behind perched blocks, boil up borscht and noodles, settle in, try to get comfortable.

Day four: When I open my eyes in the clear dawn, I discover why it has been a draughty night. An icy breeze is venting upwards from a 4,000-foot hole in the world just over my left shoulder. Above us, like a golden ice cream cone, 3,000 feet of new wall awaits, basking in the morning sun.

The climbing is pleasant, up a mixture of slabs, short rock walls and melting icefields. At times, we scramble together unroped to increase speed. In this way, we gain 2,000 feet and stop in the late afternoon to take an early bivvy on a comfortable and safe ledge. It is time to catch up on eating and sleeping, which have been in short supply the past three days. Once again, we share our three-man bivvy sack.

Day five: The weather remains perfect, but the wall steepens into more technical ground. At breakfast, I bandage my fingers with tape to cover the deepest lacerations. Once again, Alex takes up the rear and jumars as Voytek and I take three leads each before swapping over, repeating the routine as the mountain falls away beneath us. We are rising above the surrounding peaks. The seemingly endless ridges of the Hindu Kush march in ranks toward the two main peaks at the eastern end of the range – Noshaq and Tirich Mir, 80 miles away as the eagle flies.

We still can't see the final icefield and the fearsome summit cornices. They are hidden behind a 200-foot wall that caps the lesser icefield we are now climbing. The sun swings away; the rock cools noticeably in my hands. We pull down jackets from our sacks. My last three leads of the day end halfway up the wall. Voytek turns the overhanging lip magnificently on the right. In the evening glow, we reach the 65-degree summit ice and hack out a ledge big enough for the three of us to make a sitting belay. The ritual begins as we pass the pot of food back and forth between us, each taking two spoonfulls of instant potatoes and cheese before passing it on, content and amazed by our bench in the sky at 21,500 feet. Then Voytek has to spoil it.

"You see there the Pamirs? That one big peak on the far left? Last year two Russians climbed a big face for three days and couldn't get through the cornices at the top, so they had to go back down."

"Well that's great, Voytek, we've already established we can't get back down from here."

Day six: Dawn breaks slowly behind the great peaks to the east, gently gathering pace and strength as it scrolls through a spectrum of pastels. By the time the sun splits open the horizon, we have nearly finished our porridge.

The summit icefield is like *The Shroud* on the Grandes Jorasses, steep but straightforward, except for one rock step, which I tickle over on front points. The overhanging "frog's eyes" seem to stay motionless at first, but after eight pitches we are passing up the bridge of the nose between them. There is one final unwanted surprise. From base camp, we thought the frog's eyes were the summit cornice. In fact, they hide from view a final cornice now hanging over our heads.

I remember Voytek's words from the evening before, but none of us says a word.

The ice has now hardened into the familiar black steel of a winter alpine face and has steepened. Voytek and I are debating the options when Alex arrives at the stance. Voytek thinks it might be possible to go left, I wonder what happens out right. Alex clips onto the ice screws, smiles and, looking up, says: "My turn guys."

Alex has woken up. We are now in his domain.

"You are like the fabled monkey," Voytek says, "or maybe just joker in the pack."

Alex takes the ice screws, organizes them carefully on two kara-biners on either side of his harness. He takes four deep breaths, exhaling like a locomotive gathering steam, then makes a perfect placement with his axe in the ice above. He leads nearly a full rope length with one screw for protection before he cuts a narrow stance in the hard ice and brings us up in tandem.

We are now only 20 feet below the bottom of the cornice. It looks impenetrable. Alex takes the recovered ice screw and sets off again. With a grin, I agree he is a bit like a monkey. His front points barely scratch the surface as he tiptoes up near-vertical ice. Unexpectedly, he finds a hole at the base of the cornice, climbs in and rests. While gazing at the unlikely prospect of ice now stretching 20 feet out over his head, he spies a slice cut deeply into the cornice, which leads diagonally up and right. It ends in a wedge of deep blue sky.

Alex shouts down his news and begins to squirm and chimney up and out toward the lip. Thirty feet later, he is looking down through a hole at his alarmed companions. To him, we appear as red-jacketed gnats on a vertical mirror. Then Alex rolls onto his back, swings his Terrordactyl and takes a comforting bite into the hard ice above. His arse hangs in space for a moment, then he gyrates up and out of sight. There is a shout of elation.

I am last up and roll out onto the broad summit plateau. I am facing a new horizon at last, new ranges of peaks tumbling away to the west and south.

"Bloody hell," I say, "it's as flat as the top of Ben Nevis up here."

Voytek and Alex are 30 feet back from the edge with axes sunk deep for a belay. I stagger toward them, arms dragging, spirits flying.

"You look like you've just seen heaven."

"I guess this is as close as we'll get, kid."

We stay too long on the summit, brewing a drink, watching the vast shadow of Bandaka reach out toward Tirich Mir and know a summit bivvy and early start down is now the best option rather than face the collapsing *penitentes* of the south ridge. The intense cold that night keeps me awake shivering, but dawn comes with a splendid warm sun and a full day to descend.

Day seven: By late afternoon, we have reached the col at 20,000 feet and retrieved our cached food and gas. We celebrate another night on the mountain with an extra bowl of borscht and noodles and then sleep well before starting our eighth day early in the morning, descending the south side of the mountain before making difficult crossings of glacial torrents in the valley.

Alex falls into a thorn bush. I wait for him when I reach the traders' road. In near darkness, we stagger up to the pass where we first saw Bandaka, then turn the corner onto the flat, sparse grass of Bandikhan. Dogs are going mad, trying to get at us when we reach the now occupied mud hovels. We are greeted by many unintelligible questions from the people here. One of the shepherd women gives us *naan* to eat, cooked straight on the firey embers of dried goat dung. We pull out our mats and settle into our sleeping bags. I chew the last of the delicious bread slowly, wishing for something more to eat. It is not long before the dogs quieten down and the lights go out in my head.

15

SULTANS OF SWING

Two days later, we were back down at Bandikhan, having collected all our gear from base camp. Until an hour before, it seemed we were safely on the road home.

"Are they going to kill us?"

Alex was half-sat, half-slumped inside our small dome tent. He looked very tired, but more curious than scared. My stomach churned with uncertainty. Voytek was sprawled unconscious across a greasy sleeping bag beside Alex. Three turbaned men squatted in the dust a few feet away among the litter of soup packets and sardine tins marking the boundary of our civilization. One of them had a rifle.

"I don't know what they'll do. It seems in the balance. These younger guys are really pissed off."

I recalled the tale of three British climbers travelling overland to the Himalaya who stopped to rest by the road near Band-e Amir in Bamyan. They laid their sleeping bags out side by side and fell into a heavy sleep. In the morning, the guy in the middle woke up, puzzled to find his friends had swapped places in the night, before confusion turned to horror as it dawned on him it was only their heads that had switched. This was one of the more sanguinary practical jokes in the annals of climbing lore, but at least the remaining climber made it home to tell the tale. We were in a far more remote and wild part of Afghanistan than Band-e Amir.

Having descended to Bandikhan, Voytek and I had made a final journey up to base camp, leaving Alex with our gear. It was an exhausting haul up onto the glacier. The only relief was the pleasure in seeing the massive wall we had climbed rearing up as we approached. We found base camp completely intact and untouched. The sight of the tents made us whoop for joy. We had half-expected it would all have been stolen.

Opening the food barrel, we got out a tin of bread, sardines and chocolate. When I was a kid, there was a disc jockey on WMEX in Boston who raved about how good sardine and chocolate sandwiches were. I made one for the first and last time. We drank coffee and then I packed a sack of food to take back down to Alex. Voytek stayed behind to break camp and pack loads for the porters who were due to come up the next morning.

As it turned out, I got benighted and then lost, but that's another story. The real action was back at base camp, where Voytek was busy negotiating on his own. The deal was this: two tents, the leftover food and our ropes in exchange for a fist-sized lump of lapis lazuli, the elegant blue semiprecious stone that we'd seen covering the mosque in Mazar-i-Sharif. It is an unforgettable sight, the holy stone, dug from the mines of Badakhshan, prized by Titian and Vermeer as the source of ultramarine pigment inlaid into the death masks of the pharaohs. To Voytek, the trade was a good deal. I suspect it formed part of a game plan discussed in Warsaw months before. This was how the climbing life was financed in a 1970s socialist state.

But Voytek was now caught in a very dangerous game. The Afghanis had no intention of allowing him to keep the lapis. We knew nothing of the deal when an elated Voytek rejoined us at Bandikhan. Three porters dropped their loads near us; another trio still fully loaded showed a dusty pair of heels as they ran to the stone hovels with the fruits of the trade. We celebrated our reunion with a bowl of soup and tinned Polish bread, more sardines, more chocolate.

As we relaxed, a Pathan with the face of a mauled dog approached, the three stripes sewn on his filthy jacket supposedly a sign of authority. A turbaned henchman with a homemade rifle stood nearby.

"Hand over the stone," he said in Pashto, gesturing with one hand and pointing to his stripes with the other.

"What stone?" said Voytek in English, looking innocent. Alex and I looked on totally bemused as a crowd began to assemble. We had no idea what was going on, but two months with the Poles had taught us to expect the unexpected. It soon arrived.

"That stone," said the Pathan, reaching toward Voytek's jacket. Our friend's expression changed as he realized the game was up, but he wouldn't take the situation lying down; we now saw the rage of a Slav facing down the eastern horde.

"Oh, this?" Voytek said, removing the beautiful stone from his pocket. He held it up for all to see and tossed it gently in the air. Then, in one swift movement, he caught and threw it as far as he could into the thunderous rage of the glacial torrent spilling from the glacier. As if to underline how permanent this loss would be, the lapis hit a glacial boulder protruding from the river and exploded into a score of ultramarine shards. The disintegration of our hopes was complete as the pieces were lost in the opaque river.

The roar of the water was overwhelmed by the wails of the assembled crowd. Some of the younger and more foolish ones tried to jump in, in search of the lost treasure. I raced to pull one kid out before he was swept away. The man with the stripes drew his finger across his throat and men with rifles ran back toward the huts. I could already see women hastily ushering children inside. We ducked inside our tent to await developments, and Alex wondered if we were about to die.

"I guess we'd be pretty pissed off if some foreign infidel threw our village fortune into a raging torrent." Alex was right; this was exactly what Voytek had done. Soon both men were asleep. I couldn't believe they could be so unconcerned but knew that extreme fatigue can be an effective anesthetic. Maybe under such circumstances it was the best way to go, but I forced myself to stay on guard.

It was then that I saw a group of bearded and turbaned older men crossing the rough pasture toward us. They took up position in a circle on a small rise of moraine just above the tent. There were six of them. The more they talked among themselves, the more I realized our future was in their hands. They were holding a trial. Our trial.

I moved away from the tent and sat deferentially below the elders, near enough to hear their conversation. There are times when you can understand even unfamiliar languages just by closing your eyes and trying to pick up the nuances. This was one of those times. The majority seemed to argue that we had sinned against Allah, and also against their clan, by destroying the sacred and noble lapis lazuli.

There were two, and one in particular, who seemed to take a different view. They knew enough to distinguish between the *Inglesi* and the *Poleski* who did not know he would not be allowed to keep the stone. They all agreed that foreigners couldn't take lapis. The counter-argument was that the brethren had acted wrongly in a trade that had been made in good faith. The youngest dismissed that argument, saying we had no place there, that we were infidels and our riches were there for the taking.

The oldest of the gathering was, I suspected, the one mullah present. He gestured to me to come over. He pointed to my boots and ice axe lying outside the tent. I brought them to their circle. Through gestures and a few common words, he made me understand that he had seen us climb "the knuckle of Allah." He then explained that when he was young, he went on a pilgrimage to the mountain seeking the word of God.

He pointed to the col on the flank of the mountain where we had descended, a point at around 20,000 feet. Although I did not understand more than a few words, I did understand what he was saying to me. He explained, his feet sliding in the dust, that he could not find holds in the snow, that he nearly froze and comically blew wind in my face to indicate the snow and storm he faced. For us, to reach that point on the mountain would not be difficult, but this mullah tried and failed to climb Bandaka with only the clothes on his back.

"With these," I said, offering him the axe and boots, "you would have succeeded." He nodded in appreciation. He took them, inspected them, asked their value and then gave them back to me with a laugh and a gesture that said: "I am too old."

I was sent away. They talked on in hoarse, argumentative whispers for another ten minutes, then gathered themselves up and, without a word, floated in their ragged robes back toward the waiting villagers. The man with the mauled face and stripes returned, again drawing his finger across his throat, snarling. The sun fell below the horizon, its dying embers reflected briefly on the highest summit snows. Alex and

Voytek remained comatose. I drew the remaining expedition barrels around the mouth of the tent, and barely had the energy to get into my sleeping bag. The darkness and the river roared in my ears as I slipped into unconsciousness, my final thought our lives were at an end.

The heat of the mid-morning sun finally woke us and drove us from the tent. It was another beautiful clear day. A band of sheepherders stood nearby and others appeared with ponies and donkeys. It was back to business as usual and we were soon bargaining to save ten cents a day on the cost of a load.

One of the elders approached. He made me understand that the mullah had declared a fatwa in our favour. God had sent us to test the people. The will of Allah had allowed us to climb Bandaka and it was the greed of the villagers that had tried to cheat us. They had learned a lesson. Voytek charged over.

"What did that man want? We cannot offer more money, we must be very careful."

"You're right Voytek, we need to be more careful."

We were at the end of the climb and the beginning of a return journey that would lead back over the mountains and down many dusty roads through the Soviet Union to Poland. We walked out during Ramadan, which meant early starts and long hungry days. Otherwise it was pretty uneventful, except on the last afternoon when I paused to watch the string of ponies and Alex and Voytek ford a fast-flowing river an hour before Zebak. When I eventually set off to follow, I missed the exact line across the river and found myself in danger of being swept away. Alex and the Afghani drivers sat not more than a hundred yards away on the other side laughing, until Alex realized it was actually a serious situation.

"He has the Afghanis," he said to the pony men, meaning the local currency. In fact, I had all of our remaining money. Three of the men bolted to the river and crossed 20 yards upstream, signalling me toward them with warm, toothless smiles.

The expedition trucks arrived at Zebak during the afternoon after our encounter with the Afghan colonel. We were in Kabul in five days, and after a delay of another week, even the Russians relented and welcomed us back onto their train in the good old USSR.* After all, we all had return tickets.

Thanks to my bread-shopping adventure in Poznan, I arrived at Liverpool Street Station a day after the rest of the team. Jean and Alex retrieved me and I stayed for dinner. Jean laughed at some of our stories from Afghanistan but others had her shaking her head and asking: "Why do you do it?" The next morning I caught the train north to the Lake District. Alex told me he was going straight to the Alps. Some climbers might have relaxed after Bandaka, but for Alex it was just a platform from which to complete unfinished business on the Eiger. He was fit and unwilling to fall into lethargy as the autumn rain clouds gathered over London.

Alex rang round on his first day back in the UK. He heard reports from Chamonix of great deeds, including Gordon Smith and Tobin Sorenson's second ascent of the *Gousseault Route* on the Grandes Jorasses only two weeks before.** At more or less the same time, Roger Baxter-Jones and Nick Colton made a free ascent of the *Whymper Spur*.*** That meant two of the three routes on Alex's checklist were now done while he was being dragged off to Afghanistan. That left only the *Harlin Direct* on the Eiger.

Colton and Smith weren't available – Gordon had suffered frostbite on the Grandes Jorasses – but the bold young American Tobin Sorenson was still around in Chamonix and keen for more climbing. Alex went straight to Chamonix and they travelled to Grindelwald at the beginning of October. Sorenson wrote: "It is difficult to look to the Swiss for encouragement for they frown on kids trying their mountain." For ten days they sat around waiting for good weather and then on 12 October they woke to find the weather clearing and the face plastered in ice.

---

* When we arrived back in Termez, a young Russian guard wielding a semi-automatic extracted a book of American poetry from an inside pocket of my jacket and looked menacingly at me. I smiled and nodded, and moved my right-hand palm down below my waist. He understood the gesture and quickly slipped the book inside his own jacket before anyone noticed.

** A few years ago it was discovered that Smith and Sorenson had, in fact, not done the second ascent of the *Gousseault Route* but had climbed a new, more direct route somewhat farther to the right. For the full story, see *Climb*, May 2009.

*** They actually climbed the *Whymper Spur Direct* (*Directe de L'Amitié*) – the second ascent.

The *Harlin Direct* had only been climbed three times before and always using siege tactics – fixed ropes and so forth. The near-perfect ice conditions meant much of the climbing would be fast, regardless of how sustained and difficult. The pair was well matched in terms of skill and training. Sorenson had had a busy summer. Apart from the epic on the *Desmaison Route,* he had climbed several major new ice routes, each with different partners, including the *Direct* on the Dru Couloir. (This takes the difficult central line into the upper couloir rather than detouring left.)

Sorenson's report in the *American Alpine Journal* gives a flavour of the climb. He reflected: "It seemed a strange thing to take only five days of food and a handful of pitons on something that had previously taken three to four weeks. But we, more than anyone, knew there was no other way." Alex and his like-minded friends were forcing the pace of change. For the Eiger, he borrowed from Gordon Smith a single rope whose diameter was just eight millimetres, unusually thin and, at 65 metres, unusually long, for that era at least. But then he had just come from a climb using equally thin and long Polish ropes.

Despite its difficulty, the pair made short work of the route. On the second day, a Swiss guide came out of the window that leads from the face to the Eigerwand station on the Jungfrau railway to demand that they come in: "Your climb with just two is impossible." They paid no attention and with minimal fuss and shared leads reached the summit in the mid-afternoon on 17 October. Then Alex went home for a break.

When I phoned to ask what the Eiger had been like, he simply replied: "It was like Bandaka but colder during the day and safe. What's happening with the Poles and plans for next year?"

We had agreed on Gasherbrum IV when we said goodbye to Voytek at the Warsaw train station two months before.

"Voytek phoned yesterday. He tried for G4 but we were too late.* It

* Voytek climbed "the Shining Wall" – the west face of G4 – with Robert Schauer in the summer of 1985. The extremely difficult mixed route took nine days and has yet to be repeated. They were caught in a very bad storm just below the summit and, after several days barely surviving, they were forced to traverse to the north ridge and had a near miraculous escape in a continuous storm. Despite the fact that the summit was not gained, the route remains for many the finest achievement ever in the Greater Himalaya.

was already booked. But the good news is he's got something else. It's the south face of Changabang. What do you think? It's a bit of a well-trodden mountain with three ascents already, but we need to agree something soon."

"What's the face look like?" Alex asked.

"I haven't got a clue. Voytek says it looks fantastic, a big mixed ridge like the *Walker Spur* followed by El Capitan and starting at 20,000 feet."

"Sounds interesting; I'll come up this weekend. Can I borrow a suit for the BMC interview?"

Alex had applied for the vacant national officer's job at the BMC. Peter Boardman had just taken over the International School of Mountain-eering in Leysin after the death of Dougal Haston. The interviews were the following week. The problem was I had applied for the job as well.

"You think I have two suits? We'll have to change in the corridor."

I was of two minds about the job. I lived in the idyllic village of Boot in Eskdale and had a perfectly good job working for the county council as a project manager. Manchester seemed a poor second choice com-pared to the Lakes. I had a routine, to run or climb most evenings and climb all weekend. Still, the national officer's job was well-paid and it offered time off for an annual expedition in the contract. Whoever got the job was definitely moving into the professional ranks as a climber.

"Great, come up – we can rehearse the interview together."

We climbed that weekend, and phoned Voytek to agree on Changabang. I did have two suits, both hand-me-downs from my uncle. Alex went off with a double-breasted suit that was far too big for him, but he looked striking in it, a mix of high style and total anarchy.

We saw each other briefly at the interview. He was going in as I was coming out. Halfway through the interview with Dennis Gray and Bob Pettigrew, I decided I did not want to leave the Lake District. That came over in the interview. Alex phoned me the next day, ecstatic that he had got the job, which served us both well. He would now have an income and time off to climb.

16

DON'T GET ME WRONG

The headquarters of the British Mountaineering Council were not to be found on the 17th floor of Dennis Gray Tower as Mike Thompson had suggested in his essay, "Out with the Boys Again." They were, in fact, a dingy set of rooms situated on the ground floor of a six-storey building belonging to Manchester University. The few windows looked out onto a parking lot; if you were lucky, you would see the thieves trying to break into your car before they drove it off. The busy roads and characterless concrete buildings surrounding it made the location psychologically as remote from the mountains as any place on Earth. Alex spent as little time in the office as he possibly could.

Alex had only been at the BMC a matter of months when we arrived in Delhi on our way to Changabang. Voytek was curious about Alex's new job, perhaps expecting a more dynamic role from Alex in the long negotiations with the Indian authorities. Terry King and I had left first thing in the morning to work our way up through the bureaucracy to get the necessary permits. Alex, meanwhile, was lying on a camp bed in the sweltering midday heat, swatting mosquitoes when they disturbed his reading. Chrissie Hynde and the Pretenders were playing on his ever-present cassette player. Without sponsorship from Duracell, we would have travelled in silence.

"So Alex, tell me, exactly what does a national officer do?"

Barely stirring on his bed, Alex pondered this question for a moment, then gave Voytek one of his mischievous smiles.

"It's not like you see me here, Voytek. In Manchester, I have an office and a secretary, and lots of people to delegate work to. Here, everybody else is already too busy, so there is no one for me to delegate work to."

Maria Coffey was Alex's landlady for much of his time at the BMC. Those who know Maria's writing may find it difficult to picture her in this role, but Alex was her lodger for nearly two years, and she had a deep influence on him during the remaining few years of his life. Her grief after her partner Joe Tasker died with Pete Boardman on Everest was beautifully expressed in her book, *Fragile Edge*. It was Alex who introduced her to Joe.

Maria met Alex shortly after a phone call from Tim Lewis, who had taken over as editor of *Mountain* magazine after Ken Wilson sold it. Knowing Maria had spare rooms to rent, he phoned to ask if one was free.

"He's a really nice guy," Tim told her, "and really sharp as well. He's just got a job in Manchester. You'll like him – his name is Dirty Alex."

"He arrived and I just thought he was great," Maria said years later. "I loved his energy, his cheekiness and all those rings of hair. So he moved into a room and immediately lived up to his name."

Maria recalled going into his room the day after he disappeared on a trip. She wanted to tidy but described what she found as a "rat's nest." "I gathered up dirty clothes and thought as I went along and the pile got bigger that I might as well do a complete wash. So I pulled back the sheets to discover a half-eaten bowl of Corn Flakes in the bed completely covered in mould."

Maria and I were drinking in a pub as she told her story. Her dark eyes shone with memories and her straight, jet-black hair shook as she laughed, recalling her days as Alex's concierge. "My house became a base camp for lots of Alex's friends. I can't remember how many times in the morning I'd be downstairs in the kitchen when a bleary-eyed bunch of climbers appeared." She paused, taking a sip of wine. "Years later, I bumped into one of Alex's Manchester friends, Nicky Connelly. He told me how much he enjoyed staying at Alex's doss because he got a great free breakfast in the morning. He had totally forgotten it was me who cooked them."

There were lots of wild parties. Maria had recently started teaching in Manchester, but she still lived a student lifestyle so Alex was hardly out of place. "Alex and I became true friends. I think that came from what he learned about dealing with women from his mother Jean. He had the ability to talk openly and freely with women he liked. He knew how to respect people's ideas, if not always their sensitivities."

Maria continued: "He was sweet, really, and gave me advice, almost like a brother. There were times when I really needed to talk to someone and he would draw back and really listen. And then the lawyer would come out in him. He'd ask pointed questions like: 'Are you really happy with that guy?'"

The one thing that drove Maria mad was the way Alex would habitually pick an argument. When in that mood, whatever anyone said, he would take the opposite view. That was a consequence of his legal training; he was able to see all sides of a story. It gave him the ability to hold his own in any debate and was a key skill at the BMC. Alex was far from lazy during his BMC days, whatever he may have told Voytek. In fact, he was quite the opposite. He brought tremendous flair and creativity to the job at a turning point in British mountaineering when politicians were considering tampering with the basic freedoms of the sport.

Alex's tenure began with a visit from the past. On his first day at the office, Alex's past at Leeds University came to haunt him. Dennis Gray opened a letter from the new president of the Leeds University Climbing Club. They were applying for affiliation to the BMC.

"Here Alex," he said, "this is clearly right up your street. Respond to this letter and welcome them into the fold."

It was only three years since Alex's famous treasurer's report to the club, and only a year since Alex had been its vice-president, but a new regime was now running the club, and it was very different to the old one. The university had given club officials one last chance to put right our legacy of chaotic finances, no written records and an empty storeroom. They needed to convince the student union that LUCC was still worthy of grant support and should remain as a registered bona fide organization supported on campus. We had gone through the same trauma every year, but the new officers had clearly decided they needed a new image.

They renounced all previous anti-BMC sentiments expressed by the club in our various Leeds journals and were instead anxious to become fully paid-up affiliated members. It might have been a moment of acute embarrassment, but not for Alex. He wrote back to the new club president, explaining that now that the Leeds University Climbing Club had taken over the BMC, he was perfectly happy to accept their cheque.

Even so, Alex took a big risk with his image when he joined the BMC. It was a risk he willingly took on, because it meant he had moved into the ranks of professional climbers. He had no plans to make the BMC a career. He knew that Boardman had left in part because of the compromises he had to make between his image as a climber and his job as an official spokesman for the sport. But it was for both men an important stepping stone.

A spoof entry in the gear section of *Climber and Rambler* from March 1978 gives a flavour of the skepticism in the climbing community at Alex's appointment. Under a photo of Alex captioned "joining the professionals," the magazine satirized him thus: "Not the old style as recommended by the BMC, but the Pro model which comes a little dearer than before. No better on rock, but expected to continue to go well in the big hills … Could this be the start of lesser-performing imitators turning professional and hoping to reach star status?"

The quip about "lesser-performing imitators" makes you wonder what you had to do not to be seen as a pretender to the alpine-style crown – and he already had star status. His job would also have little to do with climbing status. A huge expansion of the BMC's remit was underway. With it came greater influence with both government and the climbing community. As part of the "Leeds Mafia," Dennis Gray's description of anyone associated with the Leeds University scene, Alex brought authenticity and credibility with the younger and more anarchistic side of the sport. That was no doubt a factor in Alex's appointment.

"Of course," Dennis said, "I knew Alex prior to his joining the BMC because of his involvement with the Leeds University scene. It is interesting how subsequently several other mountaineers from that milieu followed on in the style of alpinism pioneered by Alex and the rest of you at that time: Al Powell, Kenton Cool, Rich Cross and Jon Bracey from the present generation, are all past Leeds students."

Peter Boardman had also brought credibility to the BMC but was perhaps too well spoken and well connected to speak to the feisty new generation of top climbers emerging from less elevated backgrounds. Alex's streak of punk anarchy went down well with this community. His personality and approach were a stark contrast to Boardman's. According to Dennis, where Peter was "diplomatic and rarely animated unless provoked, Alex was thrusting, argumentative and had a cunning mind."

In 1978, the BMC was not the force it is today, certainly not in terms of staff and the number of individual members. The concept of an organization in the role of national body was still rejected by many climbers. For them, climbing was not a "sport." It was an adventure and a somewhat anarchistic lifestyle. The idea of a bureaucracy to look after the interests of climbing was an oxymoron, an opinion expressed not just by individuals but also some of the long-established clubs, including the Leeds University Climbing Club. Climbers were generally a pretty vocal group, and at times black and white in their views. The internal politics surrounding the development of the BMC's policies were horrendous.

At best, the BMC was seen as a necessary evil, but justification for its existence was becoming clearer among the better informed in the climbing community. It had firm supporters among some politicians in the Labour government of the time, in particular Britain's first sports minister, Denis Howell. He was keen on governing bodies for all sports, seeing them as essential tools to manage and develop sport. The ramblers' movement of the 1930s had left a legacy of freer access, but many crags in the 1970s were on private land, and access was limited and in some cases forbidden. So the BMC created area committees of hard-working volunteers, usually drawn from local climbing clubs, to negotiate with landowners and other agencies for improved access.

There was also a need to educate climbers in areas of environmental concern such as bird and plant conservation. A balance between the interests of climbers and other groups had to be found. Not many climbers were sensitive to these issues. Being able to argue a balanced case to the clubs was an essential part of Alex's job. Government, both local and national, wasn't impressed by the attitude of some climbers who would climb on a crag regardless. It would be a red rag to the Thatcher Government that came in during Alex's tenure. Compulsory rescue insurance for all climbers was another of the bullets the BMC managed to dodge over the years.

The biggest issue of Alex's day, however, was the role of the BMC in training and education. Among cognoscenti, a fierce debate had been raging for a decade over the role of adventure in education. Most agreed it was a good thing for young people to challenge themselves in the hills, but climbers argued that it had to come from inner "springs of adventure," not in formulaic school expeditions. Climbers naturally felt it was an individual choice and there were clubs to help develop adventurous young people. Most importantly, climbers learned their craft through trial and error. Only by making mistakes and having accidents were the inherent dangers realized by the individual. Ad Carter, editor of the *American Alpine Journal* at the time, famously reminded the American climber Jack Tackle that: "Good judgment is mostly a result of having survived bad judgment." It was all part of the essential process of learning to behave responsibly and safely. This line of thinking was promoted most effectively by Ken Wilson, but it missed the point that the opportunities to start climbing have to come from somewhere. Ironically, for Alex, that opportunity came at school.

Setting policy was ultimately the decision of the full membership of the BMC at its annual meeting. The direction of policy was steered by the professional officers. There were specialist committees, for training and access and so forth, which approved or rejected policy papers put forward by officers. The management structure was cumbersome but democratic. The membership in those days was mainly comprised of affiliated clubs represented, in turn, by their own elected officials. Most clubs, as you would expect, promoted their own regional and local interests. Key policy decisions could take years to agree. The clubs had to go back to their own members for agreement and this took time. The more politicized club representatives – many had strong so-cialist roots – played the role of trade union reps against the self-cre-ated and paid professional officers of the BMC. Very forceful and well-articulated arguments against any form of regulation of the "freedom of the hills" came from many directions. Alex's keen debating skills were essential to argue his ground for the sake of the larger good.

While the community argued with itself, a steamroller of public opinion against climbing was bearing down. The elitist and archaic practices instilled in the structure of the BMC, and the senior clubs, in-cluding the Alpine Club, were seen as out of date and out of touch. This attitude grew in the aftermath of a tragedy in the Cairngorms in 1971 when six children froze to death on a school winter excursion into the hills. "The tragedy should have been prevented," howled the press. Everyone agreed. Climbers argued that the children were put at risk because educationalists tried to put adventure on the school agenda when it was not for everyone. It was they, not the BMC, that controlled the Mountain Leader Training Board.

The debate went on for years and was often reduced to farce. One member of the House of Lords argued that "only a handful of climb-ers such as Chris Bonington could survive a night camped out in the Scottish mountains." Articles appeared, demanding that the hills be closed in winter. The same issues are played out today, but a stronger BMC is in place. Then, as now, the tabloid press attacks any activity they cannot fathom by trying to appeal to "conventional wisdom"; something the press usually creates for its own purposes. This is usu-ally along the lines that nothing can be gained by putting people at risk, and the personal choice to do so is socially abhorrent, and, in turn, puts others at risk.

Adverse press surrounding the Cairngorm tragedy meant the public not only blamed the teachers but also blamed climbers for wanting to climb. The government responded to that public concern by pushing for the introduction of qualifications for teachers taking children into the hills. Leading lights in the BMC – the president, the management committee and senior officers – sensed the winds of change blowing through Whitehall and found themselves in a dilemma. They knew that the values of mainstream sport and education were very different from those of mountaineers and adventure climbers. Yet if the BMC was not in a position to represent climbing at the legislative table of government, then things could be taken from its hands. That could result in access to the hills being blocked, mandatory insurance and certification for all climbers. The BMC's role was, therefore, to fight the climber's corner whilst not being seen as either extremist or elitist.

When Alex arrived at the BMC, arguments about the value of any qualification were raging, filling climbing magazines. A "diploma mentality" was seen as undermining adventure. For anyone brought up after the debate, it will be difficult to see what the fuss was about.* "It was the biggest dispute in the history of British climbing," Dennis Gray said. "The Cairngorm tragedy convinced a lot of mountaineers that there had to be more involvement in and moderation of mountain training activities by the mainstream of the sport."

The BMC set up a specialist group, chaired by Lord John Hunt with Gray as secretary, to do a review and make recommendations. "In retrospect we were a little naive; there is nothing like meddling with other people's livelihoods and standing to provoke confrontation." If Hunt was a formidable supporter, Sir Jack Longland led those against his report's conclusion and, in Gray's words, "put up a hell of a fight." Longland faced a vote of no confidence as chair of the MLTB and the BMC lost some of its funding from the Sports Council, which threatened it with bankruptcy. "Shortly after this the Alpine Club came up with the offer of arbitration, which both sides swiftly accepted."

Alex was quick to grasp not only all the issues but also the imperative to play politics and yet remain diplomatic. He was asked to write the case in support of the BMC for an arbitration panel called the

---

* The mountain leader certificates for summer and winter are now generally accepted as a good thing, while other qualifications – like the Single Pitch Award certificate – were forced onto the BMC training committee because the MLTB were threatening to create one, and some colleges were already trying to register a similar certificate nationally as an NVQ independent of the BMC. The BMC has steered climbing into fairly safe waters compared to some other sports. Although after Alex's time, the various climbing qualifications, from Mountaineering Instructor Certificate to full-blown guide affiliated to the UIAA, are more or less a vertical ladder of professional progression. Today, a risk-averse education system dominated by certification means debate has calmed – but only until an accident occurs.

Mountain Training Tribunal. In the end, the tribunal recommended that the two boards – the one run by the educationalists and the one by the BMC – combine. The BMC would develop its own policy for all mountain training, with professionals like wardens of mountain centres continuing to play a major role.

It was all new and exciting work for Alex. He had the chance to use his skills as a law graduate to deal with the politics and develop policy, and draw on his credibility as a climber to cope with rumbling discontent at creeping bureaucracy among the mass of climbers who in Alex's opinion: "Rightly couldn't give a toss in the short term, but it would be bad for the long term if we lost."

Alex was a fierce fighter when it came to a debate. He believed the role of the BMC was essential for the survival of climbing in the face of attempts to regulate "safety" into every activity. He would regularly go home to visit his mother Jean and update her on his role. Jean was extremely proud that Alex was making an impact and clearly enjoying his work. He also kept in close touch with his younger sister, Libby, who inherited all of Jean's intelligence and resilience, as well as sharing Alex's determination.*

Alex generally liked challenging and intelligent women and extended the love and respect he had for his mother to other women he counted as friends, including Maria Coffey and Rita Hallam at the BMC. He had immense respect for Rita, who was a powerful force in the running of the BMC. With her organizational skills and common sense, Rita reminded Alex of his mother; he would delegate work to Rita to carve out more time to go climbing.

Alex's relationship with Maria Coffey was a completely different matter. As they got to know each other, they began to share mutual friends in the climbing scene. On one occasion, when Maria's then boyfriend had gone to work abroad for awhile, Alex decided Maria had been alone long enough and needed to be set up with someone, so he phoned up his friend Choe Brooks and told him to come round.

---

* Libby became a successful businesswoman and rider. In recent years she has been able to choose her work. Alex would have been incredibly proud of his sister's success.

"Alex was really matter of fact about it when Choe arrived, sort of 'here you go, meet Colin, that's all sorted then.' He was so pragmatic about relationships, at least with me." Maria felt this was an important part of Alex's character. If he detected someone was unhappy, his caring side emerged and he tried to put it right. When Maria was going through a particularly bad time running several affairs at the same time, Alex decided this was not right.

He told her: "Dump them all and meet someone else." He had Joe Tasker in mind, and so he drove Maria up to Wales one weekend to a party at Al Harris's knowing Joe would be there. "When Joe and I did get together," Maria said, "Alex was as direct as usual. He said: 'You realise there is a one in ten chance that Joe will die every time he goes on an expedition, which means the longer you stay with him, the greater the chance that he's going to die.' It really made me think because I had never had a serious Himalayan climber as a boyfriend. I began to ask others, like Gwyneth, how they coped when their partners were away."

Maria's first experience of the uncertainty and insecurity of the woman left behind came when Joe went to Kangchenjunga in 1979. Alex was in the process of breaking up with Gwyneth. Maria recalls that one night he made a drunken attempt to start a relationship, but on his terms and only for a short time, suggesting they share some time together while Joe was away.

Maria recalled: "Alex said well, your bloke is away, and I don't have a girlfriend, so why don't we get together and you can use my car. It's better than yours. That's exactly what he said. I was sitting at the table and couldn't stop howling with laughter."

She told Alex that she really didn't think so, especially now that she was with Joe. When Joe returned from Kangchenjunga, Maria recalled that she was driving him back up to Manchester and "just yakking" about all the news and mentioned Alex's approach, thinking it would be something else to make him laugh. But the opposite happened.

"He was beside himself with anger and months later when Alex and Sarah came round for a meal, Joe went out and refused to speak to Alex. There was tension between them for the remainder of their lives."

17

DON'T TAKE ME ALIVE

Voytek had a list of faces he wanted to climb; Bandaka was only the first. We deferred to him to find us another objective once we failed to get Gasherbrum IV in Pakistan's Karakoram. Changabang was the second peak in India Voytek applied for; our friend Terry King had already taken his first choice – Nanda Devi's northeast face. The Indian Mountaineering Foundation suggested Changabang as an alternative.

The name had a nice familiar ring to it. An Anglo-Indian expedition led by Chris Bonington had made the first ascent in 1974. In 1975, Joe Tasker spotted the stunning challenge of the west face while climbing nearby Dunagiri. The following year, he and Pete Boardman made a remarkable capsule-style ascent of that face. It was a tremendous climb, achieved after several enforced retreats from the face in poor weather. It also demonstrated that big-wall tactics applied by a determined and skilful two-man team could succeed on a truly high mountain. Doing the south buttress alpine style would move the marker up a notch or two.

Raising the sponsorship and cash for our Anglo-Polish attempt on the south buttress of Changabang fell to me, as did most of the rest of the organization from the British side. Alex was impressively busy at the BMC and I, at least, had my evenings free. This year my dealings were not with Andrez Zawada but with Voytek. Our Bandaka climb had made its mark in Poland; his expertise not just as a climber but also as an organizer of alpine-style trips was fully accepted. For this trip, our main sponsor was not the Polski Zwiazek Alpinizmu. It was happy to loan equipment, but Voytek had negotiated with his local club and the town council of Zakopane, the mountain capital of the Polish Tatra, to give us support. It was the 400th anniversary of its incorporation, and for reasons never quite explained, our international expedition was seen as the perfect way to celebrate.

After our humiliating experience the previous year, having to skimp on every aspect of the expedition, I hoped to do a better job raising finance for Changabang. But to get private support for equipment and food, we first needed grants from the Mount Everest Foundation and the BMC, the stamp of approval that opened up opportunities for additional support. We only had limited personal funds to contribute. Since there were no trains from Poland to India, we needed enough cash to fly.

Alex argued I was more acceptable than he for the presentation of our submission to the Mount Everest Foundation (MEF), since I owned a suit that fitted, had a phone at home and could not possibly be working as hard as he was.

"Come on John, you have the experience of organizing last year's trip."

I knew Alex was flattering to deceive, but his next point was a clincher.

"Besides, as national officer of the BMC, I'm responsible for administering the BMC grants that come as part of the package once an MEF grant is awarded."

There clearly was a conflict of interest. However, like Alex, I was incredibly busy at my day job. I had seen pictures of Changabang in profile, but I didn't have time to bother with much research. Changabang is one of the most beautiful mountains in the world, with near vertical walls on the west, north and south sides. Only its east ridge, line of the first ascent, and southwest ridge offered easier alternatives. I also knew that a strong Lakes team had tried and failed the year before. That was the sum total of my knowledge. I decided that the old privateer adage of "get there and you have a chance" would suffice. Anyway, our track record alone should get us a decent grant.

I prepared an application to the MEF and sometime in May found myself in London for the screening committee at the Royal Geographical Society opposite Hyde Park and the Albert Memorial. I had never been before and no one had warned me I should come well prepared. Entering from Kensington Gore, the building has a kind of imperial grandeur from an era when exploration meant national glory. Its location, near to the Albert Hall and the great collections of the Victoria and Albert Museum, puts it in that part of London that captures the swagger of the British Empire.

From her perch in Hyde Park, Queen Victoria stared blankly at my back as I passed through the wrought-iron gates. I received a curt nod from the porter when I explained my reason for being there. I guessed he saw more grandees pass by than the average climber had hot dinners in a month. Someone had told me that the corridors echo with the ghostly tramping feet of a thousand famous expeditions, and walking those corridors I found myself suddenly overawed. The portraits of Victorian heroes hung here and there, their expression one of determination and distinction, but also something else. Having travelled with a similar set in my own era, I detected a mixture of lunacy, larceny and lust for the unknown. Surrounded by names like David Livingstone, Sir Francis Younghusband and General Bruce, who would not be awed, if not overwhelmed?

I tripped going up the stairs; it was almost a sign of respect. I was too intent on taking in my surroundings. Leaving the bustle of London just 50 yards behind for the glories of British exploration, I realized too late my quest was unfocused and potentially doomed. I needed to impress. In the hallway, a few other young men sat clutching thick, neatly ordered files and maps neatly rolled and stacked on their laps. I carried nothing. I had a flashback to one of those schoolboy nightmares of having forgotten to do essential homework before an exam.

This was my first visit to the MEF. Peter Holden had made the pitch for the previous year's Anglo-Polish expedition to the Hindu Kush. He was a veteran at these screenings. All I knew about the MEF was that it was very venerable and almost impenetrable; this was also about as much as I knew about our objective. Alex and I prided ourselves on our cavalier attitudes in those days, so much so that we did not recognize it as anything unusual. Why get frightened before you got there? Thirty-five years on, that attitude seems naive and even disrespectful. I had no idea who might be on the panel or what questions they might ask. I thought to myself: "Just look earnest, answer questions politely and we'll get a big grant. I'll be back on the train north within an hour or two."

I was right only about the venerable bit. When I entered the room, a large assemblage of what could have comprised an entire pre-war Everest expedition looked up from the long polished table. Without knowing who they were, I guessed quite a few of them must be among my boyhood heroes. The only faces I recognized were Doug Scott and Bob Pettigrew, the only two not dressed for Tibet in 1921. I suddenly realized bluff was going to be more important than sincerity and good manners.

The first part of the interview went well. I got our names and destination right, and produced a scruffy piece of paper from my pocket on which I had calculated the various costs, which were not a lot because Alex wasn't accustomed to spending money. We had to assume that the Poles would fly us out once we had cashed our assembled dollars and pounds on the black market. However, we had the peak fee to cover and porters to pay, as well as food for base camp. We would sell whatever excess goods we could get on the plane for additional Indian rupees and cash more hard currency on the Indian black market to get a bit more. That was the way to leverage our dollars. It seemed straightforward enough, but the stern expressions of the screening committee suddenly matched those of the portraits of the venerable explorers hanging on the room's walls. My story must have been hard to swallow by anyone who had not been on a Polish expedition, and that meant everyone in the room except for me. It was all very un-British.

Then things got even more difficult. "Where does your route go, youth?" Doug Scott asked, floating a black and white photo across the table at me. I picked it up and was confronted by an image of a Dru-like peak but nearly twice as high. "Bugger me, that's steep," I thought to myself, trying not to reveal my sudden consternation.

Using a borrowed pen, I started somewhere near the bottom and drew a rambling line upwards, a bit like a 3-year old trying to connect the dots on a page before being able to count. At the same time I tried to appear distracted by a question about transportation from Delhi from a very distinguished gentleman from the end of the table. He implied enormous distances and hardships were involved, which did not stack up with my image of taxis with overly full roof racks. It was enough time to complete my doodle and casually float it back to Doug. Had I impressed him with my choice of route? He remained silent for the remainder of the interview.

I concluded with an inflated summary of our skill, the need to push out the frontiers of lightweight style and the importance of East-West relations during a time of world crisis. I smiled and thought that was sure to win them over. I got a few knowing nods and encouraging grunts for my efforts. Then it was over. I semi-bowed and Doug escorted me out into the corridor.

"Nice one, youth," Doug said half under his breath. "You chose the only definite chop route on the face."

I half-stopped, stunned by this revelation of my own incompetence; I tried to get an intimation from Doug whether or not I had totally blown it. He smiled and turned back into the room. A small group of climbing professionals well equipped with maps and papers brushed passed me. They were welcomed with hearty and familiar greetings from the MEF committee. I headed for the train with my tail between my legs.

I didn't know it at the time, but we'd got the cash we needed – just – to make a success of the trip. Nor did I know that the following year I would make an even bigger plonker of myself in front of the MEF. In those days all we hoped for was a chance. There was really very little point in planning for the big mountains. Too much could go wrong. The important part was to get there.

"The whole thing will be a miracle if we pull it off," I told my diary on 27 July 1978, the day we left Millom. "We are a strong team doing an obvious thing just short of the impossible ... the details are less important than the fact of going."

So the second détente expedition was underway, although the marketing value of "détente" had lost something in the face of increasing tension between East and West. There were rumours in the press that the USSR was planning an invasion of Afghanistan – something we knew from first-hand. My good friend, Peter Clark, and his then wife, Julie, agreed to drive me out to Krakow, where I would meet Voytek to sort out the Polish paperwork for the expedition. We would then go out to India ten days early to clear the bureaucracy before the rest of the team arrived. Alex would be on his annual expedition leave from the BMC for two months. My contract with the county council had come to an end, so climbing was all I had to worry about.

I had persuaded Pete and Julie that taking me to Poland was the perfect way to start their summer holiday behind the Iron Curtain. Pete's Alfa Romeo was stuffed with as much of the expedition's free booty – food, gear and whisky – as we could cram in. A small cubicle on the back seat surrounded with stuff sacks was just space enough for one of us to sit during the set rotation of the journey: two hours driving, two as passenger and two in the back. I did not share their concern that getting through East German and Polish customs might be a real problem. The entire expedition budget of $3,500 cash was in my wallet. During my times in the back, I wondered what amounts we might have to shell out in bribes.

It took four days from Millom to Krakow. The lottery of border crossing checks worked in our favour as we entered East Germany. Eight anxious hours lining up behind beat-up wagons and Trabants came to an end when we were summarily waved through on the check-every-other-car basis. All cars travelling the other way were searched thoroughly, the logic being that no one was coming to East Germany to set up shop. We followed the cobblestone motorways built during Hitler's 1930s rebuilding program, the same roads the Wehrmacht took to invade Poland in 1939.

At the Polish border we spent a further five hours waiting pointlessly before an animated guard explained that we had a "special visa" and should not have waited in line at all. The paperwork from Zakopane submitted with our passports to the Polish embassy in London must have contained this special request. So we entered Poland late in the evening with everything intact, no bribes paid and nothing confiscated.

After an hour's driving, we took a hill road to the small fortified town of Zory, hoping to find some food and a place to stay. Everything was dark in the narrow, cobbled streets and there was little sign of life until we happened on a large hall, which turned out to be hosting a wedding reception. When the joyful and inebriated guests realized three Brits were at the door, we were welcomed in with much slapping of backs and given a place at the top table. Food and plenty of vodka were placed in front of us. Some of the older men reminded us of the special relationship between Poland and Britain. Some had worked there, and one said he had been a mechanic in the free Polish Air Force. It was a lovely welcome back.

Next day we drove southeast through rolling farmland until, at noon, we entered a hellish landscape of tall chimneys, belching smoke and the apparently endless steel works, factories and tower blocks of Katowice.* The choice of Pink Floyd's *Animals* on the car cassette player seemed perfect for the surroundings.

Voytek met us in Krakow that same evening. Having run out of zloty secretly stashed from previous trips, I delegated Pete the job of changing some pounds with a man in a leather jacket outside Saint Mary's Basilica in the main square.** I reasoned that since Pete and Julie were touring Poland afterwards, they needed the practice of a black market exchange to make their money last. I could not afford to get caught by the special police.

When Voytek arrived, we had a meal in a cellar restaurant to the sound of gypsy violins. We agreed on the amount of dollars he would need to cash for zloty and what should be kept to cash in India, where we would again be able to change hard currency on the black market.

---

* The tall chimneys and factories provided highly paid but difficult, high-access work for many Polish climbers. They came to Katowice for better pay and to be part of the scene led by the rising star Jerzy Kukuczka.

** In 1976, on our way back from our winter exchange, our plane was routed from Warsaw via Krakow, where on landing we skidded on sheet ice off the runway into a frozen cow pasture. Looking down from the window, my eyes met a cow staring up at me with a "not again" expression. On entering the terminal building, we were told we must stay in the departure lounge until further notice. There was a snack bar selling food and drink, but it only accepted zloty. All zloty had to be exchanged before entering the international lounge and this we had done in Warsaw. At the bar in the lounge, we spotted a group of men buying loads of beers and sandwiches with zloty. They were conversing in a mixture of Polish, Welsh and English. The Burgesses struck up a conversation with them and soon we all had beers aplenty. They were a Polish-Welsh rugby team on tour in Poland. When asked why they had so much zloty, they said they always kept some for emergencies should the plane be delayed or crash. Lesson learned.

In Poland we could expect ten times the official rate. In India I managed to get about 20 per cent above the bank rate but in much more dangerous exchanges. The good news was that LOT, the Polish airline, was flying the entire expedition to Bombay at a greatly reduced price.

The next day we drove down to Zakopane where we met the other Polish members of the Changabang team. Krzysztof Zurek had a stature similar to Joe Brown, small, compact and powerful. He had run up and down the 7000-metre peak Noshaq in 11 hours. His black unruly hair was a bit like Alex's. He had a straightforward manner, lacking pretence or any need to impress. He was immediately likeable. Our doctor, Lech Korniszewski, was a nimble, intelligent man, with a dignified carriage. Lech was a Himalayan climber in his own right and like Zawada was part of the Polish upper classes, an extremely well-known and respected doctor who later gained international recognition for medical research.

As part of Zakopane's 400th anniversary celebrations, the town held a boisterous civic reception in the elaborate chambers of the town council. As we sat waiting for the speeches and first course, Lech came round with a huge jug in his hands and said: "Would you like orange juice?" Expecting a dry affair of long speeches, we had primed ourselves with a few beers in a local café. How wrong we were. Lech filled our glasses with a knowing smile. This orange juice was 50 per cent pure spirit. By the evening's end, the numbers of speeches made were equalled by the bottles of vodka consumed. I gave a thank you speech using my minimal Polish, much to the amusement of the mayor and his councillors. Fortunately, we had a couple of days climbing in the Tatra to recover.

Voytek and I flew to Bombay, the only destination in India for which you could buy a ticket in Poland. We took the slow train to Delhi next day, second-class. The monsoon heat makes everything oppressive in August. We were also very hungry. Part of Voytek's acclimatization to the local germs and environment was to eat nothing for the first 36 hours. Our first real meal in two days was at the Polish embassy in New Delhi. We had expected to stay there as we had the year before in Kabul, but now the atmosphere was more difficult thanks to increased tension between East and West. I moved into a cheap hotel just off Connaught Square.

Voytek waited at the embassy for our equipment to arrive on the truck coming overland from Poland, the "Makalu Truck." I happened to be at the embassy when it finally arrived, four days late, and saw what I should not have seen. The seals on the truck were broken, our gear unloaded and various other items loaded on for the onward journey to Nepal.

"This is normal," Voytek explained. "Our drivers have seals for all the countries they go through." The opportunities for import and export through these legations were clearly limitless. Our equipment was all in order and with no bonds to clear, thanks to the Makalu Truck, we should have been ready to head for the Garhwal as soon as the others arrived. But negotiations with the Indian Mountaineering Foundation for our permits for Changabang were at a stalemate. Polish wheeling and dealing was nothing compared to the CIA's shenanigans with spy stations on Nanda Devi a decade before; we were now caught up in a legacy of intrigue that looked likely to end our adventure before it had really begun.

I met Alex, Krzysztof and Lech at New Delhi station the next day.

"When do we leave?" was Alex's first question.

"Maybe not at all – it's complicated. Let's get to the hotel."

Above the noisy puttering of the rickshaw and the roar of Delhi's traffic, I asked Alex if he had heard of the American Nandi Devi expeditions of 1965 and 1966. He hadn't.

"Well, they were covers for a covert CIA operation to plant a nuclear-powered listening device to monitor the Chinese atomic-bomb tests. But the 1965 expedition was stopped by bad weather, and they left the monitor bolted to a ledge. When they returned next year, they found no trace of it. It had been avalanched into the source of the Ganges. News has just broken here in India. Seems one of the 1965 expedition members had a guilty conscience and wrote a story for a Seattle newspaper. The thought of radiation in the Ganges has caused uproar. The Indian authorities have closed the Nanda Devi Sanctuary to all expeditions. Voytek went ballistic with the IMF staff."

"Hmm," said Alex. "Now I understand what that Russian meant yesterday on the plane when he told me: 'It is an Ilyushin you are flying, and an illusion if you think you will climb in India now.' He didn't get it when I said: 'Strange, I'm sure we are off the ground.' How serious is it?"

"Very, but Terry King and I have a plan."

Terry King and his climbing partner Paul "Matey" Smith were caught in the same stalemate. They had permission for a new route on the northeast face of Nanda Devi. Like us, they had to get into the Nanda Devi Sanctuary to get to their route. Terry and I worked out our tactics after our first fruitless meeting with Mr. Ram, the administrator of the IMF, in his stifling, cramped, little office near the Sansad Bhavan, India's parliament buildings. He was a small, polite man and rather frail and timid. Terry, like Voytek, had no patience or sympathy for the system that had first granted us permission and then withdrawn it through no fault of ours. It was completely unfair. We played on the theme.

"We're here in good faith, you've taken our money and now you refuse our permits. We will speak to the Alpine Club, the BMC and all the magazines and make sure that no British climbers come to India ever again. Blah, blah, blah," we ranted on. The poor man simply nodded his head and kept saying, "*Accha*, but why not go to Devistan," a mountain that sounded to us about as interesting an objective as the beach at Blackpool.

Suddenly, Terry lost his temper completely. He grabbed the IMF secretary by the scruff of the neck, lifted him in the air, swore and then dropped him back in his chair. He turned and stormed out of the office. The stacked mountains of yellowing paper all around the office threatened to avalanche as Terry's retreating steps echoed in the stairwell. I sat stunned for a moment and then said:

"I am sorry about Mr. King. You see Terry King is a famous actor with the Royal Shakespeare Company at Stratford-upon-Avon. All actors have terrible tempers as you know." It was a half-truth. Terry taught stage fighting with lots of repertory companies including the RSC.

Mr. Ram was clearly interested in this news. "Ah, an actor you say?" Light was dawning in the secretary's face as he saw a way to escape another tirade. He reached for a pad of paper and wrote down a name and telephone number. "Go and see Mr. Singh tomorrow at the Ministry of Interior. He is a big fan of British actors so maybe he can help."

And so it began, our little act – the good guy/bad guy routine with a twist. Early each morning for nearly a week we travelled in rickshaws to offices and met with government bureaucrats, moving slowly up the ladder. We would inevitably be referred to someone else and in the stifling afternoon heat wait at the door until we were told to come back in the morning. As we climbed ever upwards through office blocks to larger offices, Terry's reputation as an actor spread. He could well have been cast in the lead in the RSC's next production of *Hamlet* the way his performances countered "the slings and arrows of outrageous fortune." And so I explained to Alex and the rest of the team that in three days we had an appointment at the very top, at the office of the prime minister.

So it was that early one morning Terry and I found ourselves outside Morarji Desai's residence, entering the office at the gates to the quiet grounds. The receptionist asked us to sit down, and so we sat, anticipating the usual long wait. But after just a few minutes, a tall, distinguished man wearing a smart collarless white suit appeared. He was the prime minister's personal secretary.

"Good morning, gentlemen. No need for any amateur dramatics from you today, Mr. King. We have accepted that you will be better off doing what you came here to do than making any further trouble. Your expeditions will be the last in the Nanda Devi Sanctuary for the foreseeable future. You can tell that to your magazines when you get home."

We made sincere and somewhat sheepish expressions of gratitude, knowing our act had been seen through. We walked out with our newly stamped permits for our respective routes. The cool mountain air was only days away, and we headed back to our teams with the news of our release. Later that afternoon, a slim Indian captain in his mid-20s strode into our campsite at the northern end of Delhi and introduced himself.

"Hello gentlemen, I am K.T. Gadgria, your liaison officer for the expedition." K.T. turned out to be one of the best LOs any of us ever had the pleasure of meeting and an integral part of our success. That evening, he took Krzysztof and me to see the Diwali celebrations in Old Delhi. Next morning, he and I returned for the last time to the IMF to file our final plans. I said goodbye to the long-suffering Mr. Ram and gave him a small gift of English chocolate. "Dhanyabhad. I am glad you are going to your mountain. *Thik, thik.*" I think he was pleased by the unlikely outcome and this final courtesy.

We caught the overnight train to the holy city of Haridwar, where the Ganges meets the plains. In the morning, Alex, Krzysztof and I hired a taxi to go straight on to Joshimath in the foothills of the Himalaya. We would go ahead to buy food and fuel and organize porters. Voytek and Doc would come later with the bulk of the equipment in a truck.

By now, money was tight, but the wasted days in Delhi weren't critical. None of us had any particular date to get home, and we soon discovered the lingering monsoon was creating havoc with the mountain roads. Our taxi team managed to get within 70 kilometres of Joshimath before a landslide 400 metres wide stopped our progress. It would take a week to repair. We debated waiting for the others but decided to press on, walking to the other side of the slip to hire new transport as others came through to hire our now empty truck. Only later did we discover the scale of the problem we had left for Voytek and Doc. They arrived at the same impasse a day later but had to guard and at the same time ferry 300 kilos of food and equipment around each section of blocked road to a new vehicle. Two landslides and two days later, we finally reached Joshimath. The equipment arrived two days behind us and carried straight on to the village of Lata. Voytek stood up in the back of the truck as they passed us to shout his annoyance at being abandoned by Alex and myself.

Weather-wise, Joshimath was like late summer in Chamonix. The snowline had dropped to cover the pines a few hundred feet above the misty village. We completed our shopping for rice, flour, dal, tea and *bidis* for the porters and now had enough staples to last four or five weeks at base camp. We loaded it onto a bus travelling up to Badrinath and set off to join Voytek and Lech two hours up the road where the trail to the sanctuary began at Lata. The deep rumble from the swift, grey waters of the Ganges could be heard anywhere in the valley up to 10,000 feet, and it filled our days and nights as we waited for the rain to cease.

For three days we camped on the side of the road beneath the village. At first light on 5 September a weak sun appeared, dispersing the river mists, and the porters from the village arriving under the leadership of our newly appointed sirdar, Sher Singh, who had worked for Joe and Pete two years before. We hastily packed our bags while sharing the responsibility of getting the porters away with their loads. Even with just a six-day walk, we realized we were hiring many porters just to carry food for the other porters. Voytek decided we could save money if we hired sheep that were going to be travelling up with us to grazing sites high in the Rishi Ganga. The strongest sheep could carry around five kilos, and they were much cheaper than the porters, who cost around five dollars a day. Shortage of cash meant each of us had to carry full loads of 25 kilos and more.

Alex and I set off at the front, intending to check the porters in at our next camp some 6,000 feet above us. As we passed through the village, an ancient crone beckoned us toward her house. On the small balcony sat two girls in their teens. "Changabang? Changabang?" she repeated several times, saying the word with a variety of intonations, so that it sounded a bit like "chang or bang?" To my amazement, Alex nodded and said: "Both please," and vanished into the black hole that was the goat shed. "I'll catch up with you by tonight," was all he said. He never did tell me the full story, but he definitely had a bad head from the chang that night, although the relentless climb up from Lata to the top of the ridge at Lata Kharak can't have helped.

Late in the afternoon, as we counted loads, we realized that two were missing. Two teenage porters had not arrived at our high alpine meadow and it was nearly dusk. An older brother volunteered to go find them. I emptied my Kelty pack frame, threw in a couple of head-lamps and together we descended steeply back through the rhodo-dendron forests slick with mud. We found them nearly 2,000 feet be-low. One of the boys was clearly struggling. He had taken on a double load of 60 kilos even though he had a bad cold. Alex appeared at the same time, and we broke down the load, divided it between us and climbed back up to our camp on the grassy ridge by headlamp. Their friends cheered as the three Lata boys arrived for their late supper. Next day, they all seemed well enough to carry on.

As we traversed the delightful high ridges on the morning of the sec-ond day, a mist came in. Within an hour, it began to rain heavily. An hour later, it was snowing. The route that day was at 13,000 feet for much of the way, finally crossing the Dharansi Pass at 14,000 feet be-fore dropping 8,000 feet back down to the entrance of the Rishi Ganga. It was a miserable trek for the porters. The combination of the altitude, the cold, double loads and covering two stages in one march resulted in a midnight arrival for the stragglers at Debrugheta.* Next morning, the porters went on strike.

K.T. and Sher Singh spent the morning negotiating. We stayed out of the way. Fortunately, the sun rose above the enclosed valley and quickly warmed the atmosphere, drying clothes, tents and blankets, reminding the porters that their goddess Nanda was waiting to grant wishes only three days away. We agreed to two days of single stages and an extra allocation of *bidis*. Fortunately, the sheep were not smok-ers and weren't on strike. The porters had an early lunch and by noon we were winding along the initial south walls of the famous Rishi Gorge.

We crossed the river, but after Ramani, the next camp, we faced a problem we had not anticipated. The sheep could go no further as the walls of the gorge steepened. We recruited some of the porters who would have returned at this point and increased our own loads to

---

* Porters were paid double for double loads but nothing extra for two stages in a day. However, a double stage did mean they had a food and *bidi* allowance spare.

around 40 kilos. Then it was steeply uphill and across the slabs that Bill Tilman had pioneered in 1934, tottering high above the roaring Ganga. It occurred to me that Calcutta was 2,000 miles away, but to begin the journey, you had only to drop a thousand feet.

Two days later, we arrived at a meadow of delicate flowers and grass, strewn with granite boulders. It was immediately opposite Nanda Devi's impressive northeast face. A glacial river sped past between our camp and the Nanda Devi glacier opposite. We paid off our now happy porters and they immediately began the run back home. The meadow became even more colourful when the contents of the barrels were spread out to dry. One of our barrels, holding flour and dal, had already gone missing, but we had enough of that. But now we realized that a more crucial barrel containing most of the ropes and much of the hardware had also disappeared. Our initial high spirits, prompted by arriving at such a magnificent place, evaporated as the afternoon mists descended.

Early the next morning, we spotted three figures hurrying toward us and immediately saw one was carrying a barrel. It was the barrel with the ropes and hardware, brought by the two teenage boys and the older brother we had helped on the very first night. We laughed with relief, made them tea and rice and gave them each an extra day's pay. It was not worth asking how the barrel had been left behind. They set off at speed toward home and would probably still have managed to cover three stages even though the day was half-gone.

Over the next three days, we rested and checked equipment. We suspended one of the as yet unproven hammocks Alex had designed and Troll had made for no charge on a nearby boulder. Getting in and out of it even here seemed challenge enough. We debated every ounce of what to take and the days we expected to be away. There is a delicate balance in the planning for a climb where the more stuff you take, the more time you need and consequently the more stuff you need. The concept of "lightweight" is a misnomer when a route is going to take more than a week to climb. Thirty-five kilos on your back at altitude does not feel light.

On the second day, I walked up toward the Changabang Glacier to look at the face for the first time. We all made this solitary trip to clear our minds. The peak stood serene at the top of the glacier, a granite needle gracefully pointing toward heaven. Through compact binoculars, I looked at possible routes. There was the obvious left-slanting line I had drawn on the photo at the RGS. I saw immediately what Doug meant. It looked shattered and led to the ridge too far left from the main summit. But the centre of the wall from this distance looked nearly blank. On that same photo Doug had left with me, Alex had spotted a chimney system leading from mid-height on the headwall all the way to the summit ridge and that looked feasible. There was also a thin line leading right into the centre of the upper face from near the start of that chimney line. Something told me that going right would be best, but the way could not be confirmed until we got there.

After two days of staggering across shin-scraping moraines, we reached the face for acclimatization and a recce. We didn't waste time looking at the options but decided to start from the toe of the buttress. We knew the team from the Lakes that had failed in 1976 started somewhere up the slabs further right. We needed to be completely independent. Voytek led the initial wet, overhanging wall in immaculate style and we then climbed steep mixed ground in a couloir for a further four pitches. That evening, we left any remaining equipment at the base and raced down the glacier by the light of a full moon.

For two days we binged on food and daydreamed about anything except what horrors the climb might hold. Rain and snow fell sporadically. In the dark hours, our dreams were spotted with anxiety. Gusting gale-force winds roared unexpectedly down from the mountains. I lay in my sleeping bag, kept awake by fear and indigestion. Tomorrow we would start on the wall.

18

ALWAYS THE SUN

On 6 October, in one long haul up the glacier, with Lech carrying some of the gear, we arrived at dusk at the base of the wall and settled in. I felt magnificently at home, our isolation complete. The face glinted in the icy starlight. At dawn, we started up in two teams: Voytek and I, and Krzysztof and Alex. The first day was a hauling day for us, having drawn the short straw. The five initial pitches we climbed before, plus seven new ones, were done twice, since we each had two rucksacks to carry. It was midnight before we had eaten and settled into our pits.

In the morning, a beautiful pink granite dihedral led up to the right. It was our turn to lead. While cleaning the first pitch, I dislodged a block that dropped 50 feet, clipping Krzysztof's shoulder on its way to the glacier. He screamed in pain. I shouted apologies. No way could he haul a sack, so I was relegated to the ropes again. That day we climbed only six pitches and weren't in bed until ten at night. I was miserable reflecting on the enormity of what might have happened. How many times could a big stone fall without it killing someone? I apologized again to Krzysztof. He was okay. Voytek told me to just calm down and concentrate on what we would have to do in the morning.

Day four: Now the routine begins to take hold. Leading is best, and exciting; hauling offers only pain, hard work and the uncertainty of wondering if the lead pair are choosing the best line. Each day around noon, clouds begin to form and by mid-afternoon a gentle snow falls, making every move tricky and the ropes icy. They become stiff, almost unmanageable and scary to jumar. But every morning brings clear blue skies and the sun breaking over the chaotic mass of peaks that ring the Nanda Devi Sanctuary. Alex and I sort gear, grateful to be packing without freezing our fingers. For a few glorious hours we can climb in comfort, before the noon wind blows in the clouds and the snow begins to fall.

Alex leads steep mixed ground to the top of the initial buttress and I add two hard pitches up the slabs above. The granite is incredibly compact and gear placements marginal. Alex clears one of my belays, comprising three pegs, with two taps of his hammer. The third peg he pulls out with his fingers. We warn the other pair not to bounce on the ropes as they jumar. We get five hours of sleep that night, the last decent sleep before the summit bivvy.

Day five: We wake in stages, opening one eye, then the other. I reach with a thumb to pry open the icy hole in the hood of my sleeping bag. It is my breathing hole in the frozen ocean of the night, allowing in just enough air but not too much of the 20-degree frost. The dawn light beckons. Like larvae knowing it is time to metamorphose, twisting and turning in our sleeping bags, we rustle into action, retrieving boots, gloves, water bottles, clothing, all our stuff shoved deep inside to dry. Through the widening hole in my cocoon, I can see an ice-caked wall looming 3,000 feet above us, like a skyscraper. Everything is frozen solid. The wall turns from pink to white as the sun gains strength and its light swings down the face toward us. Time to move.

From the top of the slabs, Voytek breaks out onto the headwall, a single, wide crack above the overhang showing the way, like a giant keyhole in a door of vertical stone. I jig for joy on the stance beside Krzysztof.

"This is the best climb ever," I laugh.

"You think? But maybe not yet, eh?"

Then I rappel for the next load. The hours pass as they do each day; we follow the routine, not making mistakes, dismissing moments of desperation. After the Poles have done four pitches, it begins to snow heavily. This makes things tricky. Alex and I struggle up the frozen ropes on jumars with the two purple rucksacks carrying the Poles' equipment. They wait in the early evening beneath an overhang, the obvious place for our first bivouac on the wall using the hammocks. We drop back down two rope lengths to fetch the remaining sacks and jumar back up by headlamp.

Snowflakes dance in the lamp beam like moths. The jumars lose traction on the icy ropes and I fall, my heart leaping with fear. There is the sense of zero gravity for ten feet, then a jarring whipping snap as the clamps bite the rope again. It happens several times, each more alarming than the last.* Finally, I reach the bivvy site, fix the rucksack on a rope looping the breadth of the overhang and, standing in etriers, begin to boil water for Alex and me.** Voytek and Krzysztof have already disappeared into their pod-like hammocks. The snow settles then slides off the outer covers with a hiss.

"How good are the anchors here?" I enquire nervously of the nearest pod.

"The rock is very funny, no good cracks." It was Voytek, speaking from inside his cosy pit.

"Thanks for the reassurance."

Far below, Alex's headlamp sways dimly in the blowing snow, like a distant freight train, shunting upwards. Three hours later, at midnight, I finish making soup with powdered potato and then make hot chocolate, passing a final drink to Alex in his hammock. Aching with cold, I place a single "Friend" in a flared slot in the rotten overlap above and hang my hammock from it, there being no possible piton placements. This is the first time I have ever placed a Friend.*** It seems a miracle tool. It takes 30 minutes to arrange the hammock, set the flysheet and then carefully transfer all my hopes for comfort and survival – my sleeping mat, my bag, my spare clothes – from my sack into the

---

* We always jumared with a prusik knot above the top jumar in case one jumar detached from the rope. The advantage of this early version was that it could easily be opened and moved above a knot in the rope. Knots became more frequent the higher we got on the route when it became necessary to cut out frayed sections of the ropes and then tie the remaining ends together.

** Etriers are long slings, usually with three or four loops tied into them in which to stand. They are used in aid climbing; moving from the bottom loop to the top loop, hopefully making it possible to climb higher.

*** These brilliant innovative protection devices, designed by Ray Jardine and brought to the market by Mark Vallance of Wild Country, involve sprung cams. They can be used in parallel or even flared cracks.

canoe-like hull. Once I have manoeuvred inside, the hammock seems warm and secure, held open by hollow spacer-tubes. Over the next few nights, these tubes are sometimes dropped during assembly and go ping-ping-pinging down the face. Expletives, either in Polish or English, tell us which hammock occupant has lost a spacer. Fortunately, this is all we drop. A boot, a stove or crampon would spell disaster.

Day six: We emerge like misshapen storks from our eyrie. I have had a bad night of stomach pains, but Krzysztof is worse. Alex and I head up a chimney, the obvious route that we all agree on. Alex leads a pitch of very steep ice, graded Scottish v or vi, which takes him into a shattered hole. Voytek shouts up concern as plates of ice accelerate past the jumar rope like circular saw blades. As he is placing a peg, the sharp pick of his ice hammer unexpectedly shatters and like a bullet rebounds into his face just missing his eye. He is lucky. When I reach the belay, we look up at the overhanging brown dyke of shattered rock. It is a dead end. I remember the thin crack I had spied through binoculars a week or so before and teeter across the unsupported flakes to the right and break out onto a pocketed wall of perfect granite complete with just enough holds.

A 30-foot traverse brings me to the crack and we follow it upwards for 300 feet before it is absorbed into a confusion of overlaps on a near vertical wall. The next pitch is the critical one.

Wishing I had rock-climbing shoes rather than clumsy double boots, I manage to force the first hundred feet, a mixture of free climbing at around E1 and aid on RURPs, crack tacks and skyhooks.* I fall off three times, held twice on the same tied-off small peg. The other pitons rip and slide into my lap when I stop. Much higher up the pitch, I have a final huge fall when I run out of strength trying to free climb up a very difficult scoop. A small angle piton tapped an inch into a crystal pocket somehow stays in place and holds me.

"John you must be very careful."

* RURPs and crack tacks are tiny aid-climbing devices developed in Yosemite and the Black Canyon of Colorado. They can be placed in incipient cracks just well enough to hold your weight but not stop a fall. Skyhooks are even more precarious. They are hooked over tiny flakes, and you hang your etriers on them and slowly transfer your weight, hoping the hook doesn't pop off.

It is Voytek's mantra, directed up at me from the assembled team watching my antics from below. One of my etriers snakes gently through space on its 5,000-foot descent to the darkening glacier. It has had enough. Alex lowers me in the semi-dark. I am chastened, my forearms are running with blood and my knuckles have been opened to the bone. Fortunately, there is enough snow on the small ledge to make dinner. We pass pots of food and tea from hammock to hammock in good spirits before closing off the world and the gentle snow that is falling.

Day seven: The sun drives us from our hammocks into a blistering blue sky. Mountains glisten above the sanctuary's outer ring far to the east. Alex and I lounge in our hammocks, while Krzysztof fashions a belay 40 feet above my high point. The morning is still and calm, but we hear animated shouts in Polish between Voytek and Krzysztof. We do not understand what is going on but looking up we see Krzysztof tumbling through space accompanied by a shower of pegs. As one pings past in space, I foolishly try to catch it.
"Ow!"
"That's less weight for us to carry then," Alex drawls.
Years later, Voytek described what happened:

> After time-consuming aid climbing, Krzysztof decided to my surprise to start fixing a belay a bit prematurely. He still had at least ten spare metres of rope. Progress fixing the stance was very slow. Finally he informed me that the stance was ready and ordered me to climb up. I started sorting out the gear but then I sensed a strange inner resistance to move up. It was weird because Krzysztof didn't say a word about the quality of the stance, except that he was knocking and tapping the pegs and the rock with his hammer [a] strangely long time. When he urged me to move up I suddenly felt glued up to my stance. I didn't know what to say. I was simply scared. I felt terribly ashamed because I couldn't invent a reasonable justification to refuse to climb up. Never in my life had I refused to follow my partner. But this time for no special reason I was scared to

death and I could not go. Shame … real shame. Finally I stammered a question up to Krzysztof:

"Hey Krzysztof the stance is ready?"

"Yes, yes," he reconfirmed, somehow too eagerly.

"How many pitons you put in?"

"Oh, there are many pitons," he answered again too reassuringly – and then the silence followed.

And from somewhere deep within came a feeling, "no way, I will not go. Too many pitons, every one tapped and knocked a hundred times. No way."

"Hi Krzysztof, sorry, you better climb up a bit more, you've got enough rope."

Then there followed another long silence. Not a single word of comment. I sensed I was growing red with shame.

"Okay, Voytek. I will try." The surprisingly agreeable answer finally arrived. I was a bit surprised at my easy win.

He restarted the climbing. The progress was minute and it was even slower. He asked once or twice for a special attention. Finally there arrived a familiar ominous noise as he fell, followed by multiple clang and ping of pitons as they bounced into space. It was a suspiciously long fall. It proved he ripped off all the pitons from the prearranged stance. At last the red colour of my face faded away. I came to terms with my shame. Poor Krzysztof, he had to restart the final part of the pitch one more time. He finally reached a much better and safe stance. The next day he grew sicker and with that came a new fear. *

Cursing, Krzysztof has to repeat the crux, this time climbing higher still to find a safer stance. I cook as Voytek jumars up to Krzysztof and then leads through on the continuously steep rock above. We hang the sleeping bags out to dry before the clouds roll in. It is slow progress today, this is the hardest climbing so far. There are no safe pegs to jumar

* This story was sent to the author by Voytek after reading the English first edition. Kurtyka is often heralded as one of the finest alpinists of this period with an unequalled record. This story reveals that he was also one of the most intuitive and perceptive. Perhaps this helps explain why on his scores of expeditions, he was never involved with a fatality.

to the next stance so Krzysztof carries on. At last, he finds a decent crack and two ropes are tied together and lowered for us to start up.

The nine-millimetre Polish ropes stretch alarmingly.* I stay put on the ledge despite pulling 20 metres of rope through the jumars. When it is about the diameter of a pencil, I suddenly spring off the ledge into space and yo-yo a bit before daring to start. The rope squeaks like chalk on a blackboard each time I push the jumar upwards. It is all very disconcerting.

"Polish special technology – it's normal!" Krzysztof shouts down.

The daily afternoon storm wraps itself around the face by the time we have made the first carry up to the stance. The wind is blowing the abseil rope and it swings out of sight where it might snag. Alex and I haul up the rope, coil it and tie it to the peg. The Poles are out of sight above. We continue to the next stance, where Krzysztof is belaying Voytek on the last pitch of the day.

Alex and I descend to fetch the remaining two Haston rucksacks, named after Dougal Haston who had been killed in a skiing accident the year before. We had known Dougal. His ascents of *Eiger Direct*, Annapurna's south face and Everest's southwest face had put him at the top of the British alpinist charts for several years. The purple rucksacks are state-of-the-art. Each is treated with great care at every stance and handover point. To drop one would mean disaster. That is the reason we jumar with them on our backs rather than risk hauling them over overhangs of rough granite.

On the last rappel, Alex makes a terrible mistake. He gathers the coiled rope where we stored it and clips on with his descending device, intending to unravel it on the way down to avoid the danger of the wind taking it off line. But he has clipped into the bottom end and, before he realizes his mistake, he steps back into the abyss. There is a high-pitched shriek and he is gone. The rope hisses off the edge. It is terrifying. For a few seconds, time is measured at a rate of 32 feet per second. The rope is taking a sounding of the void beneath. Then it is

---

* There was value in the Polish ropes after all. We started with two 30-metre jumaring ropes, and both became damaged and frayed. Yet because they stretched so much, we always seemed to still have two 30-metre ropes regardless of how much we cut off.

gone from the ledge completely and the impact of Alex's fall hits the piton with an explosive snap and twang. It holds. I immediately shout like a madman into the empty cloud beneath but realize even if Alex is okay, the wind is too strong for him to hear. I try to lift the rope, but it carries Alex's full weight and there is no chance of me pulling it up. I wait a minute and try again, wait and try again. The rope is still weighted. Ten minutes pass. I am attaching prusik slings to the rope to descend when the rope suddenly comes free. He has either fallen off the end or is there somewhere, probably badly hurt. I can do nothing but rappel down as fast as possible to find out.

There is no sign of Alex near the bottom of the rope, only the safety knot gently slapping the wall. But then there he is, a short pendulum away, draped over the remaining two Haston sacks, as pale as the snowy mist that surrounds him.

"Christ! Alex? Are you alright?"

He looks up at me and whispers: "I don't want to play this game just to have a rucksack named after me."

Day eight: Proper granite cracks at last. I make good progress for three pitches at around HVS or E1 with a couple of nuts for aid to surmount bulges. At the end of my sequence of leads, I am pleased that the over-hang above with a dodgy looking icicle on the lip has fallen to Alex in the rotation. Staring up at the bottom of his crampons, I can tell the climbing is desperate. Alex hangs a sling for aid from his ice axe and steps into it. He swings alarmingly but, stretching up, hangs on long enough to get a secure placement with one Terrordactyl high on the icicle. He manages a one-arm pull-up and exits over the top. The icicle collapses and pummels me painfully. Now we are on the "Cyclops' Eye," a steep snowfield at 22,000 feet in the top centre of the face. We climb diagonally up to the left and exit via a pitch of awkward mixed ground before fixing the rope and descending in the afternoon storm to the sitting bivvy Voytek has excavated in the hard snow.

"We have a problem," he says. "Krzysztof is worse today – he thinks he's in Poland." The night is cold and starry. For the first time on the climb we sat together in bivvy sacks and gained warmth and strength from that. But for Voytek the night is a torment. He does not tell us but he wakes often to touch Krzysztof to make sure he is still alive. In his head, he is going through a classic alpine horror story; what to do with Krzysztof's living yet powerless body if he is unable to climb in the morning?

Day nine: In the morning, although he is slow and weary, Krzysztof is able to climb, as if he knows this is the only thing that will save his life. Voytek leads five pitches of mixed ground to the summit ridge. It is some of the hardest technical climbing of the climb. I jumar up close behind Krzysztof, watching his every move and helping and encouraging him as best I can. We reach the summit ridge at around four and our horizon broadens into a wide vista of big mountains – so much space after so many days focusing primarily on the two dimensions of the vertical plane. Views of the high Himalaya open up to us in all directions: Trisul, Devistan, Dunagiri, Kalanka and the massive ever-present goddess, Nanda Devi. We traverse the summit and descend the steep soft snow on the ridge between Changabang and Kalanka. Krzysztof is behaving irrationally.

"Now we must glissade, faster, quick down." He points toward the glacier 6,000 feet below. There are ice cliffs, rock buttresses and crevasses in which we would tumble like clothes in a drier before they swallowed us up, but in his pain and delirium, he sees only the hundred feet of 55-degree snow.

Voytek angrily reprimands Krzysztof in Polish. I notice that Alex has untied from the rope and retied with a screw-gate, not closed. If Krzysztof or any of us fall, he will quickly unclip. I follow suit. Voytek warns us to keep Krzysztof on a tight rope on the tricky descent down a steep and corniced ridge. As the light begins to fade, we safely reach the col between Changabang and Kalanka and cut a comfortable platform under a rock overhang. We are now running short of gas and food, so supper is minimal. This is the first day it hasn't snowed. A golden sunset saturates the clouds resting quietly at the feet of Nanda Devi. It is our stunning reward. But during the night we are filled with anxiety as the wind increases: the weather is changing and Krzysztof is not at all well.

Next day at dawn, we have a quick brew and begin the descent of the face between Changabang and Kalanka, the line more or less that of the original ascent in 1974. I lead, followed by Alex then Krzysztof and Voytek. I make slow progress and soon we are plunged into cloud. Fatigue takes hold of me. My stomach begins to cramp. A sudden tight rope from behind often stops me from going further. I am totally unaware of the difficulties Voytek is having to keep Krysztof moving, two ropes behind me. He is continually collapsing to gain his breath and needs to be pulled into action by Voytek each time.

Uncertainty brings me to a halt as a maze of seracs and crevasses appear in all directions. I am without a clue which way to go. There are shouts behind and suddenly Voytek is at my side.

"I will lead. You go to the back."

As Krzysztof goes past, I note his face has gone hollow, without any expression or recognition. Alex says a few words of encouragement when he arrives, then he, too, soon vanishes into the foggy depths. When the rope goes tight, I follow in a now well-worn channel.

The difficulties increase as we descend. Occasionally, I have to stop to remove a running belay, an ice screw or a snow stake. The route goes right, then left, then back again beneath the seracs and around crevasses. Voytek is using some intuitive magic to bring us through these horrors. I am too tired to appreciate the danger of the situation until much later. In the late afternoon, we reach the glacier. Alex and I traverse across to the bottom of the route to collect food from the cache we have stashed, having run out of food on top. The glacier is heavily fractured and we both fall briefly into holes. Returning to Voytek and the semi-delirious Krzysztof, we cook a big meal and enjoy our best sleep for the past ten days. We are released.

It would take us two more days to reach base camp. I drew the short straw to stay behind for a second night partway down the glacier to care for Krzysztof, who was now quite weak. Next morning, Lech and our liaison officer K.T. arrived at our bivvy in the moraine with a Thermos of tea and cooked porridge. All was now well. Krzysztof seemed to come round. K.T. took my rucksack and Lech took

Krzysztof's. We staggered down for the last few hours to base camp. The meadow was dressed in autumnal colours and a large herd of blue sheep grazed unconcerned as we passed.

A mixture of euphoria and exhaustion now overtook us. We lounged around for a couple of days. The mountain had absorbed much effort but far less time than expected. We had 20 days before the porters were due to return, time for at least one more peak, but it was now my turn to become ill. I couldn't keep any food down for six days and I suffered extremely painful stomach cramps. I lay in the tent moaning. This was too much for Lech, so one night he gave me a shot of morphine in the backside to shut me up. It did. For a couple of days, I really doubted I would ever leave the sanctuary. I took a short walk one day and found the perfectly intact head of a bharal sheep staring up at me open-eyed. The rest of the body was nowhere to been seen. A snow leopard had been near. It can't have been more than 200 yards from our camp.

Alex and Voytek set out to attempt the northwest face of Nanda Devi, but when they got to the start of the real difficulties at half height, they were without enough equipment to carry on. They also realized how tired they were. While they were away, I discovered the root of my stomach problem. We had been cooking with water straight from the river, which was full of sediment. I found a small spring and, using its pure, clear water, I quickly recovered. Why weren't the others ill? I'd thought I was tough.

On the fourth evening after setting off, Alex and Voytek returned to camp and collapsed into their sleeping bags. Next morning we did some calculations. The food was running out and the porters were not due for 12 more days. Someone needed to go and get them. Krzysztof was still not right and apart from looking like a stick insect, I was the most rested. It was agreed I would walk out on my own. It had taken eight days to get in. Four days should do it going out.

Long solo walks in the mountains are good for the soul, a chance to reflect, to get back to normality. Our climb of Changabang was possibly the hardest technical climb yet done in the Himalaya, but I wanted to put that behind me as quickly as possible and take in the mountains without the risk. I left at dawn in the hope of completing four stages in one day. Darkness caught me halfway across the Tilman slabs and by the light of my headlamp I scrambled precariously up a hundred feet to find a small grassy ledge. A leopard's scream echoed suddenly in the gorge, punctuating the continuous dull road of the Rishi Ganga. Rishi I knew meant "holy scribe." The Ganga was etching its path through the world. I munched some sweets and then subsided into a truly deep sleep. Nourished by the rich air of these lower altitudes, colourful dreams flowed through my mind.

The next morning, I scurried quickly down to Deodi. As I cooked a combined dinner and breakfast, a mongoose walked up beside me, had a good look and then strolled off. Two days later, I was back in Lata Kharak, the site of our first camp, where hallucinations overtook me, or so it seemed. The sound of pan pipes seemed to come from all around the hills. I stared through the trees, expecting to see Pan himself appear, not for a moment questioning why the Greek god of the wilds would appear in India.

As I descended the steep grassy ridge toward the rhododendron forest, the sound of music grew. Lata was still a few tiny, black rooftops thousands of feet below. The clustered houses set amongst terraced hillsides rich with golden barley ready for harvesting, a tapestry of colours that seemed sensationally rich after so many weeks in the high mountain world of black, white and blue. I realized as I stopped to take it all in that my pan pipes were, in fact, the distorted high-pitched sounds of music blaring from distant loudspeakers. Our sirdar, Sher Singh, had told us of the Nanda Devi festival at the end of October. I think he was warning us not to expect help from the village while it was on. When I arrived in Lata, I realized why.

A frantic, frenetic and mildly frightening festival of many parts was taking place in every open place. Goats and sheep were being sacrificed in a bloody and apparently endless line and then being skinned for the feast. Fakirs were walking red-hot coals, and there were climbing ropes snaking upwards, apparently without any support. I watched one fakir push a knife into his belly without showing any sign of blood or injury. All the clichés of Indian mysticism and magic were there, practised in a carnival atmosphere in praise of the great goddess Nanda Devi, a goddess that existed before the Vedas. Now the waters that flow from her are one of the sacred waters forming the main artery of Hinduism, the Ganges.

Sher Singh was at home, happy and half-pissed. I gratefully took a glass of chang while I negotiated the time and number of porters required to extract my friends from base camp, now a surprisingly distant and quickly receding place in my mind. "You must go in with your people tomorrow," I explained. "I will go to Delhi and arrange our flight for two weeks from now. The timing is crucial."

"Yes, yes, tomorrow, after the festival is over." I knew I was dealing with a concept of time that made room for gratifying procrastination.

"And the festival definitely ends tomorrow?"

"Oh, yes, tomorrow, or in a few more days, six at the most."

I calculated everything from that point forward – six days from now, one more to overcome their hangovers, four days' walk in, five out, three days to Delhi, two there, then one down to Bombay. Three weeks and one day from now – that was how I would arrange the flight when I got to Delhi. But should I now return to base camp instead? I decided to keep going; I still had the flights to organize and the bureaucracy to clear.

"You must stay. You can see festival. It is not allowed for a foreigner. You stay in my house," pleaded Sher Singh.

After the second chang it was tempting, but I left. On the way down the last of the helter-skelter paths to the road, two girls stopped me. The prettier one gestured and spoke encouragingly before opening her robes to reveal her shining brown body. I looked away and shrugged my shoulders; I had just come from the Nanda Devi Sanctuary and had been in the presence of a real goddess. I muttered, "*Angrez*, English," and ran on down the path.

When the others eventually reached Delhi, Voytek was furious with me.

"You just left us there with little food for nearly two weeks. What were you thinking?"

I explained again why I had carried on to Delhi, and the logic. Alex got it immediately, and everyone calmed down when they realized that I'd secured flights for us in just three days time, the only seats available for a month. My calculation in Lata with the help of a glass of chang was exactly right.

We had a day buying rugs and other trinkets to take home. K.T. took us to his parents' home and we told them of K.T.'s excellent work. He had been more than an LO. He had been a member of the team, humping loads and doing his share of the cooking. Later that afternoon, K.T. took us to the Presidential Hotel, where we could order "special tea" – beer that came in teapots. Public drinking was against the law in Mr. Desai's India. That night, amidst a slight alcoholic haze, we loaded endless Polish barrels into taxis and said farewell to him. We just managed to get everything aboard the overnight air-conditioned train to Bombay.

Alex and I explored the city for a day while the Poles did more last-minute shopping to fill their orders from Warsaw, and then we were on our LOT flight back. We were greeted as heroes. Radio and television interviews followed. Alex was the media's darling. Arriving just in time to go on air live and take his place in the chair, Alex was asked by the TV interviewer:

"Was it very hard to organize and do this amazing thing?"

"Yes, we had so much to drink at dinner tonight that finding this studio was incredibly difficult."

As with all big climbs in the Himalaya, the experience was strongly felt but outwardly ephemeral. At home, a general feeling of euphoria lasted for a few weeks. But it was impossible to explain to those who didn't climb, so it became internalized. Even our own breed, buried in their day-to-day lives and smelling competition, didn't respond as I expected. Joe Tasker suddenly loomed over me in a bar at the autumn outdoor trade show held in Harrogate each year.

"How come you guys managed to climb that face so quickly?" he quizzed me, looking stern.

All I could think to say was: "I guess we chose the sunny side of the mountain Joe."

19

DIAMOND DOGS

Alex and I were in Peru's Cordillera Blanca, trying to make the first ascent of Nevado III –and it wasn't going well. The first thing to go wrong was being on this mountain in the first place. It wasn't our original objective. That was the south face of Caraz I, but when we reached the bottom of our route two days before, we discovered Canadian guide Albi Sole and Nigel Helliwell recovering at the bottom, having just descended from a four-day ascent. We didn't even know they were in the country. There they were, looking exhausted, elated and a bit frostbitten, with the thousand-yard stare and animated stories of survivors.

Alex and I were deeply pissed off. We had hoped Caraz I would be one of our major ticks for the summer, but we congratulated our two new friends, even gave them some of our food, since we had already decided we wouldn't need it. Our new, unplanned choice, the south face of Nevado III, was only 1200 metres high and the summit around 5700 metres. Despite the fact that the mountain was unclimbed, and we had no time to study the face, we decided it would take us only a day. So we dispensed with sleeping bags, stove, food and all the usual extras. It would be lighter, faster, free of the umbilical cord and so much more fun.

Those who have seen Peruvian south faces – the equivalent of north faces in the northern hemisphere – will have an image of white walls like the crests of breaking waves with peculiar sculptured features and flutes like organ pipes. Looking at these, it seems logical that a bed of firm snow and ice will form a nice direct line between any pair of flutes and lead straight to the summit, or near enough, with little bother.

That is not the reality. It is difficult to explain how it forms, and how it sticks to the face, but the snow in the bed between these flutes usually has the consistency of feather pillows, while further out it is like cane sugar. This is not the rule for all peaks, but it was on Nevado III. When the mist from the Amazon drifts in over the mountains, as it seems to do most days, the stuff crystallizes. The other problem is that these flutes inevitably merge, and then there is almost always a certain amount of "fluting about" to be done. This means shifting from one flute to the next, or more aptly "sifting," since the snow has the texture, consistency and security of vertical flour. If ever there was a time to heed Alex's advice when crossing loose snow or a heavily crevassed glacier, to "think light like a fairy," it was now. But somehow it just didn't work for me; the only way I could follow him up this stuff was to pull most of it down, performing a kind of vertical front crawl.

It was some time after midnight. The moon was full, but an incessant cloud of spindrift wafted down, and its light became a dim icy halo. We had been climbing for 18 hours and were beginning to feel weary and worried. Everything looked steeper above us and there was no sign of rock or security. Thoughts of a ledge to rest on were as remote as the beaches near Lima. We had crossed three flutes already, each more demanding than the last, and after each sift Alex managed to float up another pitch or two in the hollows between the flutes before they joined again. The snow now was shoulder-deep.

Alex shouted down a warning. "It's getting very steep. Not sure how this stuff sticks." I was belayed to my two axes, and so pushed them in even further, a more or less useless gesture. But Alex was a master of this stuff. Terry King had first commented on it during their approach to *The Shroud* on the Grandes Jorasses. Alex had a knack of staying on the surface: "Pretend you are Tinker Bell," Alex advised as everyone else floundered.

Here on Nevado III, our only consolation was that if everything collapsed, it would be over pretty quickly. We were soaked, frozen and almost discouraged. It looked certain we would need to muster the energy to carry on through the night. It was now one in the morning and an overhanging wall of ice crystals blocked our passage. Alex submerged himself in the adjoining edge of the flute to the right. The moon and its pallid halo seemed to hiss down at us.

A sudden shout from Alex: "There's ice here. It's solid! Christ, a bivvy."

He brought me across into a small niche of heaven. In the darkness, we had traversed to the eastern edge of the south face, where exposure to the morning sun had worked some simple magic to create a crevasse beneath an exposed rock. We stomped down a flat area and carefully beat the snow from the ropes and each other's backs. Then we pulled our rucksacks over our feet and sat down, pressing together for warmth.

Alex and I had by now climbed together on so many occasions that we were beyond the stage of needing to enjoy it. We both knew that would come later. At moments like this, it was just a matter of getting up, or getting down, or just finding a place to sit out the night. So much in climbing depends on the state of the mountain, the state of your mind or perhaps the meal you had that morning. Each factor might be seen or felt differently by each individual. At least tomorrow's morning meal would not be a factor. We had no stove or food.

But for the moment, it was fine just to be able to sit. There was no point in imagining how much better it would have been if we had brought a stove, a pan and a bivvy bag. It was not that bad. A couple of sweets each and some ice to suck. The moon was now a friendly face, offering hope and a measure of time. We sang all night, anything we could think of to stave off the uncontrollable shivering. Mostly we sang a song to the tune of John Philip Sousa's "The Stars and Stripes Forever."

"Be kind to your web-footed friends, for a duck may be somebody's mother; lives all alone in a swamp, where it's always cold and damp! Now I come to the end of my song, and to prove that I'm not a bloody liar, I'll sing it through once again, only this time a little bit higher!" And so it went until our voices broke and we laughed. We were alive. We were the best of friends in a difficult place.

In the morning, the sun shone temptingly around the corner. We allowed ourselves the luxury of its warmth for an hour or so and even drifted off into semi-consciousness. Then we geared up.

"What shall we do, up or down?" I asked.

"Going up makes you warmer," Alex stated.

His ice axes bit into the mountain and he pulled over the top of the ice lip above our hole in a shower of sunlit ice fragments. Now we were on the eastern flank of the south face and there was real ice to climb. A vertical rock buttress gave me a chance to do my bit. To our right, the steep flutings and ice walls connecting our mountain to Caraz I were like the inside of an elaborate crystal bowl. We made it to the top by early afternoon. I should really say Alex got to the top. I sat on the last solid bit of mountain with a belay while he swam up the last pitch. Faced with heavily corniced ridges in all directions, he carefully sank back down.

"Straight down we go. No chance along the ridge."

We found our way down the east face with only one more bivvy.

Before returning, we tried to repeat the extremely long northwest ridge of Huascarán Norte. We gave up after three days, realizing we would run out of food and gas before we even got to the end of the ridge to reach the mountain proper. We descended, humbled, to the beautiful Laguna Peron and were lucky to find a taxi dropping off some Spanish climbers to take us back to the beautiful town of Huaraz. Half the population had been killed and 95 per cent of the town flattened in the great earthquake of 1970, but most of the evidence was now gone.

It was like being in Chamonix that summer. Many of our friends were in Peru.* We stood on the roof of the Hotel Barcelona with Tut Braithwaite, Brian Hall, Terry Mooney, Alan Rouse and Choe Brooks, taking in the sun. Alex and I noticed the south face of Ranrapalca (6162 metres).

"What's that?" I asked Brian, pointing to a high, distant but clearly big peak. Brian and Al had been out for six weeks so knew the view.

---

* Peru was in a state of near revolution while we were there. We were too naive and ill-informed to appreciate that things could go very wrong at any moment, but we were caught up in riots in Lima on the way home and had to stay overnight in a store with steel shutters. Tut and Choe had just come back from climbing Alpamayo. As they got off the bus, Tut said he heard firecrackers going off. Wondering what the celebration was, he looked across the square to see a crowd of panicked children running in all directions. There was a teachers' strike on and their pupils had joined in. The army opened fire on the crowd, killing several teachers and pupils. It all went back to normal within hours and the streets were again full of tourists as if nothing had happened.

"Ranrapalca," he replied. "That's the south face; it hasn't been climbed."

I looked at Alex and he at me. It was nice to have a big route to do only a taxi ride away from the nearest bar.

The idea of taking taxis to base camp had nearly cost us our Mount Everest Foundation grant that year. I followed my fumbling Changabang interview with an even more hilarious performance in front of the panel for our Peruvian trip. This time, it was a last-minute change of plans that caused the crisis. The night before I was due to appear, Alex phoned to say that a big Czech team had climbed our major objective, the south face of Salcantay, the previous year using expedition siege tactics.

Our enforced second choice was to join the boys in Huaraz. The problem was we had no time to research alternative objectives. There was no Internet and the Alpine Club library, the major resource for climbers' research, along with collections of *Mountain* magazine, was in London. Neither option was available at my house in the Lake District.

When I was ushered into the committee this time, there were no familiar faces. But at least I had a file this time, albeit containing all our Vilcabamba research, which was now totally irrelevant. I explained why the objective on the application was no longer relevant and that we would go to the Cordillera Blanca. We knew there were still many fine objectives there, but I couldn't name any. Access to peaks was relatively straightforward so we were bound to get a few new routes done.

"And where in Peru is the Cordillera Blanca?" I was asked by one of the venerable explorers arraigned before me on the other side of the long, polished table. I hadn't a clue, but I had to choose quickly. I knew Vilcabamba was in the Central Andes.

"In the southern Peruvian Andes." The gentleman referred to the huge atlas he had opened in front of him. No further questions on that one, I thought to myself, so I must be right. (I wasn't.)

"And how will you get in to your base camp?" asked another respected member.

Something Brian had told me sprung to mind and I blurted it out before I could think.

"Bus from Lima to Huaraz and then a taxi." This was not what they wanted to hear. They wanted a picture of a long line of llamas snaking up through terraced fields cultivated by the Incas with carefully balanced loads swaying gently on their backs and pan pipe music haunting the hot and arid Altiplano.

"You can't possibly take taxis to such high mountains."

"Ah, of course not, sir! I meant just a little way from the town. Then we'll hire some Indians and their llamas for the long march in." I was red and stammering with embarrassment by this point. Worse was to come.

"I've found the Cordillera Blanca," piped up my original inquisitor. "It's in the northern Andes of Peru." He looked at me down his spectacles. I knew then I never wanted to attend another panel.

Tut Braithwaite was in next after me, attaché case under his arm and full of his usual knowledgeable enthusiasm. He told me later the first question they asked him was "Where is the Cordillera Blanca?" He got it exactly right. The upshot was that Choe and Tut got a grant of £400 and Alex and I £200. I'd like to point out they got better value for money from us with two new routes and two new descents.

Indirectly, Alex and I owed British Aerospace our lives on Ranrapalca, but Choe Brooks should really take the credit. It was he who somehow wangled the purpose-made, state-of-the-art snow stakes from BAE for our Peruvian trip. They were Choe's design and the match of any of the titanium gear the Russians produced in the Kazakhstan space factories – lightweight, strong and just the right shape. They were about three and a half feet long, which made them awkward to carry, but snow stakes were indispensable in the Andean snow conditions and much more likely to see use than ice screws. Before each route you weighed up the descent as carefully as any ascent. How many abseils down that face? How many on rock? How many on ice screws? How many snow stakes to take?

"Four ought to be enough," was the almost inevitable conclusion Alex came to. "One on each side of the rucksacks."

Like Alex, Choe was a bit of a designer. We were using his newly designed tower stove as well. It was the best tower stove I had ever seen;
incredibly compact with an excellent windshield and pans big enough
to actually cook in. The only serious fault was that it didn't work. The
jet bunged up after a couple of days. If there was any flame at all, it
took half the night to make tea. Of course, the upside of this was you
could throw all the fuel away to save weight when the stove went
wrong if not the stove itself. We had faith Choe would put it right if we
brought it back. And each time he did it would once again work for a
few firings. I have a picture in my mind of Choe, sitting half-naked on
the sunny roof of the Hotel Barcelona in Huaraz, placing each tiny
part carefully on newspaper in front of him as he deconstructed the
stoves and carefully cleaned them. Behind him, the great peaks of the
Cordillera Blanca studded the eastern horizon.

The best Choe design story involved one of his cars, a knackered
Mini. On his way back from the Alps, overloaded with gear and people,
the sub frame collapsed and Choe had to abandon the car somewhere
in the south of England. In such circumstances, the usual plan was to
take everything out, remove plates and all forms of identification, go
home and report the car stolen. Choe was about to fill in the insurance
claims when the phone rang.

"We've found your car, sir." It was the police. "Can you come down
to Winchester to pick it up?" And off Choe went, armed with a two-
by-two timber, knowing he had some design and building work to do.
"And when I asked the mechanic whether I could rebuild the sub frame
with wood, he just laughed and said it wouldn't work, but he would
say that, wouldn't he? He wasn't a joiner." Choe rebuilt the sub frame
with wood and drove it around for another year.

Ironically, Ranrapalca was situated in one of the valleys where there
were no roads to service mines or hydroelectric projects. That was
probably why such an obvious face had gone unclimbed. We hired a
local Indian with his pack llamas and set off with his two sons for the
winding journey across the high plain dotted with farms. Men and
women worked the fields together in colourful skirts and ponchos
and massive hats. It took us two days to reach a lovely camp among

trees and flowers at the toe of the glacier. Choe Brooks and Terry Mooney walked in with us to attempt one of the adjoining peaks. Instead, they spent a couple of days watching us on the face, and when we didn't return as planned on day four, they descended to Huaraz expecting to have to send the worst sort of news home.

We had learned on Nevado III and Huascarán Norte not to underestimate the difficulty of climbing in Peru. Ranrapalca did not disappoint. Apart from a few places, the climbing was much more Alpine in character with little unconsolidated snow. We were able to solo icefields to cover a third of the height, starting on the right and trending left. These were interspersed with tricky mixed climbing on polished slabs, leading to ice bulges over rock barriers. There was the incessant worry of falling rock and ice, but we were fit and fast, soloing almost the entire bottom third of the face and wondering why we had the two V-shaped, shovel-like snow stakes strapped to the sides of our sacks. In a chimney between a detached serac and the rock behind we had to take these off, and lost time hauling them up.

We spent a comfortable night bivouacked on top of a massive ice tower shaped a bit like the Chrysler Building in New York but set just far enough back from the face to provide protection from anything that fell from the face above our heads. We were pinpoints in the sky – safe and able to eat and sleep well. The equivalent of the Empire State in height still had to be climbed to reach the summit.

The climbing was continuously difficult, but there were no surprises. We reached the summit midway through the afternoon the next day, having used our snow stakes only a couple of times. It was a day without cloud and we stood on the spine of the Andes. Most of the peaks were standing clear of the Amazon cloud. We ate some chocolate and confirmed our original plan. Thanks to the risk of stone fall, and our limited rack of nuts and pegs, a descent of the south face was out of the question. Descending the easy route down the other side of the mountain would put us in completely the wrong valley with a long and expensive taxi journey back around. Before we had set off, we had formulated another plan – to descend the unclimbed west ridge.

What followed was a totally bizarre and unique experience in the high mountains. All seemed well on the second bivvy, not far below the summit with a view down toward the lovely peak of Ocshapalca at the end of a serrated ridge of cornices about a mile away to the north. The only fly in the ointment was the stove, which had sputtered down to a tiny flame and our supper of noodle soup and mash with hot chocolate turned into a midnight feast. The moon shone and then the Amazon mist rose to the east like a slow-motion tsunami and embraced us in a freezing fog.

It cleared for an hour or so at dawn as we packed up and melted just enough snow for a cold drink of Tang before heading down the initial, straightforward section of ridge. We were soon plunged into thick mist, but an hour later we arrived on level snow, which we assumed had to be the col from where we needed to find the apparently broad west ridge, which swept down in a curve to connect with our glacier halfway between our peak and Ocshapalca. With no compass, we had to guess, but each guess seemed to lead to an abyss. Daylight began to melt away in the mist. Eventually, we found one drop into a deep but broad crevasse with a clear bottom. It was a point of no return. Once we'd abseiled in, we had to find a way out the other side. Our ropes just reached the bottom. We did not have a retrieval line so one of our precious snow stakes was sacrificed. We bivouacked where we landed. The stove gave up before the water was even warm.

In the morning, the stove refused even to sputter, but still we packed it, intending to repair it for the next climb. We wandered down the corridor of our crevasse until it shrank down to a climbable wall on the left. The mist was still thick, but it would lift, tantalizingly, giving momentary glimpses of surrounding peaks and, fortunately for us, of Ocshapalca moving back to our right; we knew we were headed in the correct direction. A second snow stake was sacrificed at another double rope abseil into another uncertain abyss of a crevasse, from which we emerged to teeter to the edge of a huge overhanging wall of ice that completely cut the ridge in two. We tried to descend around it on either side, but the snow was deep and dangerous with big drops beneath, so once again we abseiled off a stake. Three down, one to go.

The bivvy was cold, worrying and wearisome that night. We sang stupid songs in praise of fate and the powers that be.

The next morning, a bright sun warmed us. We were just below the mist and could clearly see the final 500 feet or so of descent on what seemed a continuous, broad, snow-covered ridge. Tired but relieved, we ploughed down through thicker and heavier snow up to the knees, then to the waist, before we came to the final mind-boggling and scary obstacle: yet another overhanging ice wall splitting the ridge. The good news was it appeared we could get onto the glacier from its base. The bad news was that it looked further than 30 metres, more than the length of our ropes. There was also an open crevasse at the bottom.

We first toyed with the idea of tying the two ropes together, but the since the glacier beyond looked like a lace doily of crevasses, we thought better of it. We would still need our ropes. Our final stake went in perfectly, at just the right angle to take the load with no chance of it popping. Like its siblings higher up, it was a piece of beautifully engineered aluminium that should by rights be part of a wing flying high in the sky over the Andes. Instead, its fate was to be left to descend at glacial rates over the coming centuries. Would we soon be joining it on its slow journey?

Alex volunteered to go first, going without his sack to give him a chance of prusiking back up if that became necessary. We were in luck. Although the rope didn't come close to reaching the bottom, the edge of the crevasse on its far side was higher than it looked and the wall he was abseiling overhung just enough for Alex to swing onto the lip and flop, with axes flailing, off the end of the ropes into soft snow. I hauled up one end, tied on Alex's sack and lowered it, but the lesser weight meant feeding through some extra rope to reach him. Then I evened up the rope, attached my figure of 8, checked everything three times and swung off into the void. I landed next to Alex in a heap. We pulled the ropes through and gave each other wry smiles.

"Nice climb, eh?"

"Could have been worse. Beer and food are calling."

I set off down the glacier in the lead and at first my heightened senses made me prod each step ahead. Telltale grey inundations criss-crossed confusingly in many directions. Then tiredness overtook us as we got through the worst of the icefall. It was no place to exhibit a lack of care and attention and disaster nearly befell us. One minute I was on firm snow, the next I was falling 30 feet into the sudden darkness of an enormous crevasse. I landed unhurt on a cone of snow that rose from the impenetrable blackness beneath. Above me I could see a hole and blue sky. I had fallen through the weakest part of the shell of ice that covered the enormous opening. This was not a usual slot crevasse.

Then I saw what was about to happen.

A shadow moved toward the hole, gaining substance as it grew closer to the opening where the snow-bridge thinned. I screamed for Alex to go back. The shadow stopped, moved slightly one way, then the other and then retreated beyond the illuminated roof above me. I breathed easier. Just as I was getting really cold, three heavy tugs on the rope told me it was time to prusik. My slings were already attached. Once the rope came taut, it cut through the ceiling above like a cheese wire, eventually halting where it met ice. I swung off and up, cutting a hole out at the top. Alex was sitting just around the corner of a big serac in which he had placed two solid ice screws for my escape from the hole.

"That must have been exciting." Then he gave me a weary grin that said "don't do that again." I didn't ask how I had fallen 30 feet when the ropes should have been tight between us.

"Did you hear me shout?"

"I think so but it was like something from a drum. Anyway, I soon saw what needed doing."

"No more please God. Let's go."

We wound our way down the glacier with a tight rope between us. My nerves were still sparking. At the bivvy, there was a note from Choe and Terry saying, "if you read this, you're lucky bastards because you're alive." More importantly, they had left food and a stove that functioned perfectly. We slept contentedly and were back in Huaraz to celebrate by late evening the next day.

20

PERFECT DAY

The strains between climbers and their partners are obvious: long periods apart, huge risks and the very real possibility that your lover might not come home. For couples, there was always the word "why" hanging in the air. Why put your life at risk when we could be together here? In those long absences away climbing, other questions emerged. Where? When? And who else?

When the worst happened, friends consoled the widows and partners of dead climbers, knowing that in the following months or years they might experience the same loss. Climbing is often described as incestuous. As a community, it is self-absorbed, fuelled with adrenaline on the crags and with alcohol in the evenings, no different to any other small, tight-knit group living on the edge.

Not many months after Alex introduced Maria to Joe Tasker, Maria introduced Alex to Sarah Richard. Alex had lived with Gwyneth for nearly five years after they met at Leeds University. She had a fiery temper sometimes, but she took a no-nonsense approach to the world and had a great sense of fun. She also seemed completely inured to the mess Alex revelled in. They were a perfect couple when it came to that. But, eventually, Gwyneth returned to South Wales for awhile and Alex's growing fame put new temptations in his way. It made matters worse that his liaisons included some of Gwyneth's close friends. When he owned up in his usual off-hand manner, it was too much for Gwyneth to accept.

"If you can sleep with all of my friends, then I am going to sleep with all of yours," she retorted. Gwyneth went off to America with some of them. With this parting shot echoing in Alex's head, our climbing in Peru in 1979 was fired up, in part, because neither of us had any commitments at home. Having split with our respective partners, we had no ties to keep us earthbound.

Sometime after Alex returned from South America, he asked Maria to introduce him to someone new. With some trepidation, Maria decided that her friend Sarah Richard might be a good choice for Alex. Maria knew her through their mutual friends in the Manchester art world. She came round to the house with her boyfriend and, as they got talking, Maria could see that Alex was smitten straight away.

Years later, Sarah and I met for coffee. She had not changed much. Her beautiful full face wore the same warm smile and her reddish brown hair hung just short of her shoulders. She was direct, honest and not afraid to speak her mind. Sarah had never been one to shy away from a challenge. She certainly took on one with Alex; that was evident from the day after they met.

"Maria had invited me around for a drink with my then boyfriend. There was this sparky guy called Alex renting a room at the house. He clocked everything he could about me, where I lived and that I wasn't working, and next day there was a knock on the door. There was Alex: 'Do you fancy a lunchtime drink?'"

Sarah agreed and as they got talking, she realized what an amazing guy he was. After a couple of drinks, Alex in his inimitable way opted to work quickly, suggesting to Sarah they have a summer fling.

"He just said: 'You don't need to fall in love with me or anything like that. I have a girlfriend and she'll be back in the autumn. It will just be for the summer.'" Sarah decided to take a gamble despite the ties of his long relationship with Gwyneth still being there. Alex was hedging.

Maria warned Sarah that she would be in big trouble if she got involved with Alex, but she wasn't to be put off. And that's how their short and intense two and a half years together began. They got on as opposites often do. Sarah was kind, sympathetic to a fault and very artistic, a perfect foil to Alex's abrasive approach to life. Sarah was a stage set designer and work took her to theatres around the country. She was used to high drama. For opposites to work, however, there has to be more than just compliance. Although not immediately apparent,

Sarah was Alex's intellectual match, someone he could depend on to put him right when he became too stubborn.

"Within a few days, Alex and I went off on a road trip together and had a really nice time. We went up to Glasgow, went to art exhibitions, then across to Donegal, stopping in Belfast to borrow Terry Mooney's BMW to travel in style." *

Somewhere during that journey to Ireland, Alex fell in love with Sarah. He explained to her how important it was to have someone who really cared for you when you were away on a big trip. And he told her his ambition was for her to fall in love with him as soon as possible and to be that person when he next went away.

Sarah and Alex moved in together almost as soon as they got back. It became apparent to Maria and all who knew Alex that his matter-of-fact attitude to relationships was changing. He didn't become a romantic overnight, but Sarah awoke something romantic within him, which he only revealed to me much later, during the frightening times just before his death on Annapurna. On all our expeditions, Alex wrote weekly to his mother, but rarely to anyone else. I noticed on Annapurna that he would follow a letter to Jean with one to Sarah.**

"During that summer was the weekend of the royal wedding of Charles and Diana, so we went on an anti-royals weekend to Wales.

---

* To a casual observer, Alex and Terry Mooney seemed complete opposites. Terry, as a successful barrister in Belfast, earned more in a month than Alex could imagine in a year. Terry was patron and mentor to Alex's successful life as a professional climber. They were very alike in what they wanted, but very different in their lifestyles, seeing the world through their lawyer's minds and able to argue any case from opposite sides. They were knowingly observant but not always able to accept personal foibles. It is also not immediately obvious, but they both shared extreme risks to their lives at different times. For Alex, that was every time he ventured onto a big climb; for Terry, a prosecutor, it was every time he ventured out of his flat in Belfast when the Troubles were at their height.

** Writing letters on expeditions was really a therapeutic exercise. Once beyond the road-head, there were no post offices, and trusting a passer-by or your porters with a prestamped and addressed letter when they left you in base camp didn't guarantee it would ever reach one. It worked both ways, as post sent from home was always to the hotel where you had stashed your street clothes before heading for the mountains. Not being in contact with loved ones took a lot of pressure off; not knowing what is going on makes it easier to settle to the task. Even in the populous Everest region, where there were regular mail runners, there was no guarantee the post would work. On my winter Everest trip in 1980–1981, one consignment of film sent out for BBC *Newsnight* was found by chance by one of the Burgesses many years later in a closet at a hotel in Kathmandu.

We stayed at Al Harris's and Alex took me climbing for the first time on the Idwal Slabs. We always went climbing when Alex got back from his trips. He really enjoyed having the opportunity to just have fun climbing away from the pressure of his peers. Alex was fun. He was the complete package, unpredictable, always making me laugh. We got on really well together."

It seemed that Sarah, despite herself, had fallen in love with Alex.

"I was terrified of Gwyneth after we got together. I always felt there was a chance Alex would go back to her. He had been with her for six years before me. She was still around the scene, of course. I decided one day just to go up to her and give her a big hug. Everyone was talking, and it suddenly went very quiet. Gwyneth just accepted the hug and then everyone started talking again. People thought that was great, the right thing. Then one of Gwyneth's close friends came over and said to me that was really nice; you two can get on now. Alex always said how hard it was to be in love with two women at the same time. Thanks a lot, I thought."

As his relationship with Sarah deepened, he was still making his mark at the BMC. Despite his own authoritarian instincts, Alex believed in the democratic process. He could be said to be a republican within the ruling family of the BMC. He wrote, "contrary to popular opinion, this is no one-man show under The Menace (Dennis Gray). BMC policy is formulated and directed by the committee of management (comprised of laymen). It tells the 'professionals' what to do."

This statement was part of the introduction to an article written by Alex for *Climber and Rambler* entitled "Democracy." It appeared at the end of Alex's time at the BMC and was a declaration of his vision for the future. In it, Alex set out his views on the need for a continuous, thoughtful and controlled change within the BMC, one that would better engage the grassroots climber. He suggested changes were needed and a new constitution. He pointed out every climber had a voice in the BMC through their area committee meetings. England and Wales were divided into eight regions where local issues could be discussed and fed back to the BMC's management committee. Alex suggested, without saying so, that these area committees were generally parochial.

As important as local issues were, the area committees, and the clubs they comprised, should in future address national issues as well as the local ones. He posed a list of rhetorical questions to make his point:

"Should the BMC try to acquire rock faces such as Bwlch-y-Moch? Should it campaign against misuse of certification? Should it institute an insurance scheme? Attempt to obtain reciprocal rights to alpine huts? Should it put its weight behind unfortunates who are threatened with criminal prosecution in alpine accidents? Should it fight the 'close the mountains' attitudes that sweep through the daily newspapers and the occasional MP most good winters?"

Alex believed the increasing numbers of people using the mountains for recreational purposes would eventually bring climbing into conflict with landowners and other sports vying for use of the same resource. Inevitably, the government would become fearful of conventional wisdom that climbing was a dangerous, anti-social activity. The solution, Alex believed, lay in a much broader-based, active membership of the BMC, whether via the clubs or as individual members. He saw the importance of the individual informed vote – values still enshrined in the BMC today.

Ironically, while many issues debated in the 1970s are relevant to climbing today, the nature and character of the climbing community have changed the way climbers think and operate. Cheap flights and a move away from risk-taking has meant that overcrowding on the UK crags has shifted to crags in France, Spain and Thailand, leaving many British mountain crags to gather moss. While it was impossible to be insured to do climbing of any nature in the 1970s, insurance is now something most people have. It is even possible to be insured for peaks over 6000 metres.*

Alex was proved right in his call to action. There has been a huge growth of membership and interest in the BMC. For the most part, it is a more democratic, accountable and professionally run organization today than it was in his years as national officer.

* The only insurance available in the 1970s was the usual lost baggage and cancelled flights coverage. The loss of equipment to go climbing would have been a difficult claim to make. Now it is possible to get insurance to bring the body of a deceased climber home. When Alex died, it was not possible to arrange for a body to be brought out of Nepal.

Reinforced by his relationship with Sarah, Alex never gave up his belief in the value of romantic anarchy when it came to some aspects of the mountains. Still, he realized that those people who called for an end to the BMC were wrong. A return to local negotiations without compromise would mean an end to national representation at a time when Thatcher was centralizing power and a new political class without regional affiliation was gaining ascendency. Despite most climbers' anathema to the idea, if national bureaucracy got a hold of adventure and activity in the hills, the lack of a representative voice would be disastrous. It was a complicated intellectual line to walk, but one that Alex managed cleverly. He won over many skeptics at area committee meetings, speaking with authority, knowledge and passion for the issues. He won the hearts and minds campaign on which the BMC has been built ever since.

Having managed arbitration on training issues, there were other tough tasks for Alex in his last year at the BMC. One was to write a paper on legal liability and climbing. This was the first time the subject had been tackled. The BMC hoped to make a case that would capture the spirit of self-help and responsibility as the core values of climbing. The aim was to reduce the likelihood of litigation spreading into climbing. It had already crept into other areas of life in Britain and was rampant in North America.

Another big issue was to find a solution to the heated debate about the plan for a national hut high on Ben Nevis. This had some supporters among guides, and it would prevent the likelihood of further deaths from exposure on the Ben. Alex wrote a balanced paper on the pros and cons, which was circulated widely and came down against the idea. But it did support the need for a hut somewhere near Ben Nevis open to English and Welsh climbers. The CIC hut below the Ben was rarely available to climbers south of the border. Ironically, the alternative solution that won favour was the hut at Onich, which now bears his name. During Alex's time at the BMC it was rented, but in 1983, after Alex died, a national fundraising effort by the BMC and the Mountaineering Council of Scotland raised the necessary finance to purchase the property.

Alex also took a keen interest in the debate raging about the future of Plas y Brenin – the National Mountain Centre. He advised the BMC that if they were to make policy decisions on training, they should not be shackled to direct delivery of training at Plas y Brenin. Alex acted as a bridge between John Barry, the centre's director and a close friend, and, from the BMC, Ken Wilson and Dennis Gray. Although it took time, eventually the centre was hived off as a separate company, thus removing potential liability should accidents occur.

Despite all his success, and his respect for Alex, Dennis Gray said to me at an event a few years ago: "You know Alex suffered from mild dyslexia. He could express himself brilliantly in debate, but he had difficulties at times getting it straight on paper. Rita and I had to spend considerable time redrafting his reports and proposals into more readable English."

I laughed when Dennis told me this but not out loud. No one else, including his closest family, ever detected any signs of dyslexia. All his articles were written in a unique, vibrant style, nuanced on various levels. Dennis said that the dyslexia was an indication of his inability to deal with the current moment. The conclusion Sarah shared with me was that Alex used this "dyslexia" as a ploy to get out of the labourious task of editing his work. Once his ideas were mapped out and dumped on a page, he would delegate the task of fine-tuning to others. That way, there would be more time for climbing and the social engagements expected of the national officer.

Alex's favourite job at the BMC was to run the international exchange meets, particularly winter ones in Scotland. Through these events Alex developed close friendships with continental climbers like René Ghilini and Jean-Marc Boivin. He also made links with potential sponsors and new partners. For example, he climbed *Orion Face Direct* on the Ben in a couple of hours with Hermann Huber, the boss of Salewa. The competence shown by British climbers on these meets, and during exchanges in alpine countries and elsewhere in the world, linked to the personal friendship with alpine guides who came to the UK, helped British mountain guides to be accepted in the international guides federation.

Dennis Gray looked back with some nostalgia at the national officers who served under him. In their own ways, they helped shape the
BMC during a period of change and controversy that required cool
heads. "I think Peter was mature beyond his years, and Alex so sharp
with his mind and tongue that you had to be on top of your game to
better him. They both worked hard for the cause, putting in many
more hours than nine to five, travelling the length and breadth of the
country. Neither ever claimed once for a hotel or bed and breakfast;
they were always content to stay with mates, acquaintances and sleep
if necessary on floors." It was a period when the habits of the privateers remained long after their move to the ranks of professional.* For
friends, it was a tremendous pleasure when Alex came to stay on his
journeys, full of gossip and climbing intrigue, always informative but
never taking it too seriously.

In early 1980, Alex put his job on hold for an attempt on the east face
of Dhaulagiri. He continued to write to Sarah when they were within
range of a post office. Sarah received a last letter from Pokhara before
the team set off for base camp.

"It was very matter of fact and it said: 'That's it, you've won and I'm
yours now so now we are together.' Before he went, I was aware that it
all could change and he might still go back to Gwyneth, but when I received this letter, I was happy. I just passively accepted the situation. I
believed we were in love."

I noticed that Alex was less argumentative with Sarah than he had
been in other relationships, or indeed with anybody. The only time
the relationship with Sarah was threatened was when Alex came back
from a trip with a girl that Sarah suspected he had been sleeping with.
That, Sarah said, was just part of the game with climbers; what upset
Sarah was the fact he brought her back.

"I was working really hard and late at night with a new stage set and I
couldn't deal with the fact that this other woman was in the house.
Maybe I got it wrong, and it was just too obvious they had been

---

* The BMC now has around 25 employees, among them one of Alex's oldest friends, "Black" Nick
Colton, with whom he did the Central Couloir on the Grandes Jorasses and many other Alpine
routes in the 1970s.

together, but in any case, I withdrew. I told him if he wanted me, he would have to make an effort, and he did. It was the only moment of volatility in our relationship. Everything mended quickly. It was very calm and peaceful. Alex rarely talked about climbing and I think he needed our relationship as a safe place away from that."

After Alex left the BMC, he rented a little place fondly called "the shack" at the very top end of Hayfield in Derbyshire. Hayfield was one of the main climbing communities in the late 1970s and 1980s. From outside their front door, Alex and Sarah could amble up onto Kinder Scout and the surrounding fells. It was an idyllic and affordable bolthole. Brian Hall and his wife Louise lived less than a mile away in Hayfield proper, where they ran the Twenty Trees café. I often visited with my girlfriend Rose for the weekend. We would climb or walk during the day and look forward to the Saturday night gathering at the George Hotel, to play pool and plan trips.

Apart from being besotted with Sarah, there was another change taking place in Alex, according to Maria Coffey. "I'd been tracking it in Joe during the time I was with him, the increasing ambition to do higher and harder things. I didn't really know about climbing but I knew what Joe and Pete were doing was very much cutting-edge. Then as I began to know Alex better, I realised that his planning and thinking was getting ever more ambitious, especially at the purist level. He really believed in that purity. He used to tell me he wanted to be famous on a number of occasions. Actually that's not quite right, not that he wanted to be, but that he would be famous. He had no doubt. He was so cocksure."

It wasn't just climbing that Alex expected would make him rich and famous. Alex had a great belief in himself and his methodology. He told me on the walk-in to Annapurna that he trained as a lawyer because that was a good basis to make another career beyond climbing. He would not only be famous but also very rich. His pragmatism covered his own belief in himself. His success at the BMC, his luck winning Sarah and his high mountain successes proved the point. He believed in a methodology that if you did a, then b, then c, what would result was x, then y, then z. It was the sort of logic that only fate can undo.

21

BROKEN ENGLISH

Alex and I drifted apart somewhat after the Andes for a year or so. He was engrossed in his job as national officer at the BMC. I spent much of the following autumn and winter in New Hampshire with Choe Brooks, working as a rock-climbing instructor for Eastern Mountain Sports and International Mountain Equipment. John Powell was running a small building company using a borrowed plant. When not guiding, Choe and I worked for him as well and slept on the floor of Powell's tiny cabin in Bartlett, paying our share when we had some income. It was all hand-to-mouth and not very satisfactory.

In January, I had an unexpected call from England, saying Cumbria County Council was trying to get hold of me to offer me a job. I had worked as a project manager on a housing renovation scheme to make money for Peru and apparently I had impressed them. They wanted me to take on a new role to regenerate the local economy and environment. I took the job based in the south Cumbrian town of Millom, not far from Bank House where I had lived in the years before Bandaka. Millom had not recovered from the closure of the iron ore mines and steel works ten years before. I did my best to change that.

I phoned Alex as soon as I got back to England. He had spent the winter tackling the last great challenges in the Alps and catching up on the newest routes in Scotland. We occasionally joined forces that winter, travelling north with Al Rouse and Brian Hall to join Mick Geddes and friends. Alex was climbing a lot with the extremely talented Gordon Smith, and also with Terry King. His skill levels on mixed ground and ice just seemed to keep improving.

His plan that year was to join Voytek and René Ghilini on the east face of Dhaulagiri. Meanwhile, Al Rouse had asked me to join a large team to try the west ridge of Everest in winter without oxygen and without any Sherpa support. I had a chance of joining the Dhaulagiri trip but chose Everest; the allure of something incredibly bold on the world's highest peak was too enticing. Alex stuck to his path of trying the hardest faces in the best and lightest style. We had, for the time being, moved in different directions.

I was a little jealous of Alex's chance to climb again with Voytek, but, at the same time, it was pleasing that our international network was intact and progressing. Their climb of the east face, although they did not summit from the top of the wall, was one of the great milestones in the progression of lightweight climbing in the Himalaya.

Not long before he left for Dhaulagiri, Maria Coffey remembered Alex sitting on the stairs shouting down the phone at Voytek, speaking English but in a Polish accent. "He said it was the only way Voytek could understand him." Marianne Faithfull's *Broken English* was one of our anthems for several years after it came out in 1979. We shared it on our single cassette player on the way into Annapurna in 1982. It was the title of Alex's account of his climb, a classic piece from *Mountain* magazine.

Broken English

"Going anywhere this summer?" enquired the brick-edge cruiser. A question well put. The whimpering white chalk haze, which might just conceivably have been going somewhere this time, hit the deck again.

"Dhaulagiri," said I.

"Where's that?" asked the youth, now revolving effortlessly around a fingernail before poising, purring.

Again, a good question. In Nepal, judging by the postmark on the card. At least it had been when I first met it courtesy of the Reprint Society's rendering of Herzog's classic *Annapurna*, via my mum's bookshelf.

"Near Annapurna."

The instant look of non-recognition spoke for itself. I qualified the statement, broadened the base.

"In the Himalaya."

The lad switched into a perfect crucifix from opposing finger locks. Orgasmic eyes eyed bulging muscles. A neat one-arm pull-up landed him on the balcony. He looked down with disdain.

"Near Bolton is it?" he said, heading for the weights.

❄ ❄ ❄

The curt "Good afternoon!" from The Lady on my right, a statement of fact in response to my cheerful "Good morning!" might have melted a more sensitive man.* Eyes front, but no relief here: the wall-to-wall grin of our recently appointed access officer being unfortunately indicative of a pre-10 a.m. presence. Behind this newly resident Cheshire Cat, splendidly isolated from its surrounds by an iron curtain of garbage and mouldy coffee cups, a fairly exact parody of my bedroom, in fact, lay my realm, that of the national officer. A recently installed telephone proclaiming to all the world the importance of this post, second only to The Menace who has two phones and even dares to ask the Lady to take dictation. A Yorkshire hum from the inner tabernacle suggested The Menace was in residence and another crisis would soon be unfolding about our heads. As the Sports Council is usually backing the other side, it is at times like these that the executive committee stalwarts can be found scrutinising the national officer's employment contract. Thus quietly did that officer tiptoe to his all too exposed sanctum to confront once again his three-tiered green wire tray. This object of despair had assumed the characteristics of a fast breeder reactor and despite a liberal dumping policy in the waste-paper basket, or on the floor, its appetite was insatiable.

This particular day atop the pile of correspondence a natty little postcard caught my eye. I had seen such a card once before, a few years ago now, on the bedsit wall of a lass who had once been an apple in an old friend's eye, and even then had been attracted to the big unclimbed face that grinned at you straight out of the 4x6, a face now obscured by a mass of lines, spot heights, arrows and exclamations

* This scene, describing Alex's late arrival at the BMC offices in Manchester, includes cameos from some co-workers. The Lady is Rita Hallam, secretary at the BMC, the Cheshire Cat is Mark Hutchinson, the Menace is Dennis Gray.

that may have had meaning for the author. The reverse side held a clue.

Dear Alex, Great chance for great days on the face you see on the card. See you in Kathmandu, 10 March. Love Voytek. PS Bring a partner.

Voytek is a sometime electrical engineer and brilliant climber whose prompt action on top of the *Walker Spur* back in 1975 saved John Bouchard's piano playing for posterity. I first became aware of his conspiratorial anti-authoritarian grin in a Russian railway carriage en route for the now topical port of Termez, the Amu Darya and the wild lands of Afghanistan. We were bound for the Mandaras Valley, but Voytek enthused me with tales of the north-east wall of Koh-i-Bandaka, a "problem for the year 2000."

At first our leader refused to share our vision but after two weeks of relentless nagging we went our separate way with their blessing and our own absent-minded co-leader to cement our friendship on that wall. Thus is explained the Polish element.

It was Christmas so I took mother, sister and card to Chamonix. The boys were there. Dire plans evolved down in Dutchy's basement. A campaign was instituted. We would wage war against the Grandes Jorasses north wall. "We" consisted of myself, Uncle Choe and Black Nick. Then local lad René appeared at the door and was promptly enlisted. An invaluable asset, he could ski, read French weather forecasts, and use a compass.*

It was an interesting jaunt. Nick dropped a ski boot down the north face of the Midi and had to take the next *téléférique* back to bed; the less fortunate three took two days to "ski" to the foot of the cliff. We reached a climax some five pitches later, three men, two hammocks and a miserable night in a shallow snow funnel. The weather, as promised, broke. In an epic retreat René played a blinder while we blindly wallowed in his wake. He took us back to Cham in masterful style. Down in the bar I put my card on the table, photo side up, picture still

---

* "Uncle Choe" was Choe Brooks, "Black Nick" was Nick Colton, not to be confused with Nicky Donnelly, or Blond Nick. "René" is René Ghilini.

obscured by a mass of lines, dots, question marks and spot heights that still only made sense to their author. We pondered the thickest black lines. I resolved to ask René along. He accepted on the strength of a hot wine, the postcard and an assurance that it was bound to be a giggle. Perhaps inside every Franco-Italian there is an Englishman trying to get out?

The team finally came together on 14 March 1980 outside the Kathmandu customs shed. The fourth member was a Polish friend of Voytek's, Ludwik Wilczynski, a musician and classical philologist. What a team: philologist, guide, computer technician and national officer, the first Anglo-Italian-Polish Expedition. Now the science of climbing Himalayan hills is steeped in lore and one of the cardinal precepts would suggest that such a racial mix must inevitably underline the inevitability of World War III. But we have not been schooled in this discipline. We were not an expedition; we were a trip, or a holiday as they are wont to call it in my office.

On the other hand we were an expedition, the first Nick Estcourt Memorial Expedition. The award, which will be made every year to one expedition going for a "particularly challenging project," comes from the funds of the appeal launched after Nick's death to commemorate his memory. We dedicated our route to his memory.

Dhaulagiri stands in central Nepal, on the west side of the Kali Gandaki river, through which valley passed the trade route to the ancient kingdom of Mustang. It is also, as far as Muktinath, a pilgrims' way. Dhaulagiri is the sixth-highest mountain in the world, a "mountain without pity," a "mountain of storms." Our objective was the east face, rising steeply out of the jumbled south-east glacier, framed between and formed by the northeast and south-east ridges.

There are two ways to the traditional Dhaulagiri base camp. For the purpose of the pre-monsoon season of 1980 they might be described as a short, silly way and a longer, sensible way. Naturally we went the short, silly way.

Some hours above Tukuche, a once flourishing town on the ancient Trade Route between the Indian plains and the Kingdom of Mustang, it snowed for a week. We put up the tents, dismissed the porters and

took to the skis. Our liaison officer fled for sanity when his tent disappeared on the second day, closely following our sirdar, and closely followed by the Poles. A passionate valley-orientated interest in preparing for "when it cleared up" spread through our team like the plague,
as the roof of the frame tent disappeared under the little white flakes,
excepting that is, that it never quite reached the Western Bloc. They
hung on with vacant grins, multiple injuries and trusting in the unruf-
fled calm of Kasang the cook, who finally called a halt to the proceed-
ings with the help of a magic potion, courtesy of a local lama, scattered
to the four winds one black night when it seemed the whole lot might
go under and we were sleeping with boots on and open knives clasped,
minds intent upon the rasping strains of Marianne Faithful.

"Why'd ya do it?" she asked.

It consequently cleared up and with a group of hardy but record-
breaking-ly expensive porters, we limped into base camp three days
later with half the gear, thigh-deep through the snows of the Dhampus
Pass and the French Col, thankful to arrive at this latter point, a most
pleasant spot which Terray had once taken a liking to as "the foulest-
looking place."

If you are alert, sharp-witted, or work at the BMC, you might have
taken cognisance of the curious fact that "alpine-style" expeditions
manage to remain absent from their country of origin for at least as
long as their more portly neighbours. Ignoring the occasional week
conveniently but quietly lost in Bangkok or Warsaw, the name of the
game is acclimatisation. This is a process much assisted prior to departure for your mountain by one of two mutually exclusive processes.
The first and, to date, financially more profitable tangent, involves the
consumption of vast quantities of garlic, making love for hours on end
in a series of two knuckle press-ups and hopping up big hills on one
toe, to the strains of Wagner from your free, portable lead-weighted
Japanese micro-cassette. This conditions the body.

The alternative approach and one better founded in reason, if not in
medical opinion, concentrates on the brain. Brain training should not
be undertaken lightly. I have even heard it said by cynics that the only
people who benefit are the breweries. Not so, sir! Climbing at altitude

is somewhat akin to going to work with a monster hangover. Once the art of operating under such conditions has been mastered, the problem is licked. Otherwise known as Mooney's Law, this approach carries other benefits. The mass destruction of brain cells prior to one's arrival in the Zone of Death leaves less for the non-atmosphere to work on and the general state of ill health attained throughout the year ensures that the body is well accustomed to the notion of oxygen deficiency, bordering on asphyxiation. Brain training is, unfortunately, expensive.

In order to evaluate our various theories we needed something to get high on. As the only thing sufficiently large enough to be of any consequent benefit – meaning "ill health" – was Dhaulagiri itself, we approached our neighbourhood Swiss who had had the foresight to come the sensible way and had set up town a couple of minutes down the glacier. They had come to climb the north-east ridge and we had obtained clearance from the ministry to approach them and ask for permission to acclimatise on the ridge. At first, and understandably, a little reluctant, they subsequently accepted our presence on their ridge and for this we owe them a big debt of gratitude.

Our plan, in the best of tradition, was simple. We would place the two natty pieces of nylon acquired for the purpose in downtown Kathmandu up on the North-east Col and designate the spot "advance base." Always a good move this. The presence of a Camp I on an alpine-style ascent can be embarrassing. (However, by dint of imaginative use of nomenclature quite a bit of ground can be gained: Rest and Recreation Camp, Operations Logistical HQ, Glacier Camp, Advanced Mountain Base etc.) From our "advance base" we would make forays up the ridge above until such a time as we had had sufficient rare air to be declared fit, whereupon we could belt up the face and go home.

Base camp life made the best of a good job, with the kitchen sandwiched between East and West Blocs. A brisk trade in détente ensued while we plotted against our common enemy, generally from a horizontal, static position, one eye on the progress of the Swiss, and the other on the cherry brandy.

The period of static acclimatisation ended, as chance would have it, about the same time as the Swiss lads managed to wade up to the col. The col is the wrong end of a nasty icefall and a long avalanche-threatened glacier valley. It is a wide, flat, featureless spot where one can wander around for hours in a whiteout looking for the tent. Needless to say no one had brought a compass and consequently we did. Due perhaps to our scorn for traditional logistical pyramid concepts our first spell at the col was enlivened by a general abundance of porridge and spaghetti and a general absence of salt and sugar. Over the ensuing weeks forays were mounted against the ridge until the team, suitably accustomed to the view (and in my case at least severe indigestion and headaches) was declared nearly, almost, possibly fit enough for the face.

For the face we had to struggle. On the col, in a vision of blitzkrieg the evening before, we unpacked the not quite bulging sacks and ejected all manner of essential items. A little after midnight we struggled out of our sugar-coated Frosties into a night of rare beauty, awash in moonlight and clear to the ends of the earth. The east face, dressed for the occasion, beckoned cold and blue. A chill breeze whipped across the col. We promptly disappeared back into the tents to repack the ejected items before disappearing, à la The Wild Bunch, four abreast down into the snow basin and away to the back of the amphitheatre in search of our climb. Daybreak caught us dallying on a compact rock buttress, trying to force a slim sliver of ice, which melted all too fast but not quite fast enough and we were through onto the slabs above, threading and twisting through this compact formation by utilising runnels and funnels and fields of snow, as we did for much of the time which followed. A midday brew was enjoyed on a small rock knoll so out of character with the rest of this face. High white wisps scudded in from the west. We consoled ourselves with our knowledge, "an afternoon deterioration, only to be expected," and carried on up while a cauldron formed on the upper wall. The thunder rolled in, the view rolled up; it began to snow. Acres of the stuff fell on the face above and the whole caboodle dumped itself on our heads. On cue the breeze stiffened to a gusting gale.

Sanctuary was sought, out to the right of the main fall line, beneath an inadequate little rock wall which failed to do its job and offered us no protection. Half-cooked ganders as some hours later in the same spot the realisation dawned that we were standing on our beds. Anxious fashioning produced little in the way of a home, for the ice adheres to the tile-like formation of this rock in no great quantity, and both teams enjoyed a poor night, speculating on the foresight of the Argentinian lads back in 1954 who had used dynamite to produce a home, or the ingenuity of the Swiss in 1958 who used bed frames to build platforms, an apparently usable solution to this commonly shared problem of sloping campsites. A poor night, but not so bad in retrospect.

The next was an absolute horror. The day had started okay, dawning sunny and hanging on in there with passing blue patches but deteriorating fairly quickly into a mean parody of a Scotsman's winter holiday. The evening crescendo left Ludwik and I stranded high, but none too dry, on steep brittle ice, battered by a fiery spindrift flow, unable to move up and unwilling to be moved off down. Forty mean, motionless, finger-frozen minutes. Then a lull let us go and a struggle put us out onto the mixed ground to the right where we had hoped to take out a mortgage on a decent doss. Nothing: no ice, no ledge, no bed, just more loose snow and compact rock.

We worked into a bitter night but to little avail. In the end René, Ludwik and I shared one two-man sack in a claustrophobic, oxygen-starved atmosphere endured in a variety of cramped, tortuous positions. Constrained in the middle and suffocated by the nylon I had the good idea of cutting open the sack to get some air but unfortunately could not find the knife. A request to René to borrow his got me it, after some mild disbelief, and a zip being opened to let in fresh air and the inevitable spindrift. Luxury! Voytek could only manage a solo effort, perched on crumbling snow and half-slumped in slings with a bivvy sack over his head and unable to get in the sleeping bag, all on a face awash with wind-driven powder.

We fled this spot at the first hint of daylight to the unwelcome sight of fresh banks of clouds and struggled on up through fresh snow to the comparative shelter of the lee side of a large rock buttress to the left of which we had to pass. Here we had a brew, standing like early morning commuters in a daze sipping lukewarm cups of tea, before shuffling on up and, finally, out of the face in the last of the evening light, stumbling over the mixed ground to a bivvy site underneath a large boulder on the ridge, and the full fury of Dhaulagiri's winds.

The summit preparations began early. We brewed through much of the night in an effort to recoup our water intake and were out of the tents by daybreak but the bid faltered. We stood where a large slab of snow had once lain and eyed its cousin through the gloom. With more clouds rolling in, this fracture line above was the straw which finally induced the camel to realism and we called it a day, bailing out and off down the ridge to the welcome arms of Kusang, cabbage and paraffin.

We went back a week later in pleasant, certifiably survivable conditions and topped out to a blue sky and a clear view, and then beating it back to Jomsom to await what is not the most reliable air service in the world.*

---

* They summited via the northeast ridge, having previously crested at around 7850 metres. The fact that they had reached that high on the ridge put the later summit climb into perspective – it was really just the icing on the cake.

LEFT Alex with his parents Jean and Hamish, and their tormented dog, at home in Beverley, North Yorkshire, not far from where Alex was born. Photo: MacIntyre Family Collection.

ABOVE Alex with his sister Libby at home at Letchmore Heath. Photo: MacIntyre Family Collection.

BELOW Snell's Field, Chamonix in 1973, with one of the ubiquitous blue vans. L–R: Bernard Newman, John Powell, the author, Alex MacIntyre and John Eames. Photo: John Powell.

OPPOSITE Alex on Lithrig, Clogwyn Du'r Arddu, North Wales, in 1974. Photo: John Powell.
ABOVE Maria Coffey, Jan Brownsort and Gwyneth Rule after a mudball fight in Hayfield, 1975.
BELOW Community transport in Afghanistan, on our way to Faizabad.

OPPOSITE TOP Alex about to work his miracle on the summit cornice on day six.

OPPOSITE BOTTOM The tough lads from Lata in the presence of their goddess Nanda Devi. The three looking at the camera on the left saved the expedition when they appeared a day after we had arrived in base camp with the missing barrel full of technical gear and ropes.

ABOVE So-called lightweight style; with a minimum of 30 kilos each, we set off for the face. L–R: the author, Krzysztof Zurek, Voytek Kurtyka and Alex.

LEFT Voytek discovers the one and only crack that gave access to the upper headwall, day five.

LEFT The author preparing breakfast on day six. Photo: Alex MacIntyre.

ABOVE Alex on the summit of Changabang.

BELOW Changabang: descending the original route at dusk.

ABOVE Nanda Devi, as seen from our last bivouac below the summit of Changabang.

BELOW Luxury transport to base camp at Laguna Peron from Huaraz, courtesy of the Mount Everest Foundation.

OPPOSITE The first pitch from the bivvy, carrying the famous British Aerospace ice stakes. Pirámide in the distance.

ABOVE The author at the last stance before the summit. Note the Karrimor sack and gaiters, and the Rohan salopettes, all designed by Alex.

OPPOSITE The moment of decision, when we turned back on Huascarán Norte.

ABOVE About to set off on a wet scramble from the Wasdale Head Inn, summer 1981. L–R: Alex, the author, John Powell, Sarah Richard, Rose Tavener, Janine Frazer, Donna Powell. Photo: Bernard Newman.

BELOW Before the route became popular with trekkers, there were many difficult river crossings during the monsoon season on the way into the Annapurna Sanctuary.

OPPOSITE On the lower slopes of the east face of Dhaulagiri, Alex oversees the assembly of his newly designed bivvy tent. Photo: Voytek Kurtyka.

ABOVE Makalu base camp after defeat. L–R: Voytek, Alex and Jerzy. Photo: Voytek Kurtyka.

BELOW A chance encounter: the Makalu team meet Reinhold Messner, who was on the north ridge. L–R: Alex, Ariane Giobellina, Voytek, Jerzy and Reinhold.

DOUG

ALEX & ROGER

DESCENT

OPPOSITE The southwest face of Shisha Pangma and, inset, the route. Photo: Doug Scott.
ABOVE From our base camp, the giant south face of Annapurna emerges after a storm.
BELOW The horrendous icefall on Hiunchuli, just before the serac collapse.

Alex descends into the crevasse on Annapurna where he and René shared their last bivouac. Photo: René Ghilini.

22

VERTICAL GRAFFITI

Through the summer of 1980, my girlfriend Rose and I would often stay at the shack in Hayfield, or Sarah and Alex would come to stay with us in Millom. They first arrived one cool clear weekend not long after he got back from Dhaulagiri. I was excited to see him and get the inside story of the climb. We met on Saturday morning and immediately set out to go climbing. I soon realized that he was not the same Alex. He wasn't different in any immediately obvious way, but there was a new depth, and his resilience and confidence seemed to have doubled. There was also a troubled restlessness and a new goal.

"I want to become one of the world's all-time great mountaineers," he announced as we were driving up to Coniston to climb on Dow Crag.

I was too stunned to respond at first.

"What, you mean like Messner?"

He scowled at me, then laughed and gave me one of his manic grins that seemed to say, "and you are doing what exactly?" I asked about the other things in life, Sarah, his job.

"I can do all that but I just love climbing. That's what I'm meant to do."

When I asked about the risks, he responded by overtaking a car on a bend. I gasped and instinctively grabbed the armrest. The narrow road that winds through the hills between Broughton and Torver was barely wide enough for one car in many places. He laughed at my instant panic. We were lucky; nothing was coming the other way.

"You see? I'm immortal now." It was a stupid thing to say and do, and Alex knew it, but his willingness to "up the stakes" was now clear.

Soon enough we were at Dow Crag and Alex was climbing as well as

I could remember. Dow is great for sound and steep rock. The Indian summer had extended into late October and the east-facing buttresses held their warmth until mid-afternoon. We did a couple of classic Extremes. A cold breeze rising from the dark waters of the tarn spoke against a third route, so we walked to the top of A Buttress to watch the sun setting over the Irish Sea, then raced down the descent gully and headed for the pub to get the craic with the locals.

When Alex and Sarah left that weekend, something of the feeling of change was still in the air. What was I actually doing working a nine-to-five job and collecting a pay cheque? Which of us was tempting fate? Was I jealous? Voytek, Alex and René had made their ascent of Dhaulagiri and so far this year I'd done nothing but work and help Al Rouse with food and finance for Everest that winter. Now Everest was in doubt as we were far short of the minimum budget needed. Was this "coming out" of ambition in Alex to be admired or feared? His friends, and perhaps me more than anyone, believed that Alex had already achieved the status he sought. But the respect of friends was no longer enough for him. He had crossed a divide; he had not only joined the professionals, he was pushing through the ranks to a higher level.

The only way to get there and to stay there was to continuously climb at the highest standards. You were only as good as your last climb. His future decisions on where to go and who to climb with would, from now on, be shaped and directed by different factors than just friends and whims. He was mapping out the faces in the Himalaya as he had mapped out the last great problems in the Alps. It's no coincidence that he left the BMC during this period of change.

At the end of October, we got a last-minute break with finance for Everest. New Era homeopathic medicines came up with £2,500. Our total budget for eight on Everest for three months was a staggering £12,000. I phoned Alex to let him know.

"Hey kid, I'm off. Look after yourself. What are your plans for next spring?"

"Makalu's west face with Voytek and Kukuczka pre-monsoon." Again, I felt a wave of trepidation mixed with jealousy; this was something

big and different. But I was off in a week's time and had my own worries and preparations to make.

Alex went to Makalu twice in 1981 with Voytek. The attempts were
unsuccessful in terms of climbing, but they provided Alex with additional knowledge that helped shape his tactics during the final year of
his life. Alex described their objective, the massive unclimbed face left
of the French Pillar, as a bit like the Eigerwand but a grade harder than
Bandaka in difficulty and higher. The pre-monsoon trip was a bit of a
nonevent. Just getting to the face was a major trudge over long moraines and not at elevations high enough to help them to fully acclimatize. After a couple of sorties to 7000 metres, bad weather forced a
close of play.

The post-monsoon trip with Voytek and Jerzy Kukuczka might just
have succeeded, but it failed because of some fundamental weak-
nesses in the lightweight approach. It proved to be a far harder climb
than the ascent of Dhaulagiri the previous year. When they reached
the difficult climbing near the top of the face, they did not have enough
equipment or food for the additional three or four days it might have
taken.

Alex had now graduated from the smaller peaks of the Himalaya and
was applying his skills to the unclimbed eight-thousander faces. In the
same graduating class but with more experience at altitude was
Voytek. It wasn't just the shift in the scale of the challenge; the two
climbers were committed to move away completely from any thoughts
of big expedition tactics.

This was more difficult for Voytek than for Alex. For Voytek, it
meant breaking from the national traditions and structures of the
Polish system. Yet Bandaka and Changabang had proven to the PZA
that the new style could also bring national prestige, crucial for continued funding from the Communist Party. Voytek's reputation was
also riding high. His achievements forced the PZA to make him a full
member without him even applying. (That way he was less likely to be
criticized by the PZA and party apparatchiks.) His model was also being followed by a number of other leading Polish climbers: Kukuczka,
Alex Lwow, Krzysztof Wielicki and others.

Alex was a perfect partner for Voytek to develop their mutual obsession for alpine style. Voytek said of Alex: "He had an aura. He was very brave in two ways; he was fearless and he broke with tradition."

Alex, like Voytek, was increasingly ambitious to apply their methods to the toughest challenges. But success for Alex put him into an upward spiral, both in terms of his ambition and his ego. This was very unlike Voytek, who continued to climb for the sake of climbing.* However, Voytek said when Alex was in the mountains he had no ego.

"He was always the unseen member of the team until required and then he would pull out something exceptional. He was a power card, like the joker in the pack."

Voytek's break with Zawada's big expedition style was now complete. Alex discussed their attempts on Makalu with Andrez at the 1982 Buxton Conference. Zawada said to Alex that their failure on Makalu proved his point. To be assured of success, Zawada said a large team was essential. Indeed, small alpine trips to 8000-metre peaks were, in Zawada's opinion, rather silly.

"Why waste so much resource and risk failure? Success is paramount," he told Alex.

But there was also a contentious debate at the time around the comparative safety of big and small trips. It went like this: Were you more likely to have an accident on a big expedition, since you had to spend much more time at high altitudes exposed to dangers? Were small trips, climbing alpine style, inherently safer because you were faster and spent less time at altitude?

Alex was very matter of fact in his response to this question. He had done his research, which made him informed and thoughtful, and not judgmental. Unexpectedly, he did not object to the big national expeditions led by Zawada, the Yugoslav Ales Kunaver or the Japanese Yasuo Kato. Nor did he seek to demean them. Kunaver's team had an impressive list of successes, and had nearly climbed the south face of

---

* Voytek has yet to write his story. When he does, it will be truly fascinating. You get a glimpse of his amazing strength in the Polish movies made about him, and also in *Freedom Climbers,* where Bernadette McDonald describes his "art of suffering" as a mixture of courage and national pride gained from centuries of fighting the Russians and Germans, and the Japanese Samurai tradition where an honourable death is preferable to failure or any wavering from the path.

Lhotse – the greatest of all challenges in Alex's opinion.* Referring to Kunaver's methods he said:

"This Yugoslav group is very cunning and very experienced, having successfully completed a number of major projects like the south face of Makalu and the Everest west ridge direct. After this type of 'training' the environment of big nasty faces like Lhotse becomes much more acceptable. They know a lot more about the environment and when it is reasonably safe to climb. They nearly succeeded on Lhotse, and when the time came, they retreated without loss of life." **

But the big worry for Alex and all this generation of lightweight exponents was that the big national teams would grab the last great problems before they got to them. Makalu's west face was on Alex's list, as it was on Voytek's, and they were delighted they had two chances to make the ascent. This was a much harder face than Dhaulagiri and the tactics had to be absolutely right.

In the post-monsoon season, Alex and his Polish companions had two sorties onto the mountain to acclimatize before venturing onto the face. First, they climbed the original north side route to an altitude of 7800 metres. On a second outing, they placed a cache of food and gas for their descent, which would be down this route if they achieved the summit via the west face. They spent one night above 8000 metres on the north ridge. They were now fully acclimatized for an attempt on the west face.

This comprised steepening ice fields, broken by rock bands, and climbing at a standard similar to the north face of Les Droites. These ice fields, 6,000 feet high, took four days to climb and led to a rock headwall. "At the top of the third ice field we just ran straight into the headwall. One minute you are on ice, the next you are pressing your nose on granite."

* As well as being one of the steepest faces in the Himalaya, the face is notorious for a number of other reasons. On 24 October 1989, Jerzy Kukuczka was killed in a fall when close to success. The following year in the pre-monsoon, the Slovenian Tomo Cesen claimed to have made the first ascent solo, but this was disputed primarily by the Russians who made what was the true first ascent post-monsoon. Cesen did not help his case by claiming that a photo taken on a successful ascent of the standard route by a friend was actually his own from a previous failed attempt on the face.

** This and all the other quotes in this chapter come from an unpublished interview Alex gave to Ken Wilson in 1982.

The team had thought a rightward slanting line would lead them through the headwall, but, as Alex reported, "we had been too cunning by half. We had pieced together an imaginary line that led up through the headwall to the top of the west ridge at 8,300 metres. The headwall was 300 metres high but ED sup not D sup as we had imagined.

"We clearly had several more days left to complete the route. We knew we would be bivouacking each night at over 8,000 metres and there would still be 400 metres to the top once we reached the west ridge. We were without the necessary gear, food and fuel to do it."

For their climbing rope, the three had chosen to take only one 60-metre, 8.2 millimetre rope. Alex described this as "quite adequate." Others might feel that on such a big face, this left little scope for hard technical climbing and the possibilities of rope damage if there was a serious fall or falling rock. With three climbers, the leader conventionally went first on a double rope and the two following climbed on a single rope. This is common practice but not without its dangers on such technical ground.

Alex explained the reason for their retreat: "I am not out to lose toes on a death or glory push. I hope to go to the Himalaya time and again, and that does temper your drive. You have to avoid situations where you might get through, but get things chopped off in the end. I am not into heroics."

It was several weeks before I got together with Alex after Makalu. When we met, he seemed much calmer and relaxed. I decided that Sarah was making a real difference to his life.

Alex had been hit by a rock during the long descent on Makalu. Fortunately, it was a glancing blow and his helmet took most of the shock. He had come home and fallen into Sarah's arms, a wounded animal needing care. He told her several times how being hit had really freaked him out. Sarah was a little perplexed. Alex seemed a different person to the cocky immortal who had left for the mountain three months before. There was, for a short time, a reversal of roles; Sarah had to deal with Alex's uncertainties. Up until now it had been he who had to deal with her occasional depression and lack of confidence.

"That was when Alex would draw things out of me, and make me feel better just by talking, by doing things." But now in her new role, when Sarah tried to laugh it off, Alex became very angry. He told her she had no idea how serious it had been. She realized he was depressed.

"He told me it was the first time he had ever known depression: 'Now I understand what it's like.' Normally he got angry with people who were unhappy or depressed. He thought it was all self-inflicted and they just had to pull themselves out of it. But now he had a new perception."

Then, one morning, he woke up as if a single night had transformed him. He was back to his normal self and said: "Let's go do something right now."

Sarah continued: "when things seemed low, that's what Alex always did, go do something then and there, no more moping. He tried to fight it, but we all knew down deep Alex was a kind-hearted person."

Being very kind to Sarah now seemed to extend to his entire group of friends. His caustic nature disappeared for a while.

I met Alex, Sarah and John Powell at the Padarn Lake pub in Llanberis one Saturday at lunchtime. We drank until afternoon closing, swapping tales, and then went for a wet walk in the hills until dark. That was when Alex invited me to go to Annapurna the following autumn. I told him I was really interested but that I already had a trip half-planned with the Burgesses pre-monsoon. When that fell through in early December, I phoned Alex the same day.

"Hi kid, is the Annapurna offer still on the table?"

"Of course – great. I've been talking to Rouse and he's up for it. René is already getting sponsors in France so that means two ropes of two which will be best on this face."

We met at an Alpine Climbing Group (ACG) dinner a couple of weeks later, but there was little time to discuss our plans. There were two main features of the ACG "dinners"; they brought together a complete cross-section of the hardest climbers in the country, almost all men, and they inevitably became very rowdy, and sometimes fractious.*

---

* I cannot recall that there was ever any food at an ACG dinner. There were fish and chips before or a fry-up the next morning.

That year's "do" was in a medieval-style banquet hall somewhere in Derbyshire. As the evening reached midpoint, one bright spark spotted the lances and shields mounted on the walls. When pointed out to the assembled drunken horde, everyone shouted: "Joust!" Jousting was a common sport; you got on the back of a mate and charged across the floor at another pair, trying to knock off the man on the shoulders. This, however, was the first time it would be tried with real lances. Alex jumped onto Rouse's shoulders, and the pair charged the opposing knights, one of whom happened to be Barry Kershaw.

Kershaw was known as the most feared brawler in the ACG. His heroic reputation was sealed at an earlier dinner in an incident after the barman called time. Kershaw had discovered there was a Hell's Angels gathering in the next room with cases of beer still piled high. Now was the time for action. He burst through the adjoining doors and said:

"Right, any ten of you outside now, and then the next ten to follow until you hand over your beer." The Hell's Angels backed down. One can imagine they took account of the hundred or so other ACG members who stood awaiting the outcome. The ACG continued the evening with the newly acquired beer.

However, on the evening in question, Alex either did not know Kershaw's reputation, or was too drunk to care. When he was knocked off, he got up and threatened Kershaw, who simply stood there laughing at him. From out of nowhere, Don Whillans appeared, pushed Alex to the floor and dragged him by his hair into a corner. Everyone witnessing this assumed it was a humiliating put-down for Alex. But, in fact, this was Whillans at his unexpected best. Guy Lee recalls him standing Alex up in the corner out of harm's way and almost spitting into his face.

"Look sonny, you may think you're a shit-hot mountaineer but if you want to live, you don't mess with Kershaw. You got that?"

This was as close as Don could get to showing real concern for someone. Whillans followed careers, and liked what he saw in Alex, an anti-establishment figure set against the likes of Bonington with whom Don had seriously fallen out after being dropped from his team for the 1975 Everest expedition.

While Alex was being put right by Whillans, the division bells had rung and a more serious encounter was about to take place as the two halves of the ACG lined up against each other in the hall. Then came a second unexpected intervention. John Barker, another man to avoid in a fight, or to have on your side, whichever way you look at it, had the wit to jump in the middle between the two armies of jousters.

"What the hell are we doing? We're all mates here, right? This is the ACG together, right? And what is the ACG doing here? Having a drink, right? And if we aren't all mates and if we start a brawl, you know what they'll do? They'll close the bar!"

There was a huge cheer, and then applause in appreciation of the brilliance of Barker's logic. The evening continued as amicably as it had begun.

The winter climbing season of 1981 and early 1982 brought great conditions even in the Lake District. A bright spring brought Alex and Sarah up to stay with Rose and me for a final weekend of climbing before Alex left for his pre-monsoon excursion to Shisha Pangma. I was jealous. It was a trip with Doug Scott, Roger Baxter-Jones and Tut Braithwaite, a very "professional," well-established crowd.

After Alex died, I asked Sarah if she ever questioned his climbing as he went off each season on a big trip, or to the Alps in winter. "No, there was never time. But also I believed that people should be free to do what they do. I think Alex liked that in me. His mother and Gwyneth had made serious efforts to calm down his climbing ambitions. But that was Alex. I wasn't going to stop him."

23

SURPRISE SURPRISE

Google "Alex MacIntyre" and you find a few entries, but they don't do him justice. Most links take you to the Alex MacIntyre Memorial Hut site, and tales of exploits from clubs and individuals who have stayed there.* This is the hut at Onich that Alex had brokered during his time at the BMC.

There are a few entries from more informed modern climbers paying homage to the boldness of his style and the clarity of his ideas. The website UKClimbing.com has a short history of the *Colton-MacIntyre* route the Grandes Jorasses. A video of a recent British ascent is followed by news that the amazing Ueli Steck has soloed the route in two hours and ten minutes. (It took Alex and Nick Colton 12 hours, climbing at night with knuckle-breaking Terrordactyls and bendy crampons. Front points often broke on crampons in the 1970s, or else the front points would just bend until they were next to useless. That happened to us all sooner or later – but not these days.)

There is also an entry on the Mountaineers Books website; it's a review of *Shisha Pangma*, the book Alex co-wrote with Doug Scott with contributions from all the rest of the expedition. *Shisha Pangma* shared the first Boardman-Tasker Award for mountain literature in 1984.

When we think of "drivers for change" in the development of mountaineering equipment, it seems to me that first and foremost it is the love of life – the need for equipment that increases the margin of safety regardless of the inherent risk of the adventure. Advances in

---

* The hut was set up largely through the efforts of Dennis Gray at the BMC and a small army of volunteers who had followed and admired Alex. Located in Onich, it is an excellent base for climbing in either Glen Coe or Ben Nevis.

every aspect of climbing – technical skills, clothing, ropes, hardware, access, training – are a process of learning from experience and applying the lessons learned to improve ways of doing things. Change is rarely that eureka moment of revelation. It is more usually a combination of shared experience and experimentation by individuals. Yvon Choiunard, Jeff Lowe, Tony Howard, Rab Carrington – these are just a few climbers known for advances in the application of ideas and technologies. All of them had remarkable climbing careers to spark their innovations.

A thesis could be written about mountaineers who understand the relationship between design, materials, manufacturing and the application of equipment. And, more significantly, about the need to develop the vision and mental and physical ability to make proper use of that equipment. Over the years I have had several discussions with Mike Parsons, owner of Karrimor and an industry guru, who hired Alex as a design consultant in the late 1970s and early 1980s.

"Alex taught me more about lightweight than anyone else – he taught me that it was about commitment," Mike said. "Going lightweight was for Alex about going on the mountain with less than you were mentally comfortable with. His audacity astonished me and set him apart from all the others."

I have no doubt that Alex would have had a place on the list of people who made advances in equipment design had he lived long enough to refine his technical understanding. He probably should be there anyway. That's also Mike's view.

"I was accustomed to working with and around great performers, like Don Whillans and Dougal Haston. I pressed them for technical advances in rucksacks, and eventually extracted some rough ideas. From a few suggestions on where to locate loops and where there was likely to be excessive wear, I designed rucksacks that bore their names. But that was it. Neither Don nor Dougal were interested in keeping the product up-to-date."

It was worse for Mike when he had whole expeditions with many different demands to equip. "Don was the expedition equipment manager on the 1970 Bonington expedition to Annapurna and

Karrimor pretty much supplied a great deal of equipment for it. I had to fill orders and design equipment on the back of a few cryptic conversations with Don and Dougal wasn't any better."

Mike is an intense and passionate lover of everything to do with the outdoors but also an engineer and designer who understands a piece of equipment that is merely adequate simply isn't good enough. He always strove for improvement and tried to express his vision through annual technical catalogues. The general theme of these was how better gear would make for better climbing. But the relationship between less-serious climbing manufacturers like Mike and the climbing community was snobbish in those early days. Peter Boardman told Mike that he could not understand what his catalogues were trying to say and "why bother because climbers will never read this stuff."

"When Alex arrived at my door sometime in 1978," says Mike, "it was a revelation. Finally, I had someone able and willing to take me on in dialogue as to what the product should be. He was bright and analytical and could see the product not merely as something he needed but also from the market angle and how it might reach non-specialist climbers."

Alex transformed many ideas in Mike's head into workable and saleable products. It was Alex's ideas and designs that eventually led to the OMM lightweight pack range. This came on the back of his design for the original Macsac, an 80-litre sack that weighed a mere 800 grams. It became much sought after by expeditions from around the world; Mike's problem was they always want them for free.

"Alex was brilliant when it came to simplifying design to a minimalist size and weight yet ensuring that it functioned as it was meant to do. What really impressed me is that he could also look at the needs of other sports' specialisms and have a go at designing for their requirements. That greatly endeared him to me."

Understanding the needs of other sports included both making suggestions on design and taking part. After just a couple of hours' instruction in Nordic skiing, the following day Alex entered the König-Ludwig-Lauf, a 42-kilometre race in Oberammergau, and completed it. Alex told Mike about it. "I was pretty much at the back of the field until around thirty kilometres. Then I got the hang of it, and began to overtake many surprised people right up to the finish line."

Otto Wiedemann, head of training for the German guides association had given Alex his Nordic ski lesson, so to return the favour, Alex took him up *Slav Route* on Ben Nevis. Otto recalled the experience. "We had one 8.8-millimetre rope, one deadman for belays and a couple of ice screws. Watching Alex above climbing a very steep gully on very thin ice with no protection, I could not help but wonder if the run-out of snow in the gully beneath was long enough to eventually slow our fall if Alex pulled me off?"

But Alex had no intention of falling off. He was in his comfort zone, even if Otto was not. Otto asked Alex after the climb how he had managed to stay in control in such difficult conditions with no protection. Alex replied: "I just switch off the usual safety thinking and feeling. Protection is a relative concept at the best of times and for the most part safety depends very much on the individual and his strength of mind."

Mike and I concluded our reminiscing about Alex's work at Karrimor with a discussion of the products that had been supplied by Mike to our expeditions together: "Sending equipment with your people on expeditions was a great responsibility and a great worry for me. I trusted Alex to be part of their creation. I gave Alex some basic training on our test machinery and then left him with my development staff. The only proviso was that I would make the final check on all items he made before he took them away. I remember going through the design and feel of the very first rucksack he made, including the stitching, with a fine-toothed comb to see if I could find any weakness. There weren't any."

Mike also appreciated the futuristic nature of Alex's vision, his ability to think ahead. "Looking back on that letter I received from Kathmandu, it strikes me how prophetic he was, in particular about future media involvement. Remember that letter arrived on my desk long before the internet, satellite phones, digital cameras and everything that is now part of our daily lives. He had a great vision of what would change and what would happen in the future."

Alex didn't just work with Karrimor. He helped create clothing for Rohan and tents and hammocks for Troll. It was always slightly un-nerving leaving base camp with a completely untested bit of equip-ment or clothing, but it always seemed to work. He was a climber and innovator extraordinaire.

What would he have made of the mountaineering scene today? I wonder if he would feel that "style" is no longer entirely a matter of personal choice; commercialism often dictates what a sponsored climber's next photo shoot or expedition is going to be. Has the pure-ness of line been replaced by the bottom line? To some extent, the an-swer is yes. If you want to become a sponsored climber, you must look good, and continuously perform at standards that require very high levels of fitness and athleticism. Furthermore, it seems to me, you need an understanding of the commercial world where performance is judged by records and numbers. This is what both the outdoor in-dustry and the public expect. How else can a company attract media attention to make films and to help brands compete? Sometimes both purity and reality are lost in the hype. There are some members of the adventure fraternity, whom Doug Scott described as "TV types," who do very little climbing and still somehow promote themselves as climbers and make a good living from the deception.

What would Alex think about the emphasis on the recording of numbers, the media attention given to the collectors of the 14 eight-thousanders or the seven summits; to be the first to ski down a peak and the fastest to solo it. These seem to be the very things Alex thought had taken Messner away from the true path of adventure. But it is these "achievements" that make climbing understandable to the me-dia and the general public as a sport; the grades, heights, hours taken, these are recognizable sporting achievements – the biggest, hardest, boldest, first, second and so on. Is this so different from the 1970s or even the 1870s? Perhaps not.

Alex would have loved many of the changes that have come and I suspect his own attitudes would have changed with the times. Looking back, I remember that we had regular arguments in the last year of his life about what changes were coming and how quickly they would come. I did not believe that expeditions would take helicopters into base camp. Even more, I couldn't imagine they would want to. Nor did I believe that there would be a revolution in telecommunications and the media would capitalize on the opportunities. Once again, I could not see, or even imagine, why anyone would want a telephone at base camp, or instant video screening. All that would be an intrusion on the adventure and allow worries from home to creep in; there would never be a time when you were completely focused on the task at hand.

I realize now that Alex not only saw the future coming, he wanted it to happen sooner. It would be part of his plan and style. To make a living from climbing wasn't part of his safety plan, having a safety plan was part of his vision for making a living from climbing. He was beginning to be good at creating tough clothing that kept you warm and dry and was designing bent ice tools that wouldn't break your knuckles. Perhaps what Alex wanted most of all was easy access to mountains and an increased likelihood of rescue and survival; these couldn't come too soon. More than anything else, he would have enjoyed the professional good looks of everything associated with the outdoors today. His vision of life was one that fits the world today.

There are at least two other key ingredients that placed Alex in the middle of the rapid advances of the period – having the right challenges and grabbing the moment. Alex just happened to be around at the right time. In the late 1970s and 1980s, there was a concerted effort to climb all the remaining major unclimbed ridges and faces on the 8000-metre peaks. The points of the compass allow for only so many, and by the mid-1970s, the race was fast developing. Alex joined that race.

Today, the media has transformed the way we look at mountaineering. There were a very few specialist magazines and a handful of films in the 1970s. Now climbing is everywhere. Brands like the North Face commission films about their own athletes. Red Bull has its own TV channel. Magazines are being replaced by material that's free online and consequently ubiquitous. There are festivals all over the world dedicated to climbing, where professional climbers meet the public.

Climbing has become an established part of the entertainment industry.

Yet the pure adventure of climbing is still there for anyone who wants it. Even now, there are more unclimbed peaks over 6000 metres than there are climbed. Some older climbers dislike the changes in the climbing scene over the past 30 years. Maybe I am one of them, believing that climbing has acquired too many of the trappings of a sport, and is too driven by commercial interests. I think Alex would definitely give me an argument about that and, perhaps, as the creator of the Kendal Mountain Festival in 1980 and SteepEdge.com in 2011 (both with our mutual friend from the Leeds days, Brian Hall), I would be on a losing wicket.

I mentioned at the start of this chapter that several websites had caught my eye when Googling for Alex. NEclimbs.com is the website of the New England climbing scene. I wonder if its creators know how much Alex learned from New England climbers? Looking around the site, I found the quote that best sums up Alex's approach to climbing in his own words: "The wall was the ambition, the style became the obsession." It comes from the second paragraph of his book, *Shisha Pangma,* and it is worth quoting a bit more from that paragraph to understand the context:

"On its southern flanks this largely unknown, elusive, barely pronounceable mountain of uncertain altitude boasts a huge, spectacular, visually formidable (and consequently tantalisingly attractive) mountain wall over two and a half kilometres high and twice as broad – an unclimbed, unvisited alpine playground. To climb it became an ambition, but not just to climb it, we had to make the ascent with style, as light, as fast, as uncluttered as we dared, free from umbilical cords and logistics. With none of the traditional trappings of a Himalayan climb."

Alex was very aware of the dangers that came with ambition. But style could counter this, a combination of lightweight tactics and mental commitment. Through the speed gained going lightweight, high-altitude climbing became safer. In many cases, this was true. A combination of style and ambition saw some stunning successes on the world's highest mountains, and one of the first was Shisha Pangma.

24

DON'T STOP ME NOW

The higher the mountain, the more the risks there are, and as you spend more and more time at altitude, the dangers are compounded. It is fair to say that high-altitude mountaineering is among the most dangerous of all pastimes. Those who take part inevitably become accessories to death. With the exception of a few other activities –cave diving, BASE jumping and wing-suit proximity flying – it is unlike other sports in that respect.

There is no shortage of misconceptions about high-altitude mountaineering today. One says it has now become relatively safe. In 2010, a stripped-down French AS350 B3 helicopter (the same type as landed on the summit of Everest) succeeded in rescuing three alpinists from almost 7000 metres on Annapurna I, one at a time – the highest rescue achieved at the time. Large commercial expeditions that place fixed ropes more or less from the bottom to the top of the world's highest peaks provide their clients with a sense of safety, an experience similar to climbing a via ferrata in the Alps, except that in the Alps there are no Sherpas to help put up tents and cook food. Bottled oxygen keeps the altitude well below 8000 metres.

It is simple enough to distinguish between adventure climbing and mountain tourism. High-altitude mountaineering in the 1970s and 1980s cannot be compared to the commercial adventure tourism that the public understands as mountaineering today: paying to climb Everest, or joining the numbers race on the eight-thousanders, or the quest to climb the seven highest summits on the seven continents. There are dozens of websites where you can sign up with a credit card to go on these trips. When Alex visited Shisha Pangma in the pre-monsoon season of 1982, it had been climbed only a handful of times, and no one had yet been to the bottom of the southwest face of the mountain.* If you Google "Shisha Pangma" today, you'll come up with pages of offers from various companies to take you to the summit.

No doubt there are adventures to be had on commercial trips. But what is the true personal value of buying a summit in the way you might buy a ticket to fly to Hong Kong? And what are the underlying risks, both in terms of the risk to personal health and safety and also the risk that the experience will be diminished because individuals don't take full responsibility for themselves?

Paul Nunn, another good friend from that era, succinctly described the real value of mountaineering for the individual as "being able to put one foot in front of the other for vast distances and at great heights in the knowledge that at some point it would be time to turn around and do the journey in reverse." The dynamic of the expedition, and the psychology of its individual members, changes when responsibility is abrogated. The commercial nature of most expeditions to the Himalaya and the client-guide relationship has changed the nature of modern mountaineering.

The ownership and responsibility for each step taken is now part of a signed contract. Money changes hands. The trappings of modernity – better access, equipment, oxygen, helicopters and medical camps – further diminish the experience. On the positive side, there is the emergence of some Sherpas as a powerful force in mountaineering, but for the most part they are just paid employees working in very dangerous circumstances to look after the every need of their clients.

When fatalities occur on these trips, it is often the guides and even the Sherpas who become implicated and are critizised in the press. They are just doing their job. It is high altitude and bad weather that kills people, even if lawsuits have tried to pin a charge of manslaughter on guides.

---

* After the first ascent of the southwest face by Alex, Doug Scott and Roger Baxter-Jones, there were a number of new routes on this face and some curious associated events. Voytek Kurtyka, Erhard Loretan and Jean Troillet climbed a new route in fine style in 1990. Kukuczka climbed a new route with Artur Hajzer, and Wielicki soloed a route on the mountain. It was beneath the face that Alex Lowe and Dave Bridges were killed in an avalanche in 1999, and, almost inevitably, Ueli Steck took the speed record of 20 hours up and down the southwest face in 2011.

Jon Krakauer's *Into Thin Air* was a good book and deserved a place on the bestseller lists and its various awards. But what is it about? For nonclimbers, its subject is mountain climbing, but *Into Thin Air* was more accurately about disaster overtaking a tourist excursion than a true mountaineering adventure. Alex made a remarkably perceptive comment on this subject in the opening pages of *Shisha Pangma*. He can see and feel the changes taking place and is very ambivalent about it.

"In the accessible big mountain ranges of the world, climbing is currently undergoing something of a mid-life crisis. The problem is that almost all mountains worth their salt have been climbed, sometimes by a whole handful of different routes.* [...] It is increasingly difficult to maintain the pioneering spirit in the face of information, the need to book a peak well in advance of a projected expedition, the probable presence of a couple of other expeditions at the base camp (and more likely swarming all over your mountain), and the multifarious trekking groups, cake shops, hotels and hippies on the approach route. The mountaineer observes himself as part of an industry, and, incongruously, it is the tourist industry he is part of."

It is hard to argue with the reading public that *Into Thin Air* is more about a disastrous tourist enterprise than it is about mountaineering. It probably sounds both dated and elitist, and perhaps it is. The way the public views mountains today has changed. Many people take up climbing with a completely different perception of what it is about. It is assumed that going to the Himalaya is expensive and commercial expeditions are the norm. Mountaineering on the highest peaks 30 years ago was far more affordable than it is today, and there were many more unclimbed mountains and new lines to attempt. Now the high-mountain nations have grasped that mountaineering is just another branch of tourism. Peaks and their routes are priced accordingly. The price tag carries with it a star system based on either high demand or the remoteness of the peak. In this system, Everest has become like

* Alex was focusing on 8000-metre peaks and those near to that elevation with great faces still to be tackled. As China and the Eastern Karakoram have opened up in recent years, there are clearly more unclimbed mountains above 6000 metres than there are 6000-metre peaks that have been climbed.

Monte Carlo, and to visit Dolpo is an experience to be sold as being unforgettable, as unique and as expensive as staying in an ice hotel in Sweden.

Ironically, the 1982 Shisha Pangma expedition had some of the features of a modern commercial expedition. It was made up of disparate members, both in terms of mountaineering skills and their reasons for being there. Getting the money together for a lightweight attempt meant that some members were seen by Alex at least as just part of the essential package to make an attempt by the lead climbers possible. Alex was being an opportunist and the opportunity came to him by chance, as Alex wrote, "in the more obscure regions of the mind of a young man from Belfast. Nicholas John Prescott is a tall eager, agitated Irishman possessed of fair, aquiline features. An irrepressible buoyancy, eyes framed in gold-rimmed spectacles, a brash and sometimes misplaced confidence and a method of speech that can reduce all but the most hard-nosed listener to a confused resignation."

Prescott, a modest alpinist with no Himalayan experience, had been trying for several years to get permission to climb in China. Very unexpectedly and many months after making an application to climb Shisha Pangma, a large envelope landed on his doormat granting him permission from the south. His elation was soon tempered by the costs and size of the undertaking, and by the assigned route. He had expected that if permission were granted, it would be for the much easier *voie normale* from the north. Prescott initially persuaded Bristol-based climber and filmmaker Jim Curran to come and help finance the trip by making a film. When this fell through, he had little time to find a replacement team capable of tackling the completely unknown face. In April 1981, he phoned Doug Scott to ask Doug to take over the permission and organization. Doug accepted immediately.

By chance, Doug had bumped into Alex at Makalu base camp in the autumn of 1981.* He had never climbed with Alex but knew his record. "Alex had earned himself a fine reputation as a young and innovative

---

* For UFO enthusiasts, Alex's team saw one from their bivouac high on the mountain, while Doug Scott's team witnessed one from neighbouring Chamlang at midday. Alex described a bright, silvery object travelling slowly through the sky and then passing around to the north side of the mountain.

Himalayan face climber but his contribution to climbing was also seen in other departments, principally in helping to establish a solid connection between Polish climbers and ourselves. He had also brought a touch of realism to the bureaucratic procedures of the British Mountaineering Council."

Doug was also very aware and understanding of Alex's nature. "Alex was 'all out front,' forthright in his opinions on matters which concerned him and about which he had given much thought; then again, when he was not sure of his ground he knew when to keep quiet, to watch and learn until he was sure."

Despite this, the two clashed on Shisha Pangma over the expedition's overall approach and fairness to all its members. To Alex, it was clear that the two least experienced members of the team – Elaine Brooks and Nick Prescott – should be left to fend for themselves while the four lead climbers – Doug, Alex, Tut Braithwaite and Roger Baxter-Jones – got on with climbing the face. Doug appreciated that these two members had contributed equally to the trip both in terms of personal commitment and finances. Doug felt they should enjoy the experience and everyone should have a chance to climb. Alex believed that any effort spent "guiding the other two" would greatly reduce the odds of getting up the face because too much effort would be spent at altitudes too low to properly acclimatize. Initially, Doug did not see Alex's attitude as a risk:

"Alex had a reputation of being very abrasive and very ambitious, saying that he wanted to achieve the status of Chris Bonington *now*, not when he was forty – and there is nothing wrong with that, providing he could reconcile himself to the competition. Problems of ambition only seem to arise when climbers seven years younger are snapping at the heels of those in the way. There is no real difficulty between those who are two generations apart, and with Alex I felt no great threat." *

The expedition was hampered very early on by a lack of finance. The Chinese authorities did not believe that the expedition had as little money as they declared, despite the fact that the budget had been set

* Both this and the above quote, *Shisha Pangma,* page 27.

out clearly in the final papers sent to Beijing. The team found themselves being asked to pay for Land Cruisers, not trucks as they had specified, and spending nights in hotels rather than camping. A corrupt liaison officer didn't help matters. But with a combination of stubbornness and hard-nosed negotiating by Doug, and the support of their young expedition interpreter, Wu, they were able to get their way.

Eventually, the team found itself in Nyalam, the last town before Shisha Pangma's south side, but with the yaks that had been ordered in a village 40 kilometres away. No one had ever approached the mountain from the south, and Nyalam was out of bounds for the foreigners, so the local party boss had assumed there had been a mistake on the paperwork he had been sent from Beijing. It was eventually sorted, but at a cost in time, effort and cash as alternative yaks were hired and the team had to shoulder much more weight themselves. It was not an auspicious start and as the delay turned from days into weeks, it preyed heavily on Alex's mind.

The bad feelings between Alex and the two less experienced members of the team, especially Elaine Brooks, came to a head during continued bad weather in base camp in late April. Doug found himself trying unsuccessfully to moderate between the warring parties. "For Alex, Elaine had only contempt, saying he always spoiled a good atmosphere with his aggressiveness and took others with him. Without realising it, they turned from sensitive beings into oafs."

Elaine believed Alex was making the entire expedition an emotional nightmare for her and others, especially Nick and Doug, while it seems Tut and Roger, known as RBJ, sat on the sidelines, secretly cheering Alex on. Then Elaine decided to confront Alex head-on about their differences and went to talk to him.

Doug asked her: "Did it help?"

"He was brutally to the point," she said.

Doug explained: "Later Alex told me that during this conversation he had told Elaine that he did not want her to come between him and Shisha Pangma. Alex told her, 'You are the problem of the trip – if you were not here there would be no problem.' … I felt like a pig in the middle ... as soon as Alex or Elaine's expectations appeared to be in jeopardy the negative energy that was generated put a dampener on the whole enterprise."

Such problems are all too common on expeditions; behaviour can become oafish. I watched it tear into the goodwill between Alan Rouse and his teams on both Everest in the winter of 1980 and on K2 in 1986. It would also greatly affect our Annapurna trip only a few months after Shisha Pangma.

Despite very unsettled weather, the team agreed to two acclimatization peaks – Nyanang Ri (7047 metres) and Pungpa Ri (7445 metres) – as suitable objectives offering the chance to sleep high and, in the case of the latter peak, a possible descent route from the main objective nearby. If Nick and Elaine were able to keep up and do their bit then that was okay. Alex felt it would be a chance to sort the wheat from the chaff, and that soon proved the case.

Nick became ill almost as soon as they set off for Nyanang Ri. The team stopped to wait for him barely an hour out of advanced base. Doug told Alex to step back and let Nick make his own decision whether to proceed or not. When he caught up, Nick asked for another day's rest to recuperate. But Alex had already done his calculations on the days remaining to the team and the days required to climb the two training peaks and then climb the face. There were no days to spare to accommodate anyone's need to recover from illness. Alex went for the jugular.

"Nick, you're clutching at straws. You don't have the years of slog necessary. I'm sorry, but charity ends at 5,000 metres."

Alex was being cruel to be kind. He realized Nick did not have the experience to make the decision that would be good for him and the team. "I thought back to the same argument underneath Makalu the previous spring, when a friend [René Ghilini] had slowed perceptively and fallen behind. Then, on the barren moraine, I had shouted to a colleague: 'Look you stupid Pole, give him a couple of more hours!' That time it had been me demanding time for a friend, but I knew him well enough to know he had already reached his decision; he only had to catch us up to tell us."

Another crisis swept through the team as they argued over Nick. RBJ now sided with Doug and said Nick should make up his own mind. Alex retorted: "Bloody hell, Roger! Don't be such a bloody amateur. These are mountains you know. They kill people." It wasn't just Nick who was struggling; Paul Braithwaite announced with regret he would be leaving the expedition. Elaine arrived at the cluster of boulders where the males were all in a state of uncertainty and argument, and made up her own mind to carry on and not get embroiled in the debate, sensing that Alex might soon question her fitness and commitment. She wrote, "The arguments were still buzzing back and forth, crowding and pushing against the timelessness of the mountains. Why was it not just enough to be here, feeling the energy of this place? ... Somehow the dream had been turned into a military exercise with no room for dreamers ... I turned and walked up the moraine before even that evaporated."

Alex now confronted Doug: "If I was the leader of this trip, I would tell Nick to go down."

"Well fortunately, Alex, we are not all like that."

"But it's bloody obvious, man. If Nick can't see this now, how the hell can you expect him to see it later? I've a lot of respect for you, Doug, but I also reckon that some of your trips have failed to realise their potential because of your happy-go-lucky approach."

With that, Alex left the others and raced to catch up with Elaine before she got into trouble on the glacier above. He shouted for her to stop and wait. At first she just ignored him, so Alex tried a different tack: "'Oi, woman!' I screamed in my most deprecatory tone; surely she would hear that. She turned and I beckoned her in my direction ... The glacier looked safe ... [but] it had a comprehensive covering of snow that could be obscuring a potentially lethal crevasse."

Elaine records the moment when they met at the edge of the glacier: "Alex was uncoiling the rope. 'Better tie on for this one.' He was smiling, the aggression gone and replaced by an instant boyish charm. It was too sudden. I groped for excuses not to go with him, but even as I did so, I realised I was a very small rung on his ladder of success that would take him to the summit of the mountain as quickly as possible."

Knowing Alex as well as I did, I can see now not just a calculating mind but also deep care for his fellow climbers. He may have been genuinely annoyed with Doug, Nick and Elaine, but his annoyance was not personal, it was because they as individuals did not see the reality of the situation. Elaine did manage to get to the first bivouac before realizing she would not be able to keep up with the remaining three. The others continued and succeeded in climbing Nyanang Ri, but not without a final fractious argument between Doug and Alex in the icy snow cave on their last bivouac.

Doug announced in the frozen darkness: "I am not going to operate in this cold calculating manner, Alex, and follow your decisions which have been inflicted on the team by force of personality."

Alex countered: "The problem is that for the first time you are not necessarily getting things done your way under the guise of democracy by the force of *your* personality."

Roger was caught in the middle and no doubt was reflecting on the value of his mantra: come back; come back friends; get to the top. "This bivouac in the ice cave saw the birth of a timetable. Gone the freewheeling approach where we would climb around our chosen mountain until one day we sensed that permission was given and the final pilgrimage would begin. This was logical but death to a certain spirit we sought in the hills."

It didn't help that on the descent Doug was less able at rapid descent on steep ice than the guide RBJ and the ice master Alex. Now it was RBJ's turn to become critical of Doug. After a period of bad weather at base camp, Alex and RBJ got drunk and very obnoxious one night. Doug began to question whether, as the old man on the trip, he wanted to climb the mountain with the two youngsters.

Alex summed up Doug's thoughts. "Was he in the way? Why was there no rapport between us? Surely he was out of sympathy with me and Roger, and if climbing the mountain was going to be an aggressive, individualistic ego-trip, he would go visit Tibet."

Alex and RBJ began to make plans to climb the face as a pair, but something was troubling Alex about Doug's state of mind that he could not simply put aside. He cared deeply that Doug made the right decision. In an honest, almost legalistic, analysis of his own response to Doug's personal dilemma, Alex reveals a great deal about himself, which he rarely displayed in conversation.

"I am not the best person to pose a question to, by someone hoping for some grasp of the underlying confusions that prompt it. My mind does not have the intuition for this. I could sense that Doug was searching for something but what? Who was I, at twenty-eight, to tell a man with his record when to climb on? I did not understand Doug's doubts because I had never shared them. I was better at walking down snow; Doug was better at climbing rock. So what? I would not be sensitive enough to feel out of sorts if I was holding the team up on the rock. I would probably demand and expect a rope. Doug, in contrast to all the teaching he had tried to instil in himself, was unable to see our situation in its overall context. He could not see his stamina, his experience, his selflessness on the mountain; he could only worry if he was fit enough to climb with the 'youngsters' (even if this particular youngster had been the least fit of the team)."

Alex and Roger realized they wanted Doug on the climb. Alex went to Doug's tent and found he was talking with Elaine. He knew she had the most to gain if Doug decided not to go on the mountain, as she would have a companion to tour Tibet. But Elaine had just told Doug that he must stay and climb the mountain. It was settled.

The expedition was now reduced to Alex, RBJ and Doug as the climbers, with Nick reconciled to the lesser role of support climber for the other three. Having dispatched Nyanang Ri, the three lead climbers turned their attention to Pungpa Ri and made an impressive ascent of the mountain. They were now resting and about to engage in the main event. In one succinct paragraph, Alex sums up his feeling of angst, explaining his bouts of anger and cross words with other team members. It stands as an illustration of his state of mind before other major climbs.

"Alpine-style climbing in the Greater Ranges is not dissimilar to some aspects of conventional, or perhaps even guerrilla warfare. Long periods of lazy inactivity lead with an inevitable sense of increasing urgency to a short, frantic, dangerous engagement on the front line, the mountain wall. The climber enjoys many advantages over the soldier; he is his own general and his own private – the carnage, the destruction, the imperative of killing does not haunt him. But the same brooding, electrifying tension is in the air, the same inevitable advance toward the appointed hour and if in the close proximity of strong minds and tired bodies, tempers become a little short and nerves a little frayed, the context must be understood."

On 24 May they left base camp for the southwest face. Alex wrote, "there was now a total unity of purpose. Nothing existed to distract us from the climb; no more ruthless decisions had to be made and problems of calendarisation, of ambition, of ego had now vanished. Individual method and madness were being channelled into a united drive, the variety of skills and experience in our three-man team could be collectively pitted against the wall."

The approach took them to the extreme right-hand end of the face. From there, to avoid losing altitude, they traversed a dangerous icefall beneath a seemingly endless ice cliff. It was a huge risk, especially for Nick who had agreed to carry some of the equipment and food to the bottom of the face. He would have to retrace his steps alone. A number of blocks of falling ice missed them; only Nick was hit a glancing blow. Alex described this traverse as "gambling time and effort against the prospects of infinity."

That night, in perfect weather, the team made the decision to lighten the loads they were planning to take on the face by eating half the food they had brought with them. At seven the next morning, they began the ascent.

They made remarkable progress the first day, although tempers flared once again when Doug decided to climb a rock rib to the left of the ice couloir that Roger and Alex climbed. Doug shouted across, suggesting the pair leave the "boring" couloir and join him on the rocky rib. Alex took that as contempt for those who preferred the ice and shouted insults were exchanged back and forth from their chosen media. Roger joined Doug while Alex continued alone up improving ice and was soon ahead of the pair now struggling on steep compact rock. He sat and ate a Mars bar and watched with amusement as the others eventually made a difficult re-entry into the couloir. Doug's detour proved to be the hardest technical climbing of the entire climb. It had also cost the team valuable time. But as Doug later pointed out, Alex had conveniently forgotten that the trio had agreed before they went onto the face that the rib would avoid the danger of stones falling down the couloir, and it would also be kinder on Doug's gammy ankles.*

Reunited, they made rapid progress to the bottom of the rock barrier that barred the way to the upper half of the mountain. To make up for his earlier mistake, Doug took over and led them up the intricate and demanding rock and mixed ground. The other two climbed together while Doug belayed, Alex taking extra care not to dislodge rock or ice onto Roger below him. When the pair arrived at the top of the final rock pitch, Doug quipped: "Well youths, you seem to have managed to second that almost as fast as the old man led it."

In the dusk, they managed to make a fairly level area at the bottom left of the upper couloir. Doug failed on the first effort to erect Alex's recently designed tent, so Alex took over. "The contraption being my responsibility, I was summoned to make a second attempt. With no backing wall of ice or rock to suspend it against, the tent had a mind of its own. The remaining, half-erected fibreglass poles flailed around the tent and disappeared like crossbow bolts. With all the doors closed, the thing was finally tamed with the remaining poles and pinned to the floor and slopes with ice screws and ice axes.**

"Next morning we remained cocooned, awaiting the sun. It is hard to grasp the splendour of this life-giving force unless you have sat frozen, waiting for the first light of the far horizon and that triumphant blaze of gold as the topmost part of the orb comes into view … Now that we

---

* A reminder of his ordeal on the Ogre in 1977, when he broke both legs just above the ankles and endured an eight-descent to base camp after his successful ascent with Chris Bonington.

** The Mac Tent had a wedge-shaped design. It worked best when the top could be suspended above and the back anchored to a wall behind with two hooped poles criss-crossing the third side to give it shape and most importantly air space inside. It was designed to sleep two but could sleep three very uncomfortably, with the third unlucky person cramped into the bottom of the wedge and struggling through the night for both space and air – we called this the doghouse.

were through the rock band, we decided to abandon even more equipment and stake all on speed. A couple of pitons, three ice screws, and our one and only helmet were abandoned, carefully tied to one of the ice screws in case we should need to have recourse to them in the unforeseen emergency of descent down this route."

They made excellent progress on easier ground and bivouacked that night at around 7800 metres. There was a worrying build-up of clouds on the horizon, but the next day dawned clear and soon they were soloing up the final few hundred metres in the freezing thin air of early morning. As they neared the top, Alex saw Doug suddenly stopped up ahead.

"What's up, Doug?"

"We're there, youth," came the reply. The trio were up, but, as is often the case, there was little outward elation. "The face was done," Alex wrote, "we were just a couple of minutes from the ridge. I sat beside them in the bitter wind, emotions numbed. So many barriers, so much work, protocol and precipice. If only Paul could have shared this with us today!"

They traversed the main summit and went partway along the ridge toward the (slightly lower) central summit to make sure they had climbed the highest and then began the long descent down the east ridge. They had one more bivvy as a storm threatened, but the next day, apart from a ferocious wind, the weather was still clear. They descended the far eastern flank of the face from the col below Pungpa Ri, abseiling down the last steep ice slopes. "Our last ice screw took us to snow deep enough and adherent enough to allow us to turn out and continue unroped, almost leaping now, down to a gap that led us simply over the serac rampart before making a last bounding dash through the snow to a place where a small trail of footprints, days old and wilting in the sun, passed across us rising left-to-right, heading toward Shisha Pangma. They were our own tracks. We had squared the circle!"

At the beginning of June they were on their way home, exhausted but triumphant. At Shigatse they were delighted to suddenly see two familiar figures, Charlie Clarke and Adrian Gordon, who were the doctor and base camp manager of Bonington's four-man team to the northeast ridge of Everest. The elation of their unexpected meeting vaporized with the news that Joe Tasker and Pete Boardman had vanished high on the mountain. As Roger recalled: "There was nothing left to do but for the survivors to get drunk together."

Many thousands of miles away, I had just completed a splendid day's climbing on the Isle of Skye. I got back to our hut at Elgol at around 11 p.m. and heard the news on the BBC as the others cooked a late supper. I went outside, wracked with sadness, and watched the last light at midnight drain from the sky over the sharp profile of the Black Cuillin. I prayed the same fate had not befallen Alex, Doug and Roger and watered my Scotch with tears.

25

WISH YOU WERE HERE

My afternoon with Maria Coffey was almost over. She had a flight to catch back to Vancouver. As we finished our coffee, she said, "After Joe died, my life was a blur and I can't remember much about how Alex reacted. Everyone was devastated. Of all the young climbers around, Pete and Joe were seen as the invincible duo."

For the first time Maria looked sombre as her memories took shape. "I do remember Alex coming around the night before I set off to go to Everest base camp. He tried hard to talk me out of going, saying it was ghoulish and sentimental. He displayed his usual 'get over it' attitude. But it was a really tense meeting, because Alex was about to leave for Annapurna and I said to him be really careful. He was just dismissive, saying, 'don't be stupid, and don't lecture me.' He was really quite harsh and angry with me. Maybe it was his own concern about what he was doing, or maybe he was worried going to Everest would hurt me more. Or maybe he was just in denial."

During the summer of 1982, Alex was focused on our plans for Annapurna and behaving with his usual pragmatism. But now he seemed to me to be caught in two minds – confident, even arrogant, one moment, but then ever so slightly uncertain about the speed at which things were happening. Back-to-back successes on Dhaulagiri and Shisha Pangma had convinced him that more success was inevitable if he stuck to the plan.

In the 1970s and 1980s, the realization that the next trip might be fatal was something mountaineers accepted. Subconsciously they prepared for the possibility each time they discovered an unclimbed project. We knew the risks but never thought it might be our friends who were killed. Increasingly, we all became aware of the emotional consequences experienced by their relatives and partners when they fell into the dark abyss of grief and loss. The climbing community that stuck to their tasks inevitably felt survivor's guilt and the knowledge that somehow we were all accessories before and after the fact.

That summer, the realization that Pete Boardman and Joe Tasker were gone put a dampener on our climbing. The Everest attempt was the first lightweight expedition Chris Bonington had led to an 8000-metre peak. This ridge was seen, along with the Kangshung Face, as the last great problem on Everest. There were only four climbers on the trip. Pete and Joe, Chris and Dick Renshaw. After Dick became ill – he had a minor stroke – and Chris realized he was not acclimatized and fit enough to move at the speed required to cover nearly a kilometre of difficult pinnacles above 27,000 feet, Joe and Pete had gone off for one last attempt and not returned. We all went to the memorial services. Pete and Joe were good friends, very different in character, but they had set a standard with their ascent of Changabang and the new route they'd climbed with Doug Scott on the northwest face of Kangchenjunga.

I talked with Sarah Richard about Alex's behaviour during the summer leading up to Annapurna. "The whole thing was odd before Alex left. It was as if we knew," Sarah recalled. "I remember speaking to Al Rouse after he'd fallen in love with Hilary and he said to me that falling in love was the worst thing that could happen to a climber. It meant you couldn't face up to the climbing with the same commitment. I had a letter from Alex from somewhere on the walk-in saying how hard it was, how cold and miserable and how he just wanted to be back with me. And he said 'remember how much I love you,' as if he was preparing himself. I detected other things in Alex, his wanting to speed up the process of getting known as if he were running out of time. Do you remember that weekend with the film crew a month before you left for Annapurna?"

Until she mentioned it, I had forgotten this rather sad and peculiar episode. I had met Alex and Sarah on Friday evening in July at the Black Cock in Broughton-in-Furness. We had a pint and a meal before going to our place in Millom. He was in a strange mood: beyond excited, more dangerously ecstatic. "Don't worry anymore about money for the trip kid. We're about to become famous. I've got a production company lined up who want to make a film about the climb. They're coming up next week to film us here making preparations. René may come over if he's not guiding."

My first thought was absolutely no way; a film team accompanying us on an alpine-style ascent of Annapurna? How could that work? It made no sense at all, big cheque or not. They would totally disrupt the flow and concentration of the trip however far they came with us. I had found it disruptive enough having a film team on our winter Everest trip the year before. On that expedition, we were a big team of eight sieging the west ridge. There were no issues with the film team itself. We got on well enough with the crew. The cameraman was a climber and once got himself up to the first camp on the fixed ropes on his own. But much energy was expended bringing all the necessary film equipment up – the big 16-millimetre Arriflex camera and tripod, batteries and rolls of film. I soon got fed up with this imposition and my solution was to stay as high on the mountain as possible to keep away from the cameras.

All this raced through my mind before I responded to Alex. "Okay, who are these guys, where do they come from, what's the story for the film, what's their track record of making films in the mountains and, most importantly, are they climbers and why do they want to make a film?" I noticed Sarah looking at me with a quizzical smile, urging me on. Go on, she seemed to be saying, talk some sense into him.

"They don't have experience but they have money and want to make the film. They tracked me down through the BMC after they saw me on TV being interviewed after we climbed Shisha Pangma. It will be fine. We'll tell them how it all works, and maybe they won't even get to base camp, which will be fine because they will still have paid for the trip."

They arrived next weekend with their cameras, a pretty alien and ya-hoo bunch, southerners with money and a new company. My friend, Pete Clark, organized a party for us after a day's climbing. After too many drinks, I agreed to get wired up, but with a plan, knowing Alex would spot the fact that he was being secretly recorded. I wanted to get his reaction and it was, as I suspected, negative. He was not going to be taped when he wasn't totally in control.

Sarah phoned me a week later. She told me with relief that Alex had dropped the idea and the reason why. After the filmmakers had completed the weekend filming us climbing and partying in the Lakes, the director had a further phone conversation with Alex, thinking he was reassuring him and sealing the deal.

"Whatever happens, it is going to be a great film and you will be the star. And if you die, we'll do a really sensitive interview with your mum and your memory will go on and on."

Alex cut him short: "Excuse me, wait a minute, if I'm killed there's no interview with my mum." And with that, Alex told the guy to get lost and put the phone down.

As Sarah and I talked through these memories, she speculated what it might have meant. "I think that final conversation with the producer sowed a seed. He was reluctant to discuss his fears with me in any detail, but he would say things like 'it's my destiny,' and he implied that he would go on the trip even if he knew he was going to die."

Sarah paused and then continued. "And it wasn't just once. It happened several times, but then he would say things like 'but you don't need to worry about me on this one, it's the next one you need to worry about.' One day it got so bad, I just left him and went for a walk."

Hearing this from Sarah, I recalled the cracks beginning to appear in Alex's armour, the antithesis of his usual brash confidence. Looking back at my notes from base camp, I realized that Alex was saying similar things to me. At the time, I was psychologically beaten trying to deal with these same questions myself.

Before Alex left for Annapurna, he and Sarah talked about getting a proper house together. Sarah told Alex she wanted to have children. She knew Alex's Catholic upbringing meant they would get married. "If you get pregnant Sarah, you're the one telling my mum, not me. You realise it will be a full church wedding with all the trimmings. My mother won't have it any other way."

26

EYE OF THE TIGER

As the flight from Delhi began its descent into Kathmandu, for a few tantalizing minutes the full extent of Annapurna's south face was framed in the window. Although gigantic, at this distance it looked perfectly feasible. We could even pick out our proposed line running right-to-left up and across the Polish Pillar. Then thick clouds swallowed the peaks as we sank into the turbulence of the late monsoon. Dropping out of the heavy cumulus, I could see tree-covered ridges rising up with frightening speed to meet us. It was still early morning. Smoke from breakfast fires hung above farms perched on ridge tops. The terraced fields dropped steeply down toward the valley bottoms in verdant stairways.

The flight to Delhi had been longer than usual. Security forces in Istanbul and Karachi forced everyone to leave the plane and have all their hand luggage searched before reboarding. These long stops meant no sleep and frayed nerves. These were tense times in a turbulent year, one that had already seen Britain at war in the South Atlantic and Pete Boardman and Joe Tasker lost on Everest. The papers were filled with endless hijackings, kidnappings, civil wars and bombings. The Soviets were in Kabul and the insurgency of the mujahedeen was intensifying. I joked to Alex that it could be worse. The bucket shop had offered me cheaper tickets on Czech Air and Ariana Afghan Airlines via Prague, Beirut, Baghdad and Kabul.

His reply got me thinking. "And you mean to tell me you chose Pan Am? How the hell do you think the terrorists get around if not by Afghan Airlines? That would have been a much safer choice."

We were on Pan Am flight 002.* It was £15 more expensive than the Ariana option but had one big advantage: our relationship with the London ground crew that Joe Tasker had established, providing free excess baggage. On this trip, I had travelled down separately and took most of our bags to Heathrow before Alex arrived from Letchmore Heath with Jean. By this time, I knew several of the Pan Am baggage ground crew staff and had phoned a few days before seeking their help. The manager was an outdoorsman and understood that lightweight was another way of saying "very little money." Having ditched the idea of a film, on this trip we had very little indeed. It was essential that all equipment and booty for sale got out as cheaply as possible. He wouldn't accept the bottle of Scotch I offered him over a coffee. He had been a friend of Joe's and that was good enough.

"You'll need that where you're going," he said.

An upgrade to business class was an unexpected bonus. After a fraught departure, thanks to Alex's late arrival, we entertained ourselves with the free drinks, games of cards and endless examinations of a big photo of the face.

Landing in Delhi at first light intensified the red-clay landscape around the airport. Customs was as fraught as expected. We had to get our bags from the international terminal (a very large shed) to the adjoining domestic terminal (a much smaller shed) and onto our Air India connecting flight without a prohibitive excess baggage charge. I was aiming for the smallest possible bribe. Security in Delhi was lax compared to Istanbul and Karachi. To get to the domestic terminal, I simply walked around international passport control and customs, went outside the building and entered the adjoining building.

I was relieved to see some baggage handlers with whom we had negotiated the deal for our Everest bags a year earlier. I walked over to explain that I had "a little extra expedition gear." They immediately went into a frenzy of gestures, telling me how everything had "changed now sahib, much harder, must be good deal." We threaded our way

---

* Pan Am launched its round-the-world flights in 1947. Flight 001 went west from San Francisco, and Flight 002 east from New York. In 1982, although the airline was within six years of Lockerbie, and a decade from going bankrupt, the service was still a continuous journey, albeit with different stopovers, and anyone wishing to do so could stay on the same plane all the way around the world.

back around airline counters, customs and passport control with armed guards giving us no more than a glance to reach the international baggage area where Alex lay sprawled atop three huge trolleys.

"How much weight?" the head baggage handler asked him.

Alex smiled. "Maybe 100 kilos."

"*Achha*. We see." His squad immediately started dragging the bags toward a scale and with every bag weighed our hearts dropped. We gave up mentally weighing up what the bribe was going to be once the total weight topped 300 kilos.

"Now you pay me $500." With the start of the haggling, our expedition began in earnest. Half an hour later, we had managed to get everything onto the Kathmandu flight for $150. With a total budget of only $3,500, every penny was critical.

Coming into Tribhuvan airport, I saw a man with a flag standing beside the runway on the third fairway of Kathmandu's only golf course. His job was to warn anyone about to tee off to wait for a moment while a flight landed or took off. My anxiety returned as we touched down. Our 300 kilos of gear and free sponsor swag would soon be offloaded into the arrivals shed. Next problem – could we get it through without it going into bond? Alex remained relaxed, headphones barely reaching around his head from ear to ear because of his thick, curly shock of hair. Anxiety was just part of my nature, as acceptance of the moment was part of his. I had volunteered to take the additional responsibility of all the baggage and bribes and he was out of it. I was the one with the bag of tricks to avoid customs and bonds. Alex's coolness in the situation was just Alex. What would work, would work.

Getting through the airport was once again fraught but not a disaster. When officials pointed to our bags and started to show interest, we responded, "trekking, trekking," and moved to the back of a long line to give ourselves time. I watched the customs men checking bags in front, and once I identified what the correct squiggles were for that day, and what was the right colour chalk, I extracted my own box of chalk and surreptitiously marked all our bags.

Two hours later, we were out in the bright sunshine with all our gear in a melee of cab drivers gesturing to us and shouting "best taxi, best price" from all directions at once. We managed to get all the bags into two taxis at a fixed price and bumped along in our small ramshackle convoy to the Lhotse Hotel. Exhaustion hit us as soon as we walked into the cool marble surroundings of our modest digs. We checked in alongside commercial travellers from India and the Middle East. The Lhotse wasn't a tourist hotel but had the advantage of being located halfway between the airport and Durbar Square and very near the Sherpa Co-operative. We showered and slept. Strange dreams overtook me, images from the journey, fleeting visions of Annapurna and the quizzical cries of mynah birds just beyond my consciousness in the garden outside. René woke us some hours later, having arrived from Paris with news that all the high-altitude clothing he had brought from France had not arrived and everything else was in bond at the customs shed. I should have gone back out to meet his flight with my chalk.

Over the next few days we had three separate tasks. René had to get the bulk of our climbing equipment out of bond. I had to clear the bureaucracy and make the arrangements with Mike Cheney at the Sherpa Co-operative to hire a sirdar from Pokhara, a cook and cook boy. Alex had his Shisha Pangma book to finish and his article to write for Karrimor and many letters of thanks to sponsors.

René spent hours each day at the airport, filling in endless triplicate forms. He came back depressed after the first two visits. "It's crazy chaos there. Just a huge shed filled with boxes, many opened. There are smashed TVs all over the place."

We needed around $1,700 to get to the mountain and back, and were several hundred short. I sold everything I could from our supplies brought for this purpose – whisky, coffee, chocolate, meat bars and cereals. The trekker hotels and bars paid a reasonable price. We pooled all the hard currency we had and gave René the job of getting it changed at the highest rate. In those days, a close relative of the king of Nepal was the head of the Nepal treasury. Rumour suggested he would give 10 per cent more than the bank for hard currency, dollars especially. René took a chance and headed to the office near the palace. He soon found himself facing a tricky situation.

The factotum of King Birendra's uncle looked at him with disgust. "What is this?" he shouted at René. "This is only $1,000. I thought you had $100,000 you wanted to change. We do not take these small amounts. It is impossible."

René persisted with promises of much larger amounts later in the year when he returned in winter with a big French expedition. Eventually, he arrived back at the Lhotse Hotel with the 10 per cent bonus.

We still had to clear the high altitude clothing from the bond warehouse. On the fourth day, Alex and I were repacking the specialist food we hadn't sold when René burst in to the room with exciting news. "The rest of the gear has arrived from France and I have agreed the amount of the bribe. I can go back in two days to collect. It is such a crazy place, you know? They just do nothing with all this stuff in the shed, only money counts."

Now we had a difficult decision to make. Should we all stay or should some of us head for base camp? René still might need us and our liaison officer Mr. Gupta to put pressure on the airport staff should they up the bribe. But we were now behind schedule and it was nearly the end of the monsoon. Our original plan had been to reach base camp by 10 September. That gave us three weeks to acclimatize before we tackled the face in October. October is an uncertain month in the Himalaya. With luck, we would have a couple of weeks at the beginning of the month before the jet stream descended and autumn storms arrived. We had already lost nearly a week in Kathmandu.

Alex argued logically that we should split up. Time was as important now as securing our high-altitude clothing. We had already considered buying used gear on Sherpa Street. There was plenty to choose from. The Burgesses had been on the successful Canadian Everest expedition pre-monsoon. The shops were full of down suits, parkas and sleeping bags, all marked "Burgess" in indelible pen. It made me laugh. It seemed the twins had managed to sequester much of the expedition's inventory to flog in Kathmandu. No doubt a number of loads had gone missing on the way out.

We decided René would wait in Kathmandu. If he failed to get the clothing from the warehouse, he would buy all we needed on Sherpa Street by credit card and we would sort it later. Alex and I would press on to Pokhara, hire porters and start the seven-day walk to base camp. René could catch up with us. We had one final day sorting and packing and bought our tickets for the early morning bus to Pokhara. The last evening in the Up and Down Bar was excessive, and when our small team assembled at the bus depot the next day, we were feeling a little rough, although not as miserable as Mr. Gupta. He took one look at us and our meagre possessions and his face fell with the disappointment of the condemned man.

"Where is all my new equipment?" he asked as we boarded the bus.

"All packed specially for you," Alex responded. The law in Nepal was that all expeditions had to supply high-altitude equipment for liaison officers and also protective clothing for the base camp cook boy. Between us, we'd brought perfectly adequate but rather patched and slightly smelly sleeping bags, down parkas and all the other requirements for our LO and crew. We could not afford new equipment. It was a sore point throughout the trip. The Nepalis were worried there might be bad karma carried in used clothing, especially when someone who had subsequently died had worn it.

Good to his word, Mike Cheney's sirdar met us in Pokhara. We hired 38 porters, issued them waterproof sheets and the low-cut wellingtons unique to the porters' trade, paid them an advance for half the stages and then had a quiet evening wandering through town, hoping the monsoon clouds might part for long enough to give us a view of our mountain.

We set off early the next morning in blistering heat. The walk-in for the most part passed in a dreamlike state of uncertainties overlaid by the compulsion of where we were going and why we were here. Mountaineering was, Alex told me, just tourism with an objective.

I had hoped that the days walking in would give us a chance to get to know each other again. We had rarely climbed together in the past two years and had been on different trips after three expeditions in a row together in the late 1970s. Disagreeing over the inclusion of the film team had not helped our relationship in the weeks before departure.

Alex admitted he had needed to borrow £700 from Mike Parsons to make his contribution. I reflected it would have been nice to have the luxury of money on this trip, but that was not the main worry.

Alex was more withdrawn than in the past. He walked more often with his Walkman as his companion than he did with me. Our last major climb had been in Peru three years before. There, we had played to our strengths, made a few ascents and failed on a few others. I suspected we would not be singing "be kind to your web-footed friends" on this trip. He was a more serious and less communicative character than the Alex of old.

What had changed? The main thing was that Alex was now a professional mountaineer. He had crossed the line. On every expedition he would be expected to build on his already considerable reputation. His passion, his style, was now his obsession. Getting to the top would never be enough. It must be done perfectly.

I was eight years older than Alex and much more cautious. Two close calls on Everest in winter the year before had taken something from my usual carefree approach and substituted it with greater respect for life and my own mortality.

The almost unbearable heat of the first three days spent winding our way up through the rainforests was replaced by continuous heavy rain and chill winds as we entered the Modi Khola valley beyond Landruk. The torrential rains flooded the paths and the thunder of the river reverberated around the gorge. Even if we had wanted to talk, the issues of managing the porters, some carrying double loads and suffering in bad weather, took time and effort. We needed to stop and talk to them, share a joke, encourage them by displaying our own massive loads. The pounding rain made it difficult for us to communicate.

The leeches were living bombs, dropping from the branches and, like raindrops, bouncing off our umbrellas. They were devious little creatures and every evening we had to do complete body searches, carefully dosing with salt or putting a lit match against the bloated bodies of those that had found a way through our defences.

On the fourth day, the weather was so foul we worried the porters might go on strike if we insisted on a multistage day. Chhomrong was the last chance for a bit of comfort before we entered the Annapurna Sanctuary, so we decided to stop at a lodge after only walking six hours.* We crawled into sleeping bags, and talked and read the afternoon away.

Despite being in my bag, I couldn't stop shaking with the cold. I'd spent too long in just shorts and a t-shirt as the rain turned to sleet. Alex seemed relaxed and assured. That night, as the rain continued and the thunder echoed around the gorge, I couldn't tell whether I slept or woke. I had memories and strange dreams that mixed all of our previous times together.

The next morning, the rain started again as we set off into the narrowing gorge. The huge forests of rhododendron provided some shelter from the wind. As we got higher, Alex began to relax and open up. In the smoke-filled lean-to where we slept that night, we talked the evening away, squatting on the floor or sitting on rough benches to eat gritty dal bhat that tasted of kerosene. Alex was on fire with his love of climbing and his need to achieve something new each year. It was then that he revealed his list.

"Two expeditions a year from now on," he exclaimed. "Once we've climbed the south face of Annapurna, I can relax for a few months. I've got Makalu and K2 on the agenda for next year. Want to come?"

I was enjoying Alex's company, hearing about the last two big climbs, seeing the scale and the style of what he had done and what he intended. I understood now why Messner said that Alex had the purest style and vision of anyone then active in the Himalaya. Alex was completely unsullied. Unlike all the rest of the British climbing community, and Messner himself, he had never been on a big siege-style expedition.

The next morning the rain lessened, although the cloud swirled

---

* This was the Captain's Lodge. As far as I can remember, it was the only accommodation in the whole of the Kali Gandaki that was purposely set up and run as a climbers' and trekkers' location. I confirmed this in 2012 when I returned to Annapurna, except this time, every two to three hours' walk, there were whole villages of hotels and lodges, each accommodating many hundreds of tourists at the same time. I'd left my mobile phone behind in Kathmandu, expecting there would be no connectivity. Not only was there mobile phone connection all the way to base camp, there was Wi-Fi most of the way, too. I did the right thing leaving my mobile, however, as there is no reception for mobile phones where I live in Caldbeck. The Nepalis didn't believe me.

around the gorge, blocking all views of the mountains we knew were there. Machapuchare is sacred to the local Gurung people and also Hindus, who believe the peak is home to Shiva. The snow that blows from its twin peaks, the spear of Shiva, is thought to be divine incense. The sign told us that all meat and eggs were banned beyond that point. I felt a twinge of superstitious guilt as I remembered our tins of Spam and meat bars and put it out of my head.

"Two more days, and we'll be in base camp," I said to Alex as we gathered pace and, with it, warmth.

"The weather better improve or conditions are going to be crap."

The rain fell again in sheets. A couple of river crossings were as scary as any climbs we had done. We took turns crossing first with a rope, climbing from boulder to boulder in the torrents of white water, and then set up elaborate double-rope handrails for the porters. Machapuchare was towering above us somewhere on the right, but Shiva offered us nothing but swirling rain clouds that, as we got higher, turned to a freezing mist filled with sleet.

We had a cold, damp night crammed together with our porters under a huge boulder. Alex was as suspicious as ever and checked the soundness of the boulder's footing. We talked about our close encounters with huge boulders on Bandaka and Changabang. I had been lucky over the years with falling rocks. Alex had twice been hit and injured, once in the Alps and a second time the year before on Makalu. As he was telling me again, my own fears found a focus.

"You will look after my little boy, won't you?" Jean MacIntyre's voice echoed around my head. But I no longer knew how to look after Alex. It was how he looked after himself that mattered now.

The sun broke through at midday and shone on the splendid white walls of the sanctuary. The south face suddenly filled the space in front of us. We knew from earlier expeditions that base camp was tucked into a fold between the lateral moraine of the glacier and the steep hillside that rose toward Annapurna South and Hiunchuli. But this was not where the porters had expected us to stop and an extra stage had to be paid for the additional two hours. What is now called Annapurna base camp, the destination for trekkers, was directly opposite the face but hours of awkward glacier away from the base of the face proper. It comprised a couple of smoky shacks made up of loosely bound branches covered in a corrugated tin roof.*

Our camp at around 4500 metres was idyllic. Late summer flowers still held their fragrance. The earth was soft and comfortable for our three-man tents. These we erected not far from a large overhanging boulder, which formed the roof for the cooking area. A large tarp was lashed around the boulder and, with a few poles recovered from earlier expeditions, we created a covered communal area. As the skies cleared, the penetrating cold transformed the remaining alpines overnight into eternal blooms, perfect in shape and detail but empty of life.

Late the next day, René arrived with three porters. He was in a jubilant mood. He had made the journey from Pokhara in just four days with all the bonded equipment. We had a cheerful meal of dal bhat and tuna fish and made our plans. Apart from permission for the south face of Annapurna, the permit stated that we could "climb on the slopes above base camp." The "slopes above base camp" led to a number of attractive 6000-metre and 7000-metre peaks, perfect for acclimatization. But first, we wanted to have a look at the bottom of the route.

René and I set off a day later to climb directly up onto the glacier from our base camp. Alex did not feel well, so we rearranged our rucksacks to take most of what he would have carried. After a couple of false starts, we gained the spur that led directly to the bottom of the Polish Pillar. This rose immediately to the left of our intended entry couloir. Steep grassy meadows soon gave way to rocky ground that narrowed and steepened as it rose into the mists descending from the face. René was ten years my junior and supremely fit. I fell behind and had to pick my way up damp rock walls and unmarked snow patches, wondering which way he had gone. The mist held tight around the spur like a

---

* This location now comprises around six lodges capable of sleeping several hundred people. Due to global warming, it is now extremely difficult to access the glacier from there. On the large chorten just above the complex, I placed the new memorial for Alex.

glove. As the angle eased, I spotted steps ahead in the snow and, finally, I found René waiting. I felt slow and tired and expected a caustic comment, but instead he simply said: "We are at the base of the Polish Pillar. This is where we will camp."

We were somewhere around 6000 metres. Once I'd dropped my heavy rucksack, my energy levels soon returned. We quickly cleared a good platform for the Mac Tent, the same one that had been used on Shisha Pangma just a few months before. We had planned to bring two Mac Tents, but when Al Rouse dropped out, we decided to share and accept the discomfort of three in a space designed for two. Tonight, at least, René and I would sleep in relative comfort. The mist cleared and the wall emerged above us. The big couloir that was the start of our route was clearly visible, but it was deeply scoured by rock fall and runnels of water running down the lower half.

"It is far too early in the season for the face," René said. He was standing looking up as the evening light left the face. Even now as the temperature dipped toward zero, there was still the occasional zing-zip of falling rocks and the swoosh of wet snow cascading down the couloir like a demented dragon.

"It's still September. We've plenty of time," I said. Above us to the right, as we looked down the glacier, the icy block of Annapurna South hung frozen in the sky. The spiky twin peaks of Machapuchare speared the sky to the left. And rising above the now tiny meadow where our base camp sat, Hiunchuli rose from a series of serrated ridges.

"That looks interesting and it's close to home."

René agreed. "We'll go down early, repack and head for Hiunchuli."

27

HEART OF GLASS

We were back at base camp by noon the next day. Alex had completely recovered and was raring to go. We quickly threw together food and equipment for four days and left early the next morning.

After slogging uphill for a couple of hours, the pleasant grassy slopes gave way to *roches moutonnées* of deeply striated granite.* We climbed up beside the braided outwash stream to the bottom of a shattered icefall and found a secure location beneath a solid wall of ice that was perfect for hanging the Mac Tent. Alex drew the short straw for the doghouse that night. While melting snow for Tang, I did something I'd never done before, I spilled a full pan of water just as it was warm enough. None of us was amused. During the night, the sound of snow sliding down the nylon woke us and by morning several inches had settled. We left everything in a cache and bailed out for base camp.

The storm lasted two days but the third dawned cold and clear. At last the weather seemed to be settling down. With light rucksacks, we climbed quickly to our camp beneath the icefall and spent a second night there; early the next morning we entered the chaotic labyrinth of seracs and crevasses above. It was the worst icefall any of us had encountered. We stopped for a mid-morning brew between two deep crevasses, but the pan of snow had only just been placed on the stove when a huge serac tumbled from above and crashed down onto the thin connecting ice bridge we had crossed just minutes before. Forgetting tea, we hastily packed up and set off up again. By the afternoon, we had negotiated the icefall and reached the upper glacier. We

---

* Also known as sheep backs, *roches moutonnées* are irregular rock formations with steep sides on the opposite side of the direction of ice-flow and can make the approach to the base of receding glaciers difficult.

ploughed through deep snow to the bottom of a couloir that led to Hiunchuli's east ridge and cut a second bivvy platform in secure surroundings.

It was another perfectly clear and still morning. Six pitches of steep ice, each of us leading two pitches, brought us to a col on a dramatic, razor-sharp and heavily corniced ridge at about 6200 metres. To our right, a three-kilometre ridge led to Annapurna South, a thousand metres higher. To our left, and much nearer, was Hiunchuli. The fantastic double and overlapping cornices reminded me of the ridge on Huascarán Norte that had stopped Alex and me three years before. But, with care, we traversed the ridge to the bottom of the final summit cone, ready at any moment to jump down the opposite side of the ridge in the event of a leader fall. We cut a precarious platform for the tent on the south side of the ridge and I boiled water for brews and soup with instant potato, tuna and cheese – a lavish meal that we ate in the fading light. René crawled into the tent while Alex and I lingered outside, wearing every layer of clothing we had, and savoured the wonders of being high on an unclimbed route.

It became incredibly calm and quiet once the stove was turned off. Many thousands of feet beneath us, deep wooded valleys were broken only here and there by terraced fields and clusters of farms and small villages. I could make out Chhomrong where we had stayed at the Captain's Lodge. The plains of Nepal and India lay far beyond, cloaked in a dark haze. A few small but steady lights shone out of it. The silence was almost tangible as the stars sparked into existence, taking over from the dying evening light.

"You see those lights way out there?" said Alex.

"Yeah, I see them. They look almost unreal. That must be Pokhara and I'd guess a few hotels must have generators for electricity."

Alex and I had debated the future of Nepal during our evenings on the walk-in. "I bet you that in twenty years there will be electricity right up this valley," he said.

"No way," I said. "What would be the point? There are only a few poor villages and the farmers just live a dawn to dusk existence."

"But is that what they really want?' Alex asked. "In any case, it will be done as much for the trekkers and climbers. You'll see. They'll be arriving in their thousands."

I wondered if maybe he was right and for some reason the idea depressed me. Alex unzipped the tent as the cold intensified and I had to get in first. It was my turn in the doghouse. Sleep escaped me most of the night as I fought to keep my body from sliding off the edge. Cheyne-Stokes breathing woke me every time I did drift into sleep. The next morning a vicious wind began to blow and clouds curled around the summits. I felt semi-relieved and said so. René was not amused. We decided we had done enough for the first acclimatization climb and set off down, arriving safely back in base camp just after dark and woke our cook boy, Pemba, to demand a late supper.

The weather was in sync with our plans. It remained bad for three days, giving us time to rest and consider our next climb. On the other side of the glacier were two trekking peaks – the 5945-metre Tent Peak and Fluted Peak (Singu Chuli) at around 6500 metres.

Fluted Peak had not been climbed from this side, but a long and attractive ridge we named Tower Ridge rose up to a plateau beneath its summit. From there, it would be possible to climb a second steep ridge to Glacier Dome (Tarke Kang, 7168 metres) and thus gain the main ridge that extended many kilometres from Annapurna. Attaining the ridge would allow us to spend time well above 7000 metres and provide a final acclimatization climb before returning to the face.

I spent the days reading or walking in the snow above base camp. Dinner in the damp kitchen area with its floor of black ice was squalid and the food generally unappetizing as we tried to conserve our high-altitude goodies. Dinner each night was dal bhat with spicy pickles and some ten-year-old meat bars left over from Antarctic supplies that a friend had donated. Alex and René often stayed on in the cook tent to drink Nepali rum while I went to read. Their conversations became loud and abusive as they swapped tales of lesser mortals. Al Rouse came in for particular criticism for having dropped out, and at one point I heard René suggesting they would be better on the main face as a twosome. I put the talk down to rum, and ignored it.

We set off on the fourth day after Hiunchuli with food for five days and a mixed rack for both rock and ice. Steep walls of gravel blocked the route off the glacier onto the face, but we negotiated these and were soon soloing up a rocky rib that felt like a Scottish scramble. At around 5000 metres we put on our crampons as the ridge turned into an elegant crest of ice and at around 5 p.m. cut a spacious bivouac platform. My two companions seemed strangely detached from me as we studied our intended route on Annapurna that now rose up in sharp profile to our left.

The next morning, interesting ridge climbing on mixed ground allowed us to gain the plateau below Fluted Peak. The snow was waist-deep in places and we agreed 200 paces each before handing on to the next person to break trail. René did his 200, and then I took over but stopped for a rest 20 short of my quota.

"You're getting old, Porter," Alex said as he went past.

"Hey, I was only catching my breath." When my turn came again, I perversely refused to hand over the lead and took us to the bottom of the connecting ridge that led to the summit of Glacier Dome. René and Alex roped up and geared up and I went to the back. Four pitches up, we came to a perfect ice sheet of around 70 degrees – it was my lead.

"Pass me the rack Alex."

"No way, I'll lead this. I'm not sure you're up for it." René laughed and I wondered what the hell was going on, but decided to stay quiet.

Alex traversed right onto the ice, which narrowed into a couloir above. He put in an ice screw about 30 feet out and then cursed and shouted down that one of his crampons had come off and was hanging by the straps to his boot. It seemed to me the gods were making a point.

"You dumb amateur," I shouted up. "Lower off and let someone who knows what he's doing lead."

The situation was too serious to continue an angry exchange. Alex tied himself off on the ice screw and, with difficulty, managed to get his crampon back on. I found myself arguing with René in the meantime, wondering why he hadn't just told Alex it was my lead.

I was still fuming when we cut our next bivouac platform at around

7000 metres. For the second time in a week, I tipped over a pan while cooking, this time losing half a pan of soupy snow just as it was ready to have powdered potato added. I had a miserable night in the dog-house, struggling for breath and listening to the mountains of the Annapurna cirque, their rumblings echoing back and forth as if in trollish conversation with each other. We were all awake half the night.

The next morning, a steep ridge led to the top of Tarke Kang where we rested and brewed up. A blanket of cloud now filled most of the Annapurna Sanctuary. Beneath us to the northeast, the shark fins of Machapuchare's twin peaks cut through the white sea of cloud lapping halfway up the great sweep of Annapurna's south face. Hiunchuli was now submerged. It was serene and beautiful.

As the stove hissed into action, I turned to Alex. "Sorry I got angry yesterday."

"Just get your shit together and no more mistakes."

I suggested to Alex that we climb toward the Roc Noir to get a bit more altitude beneath our feet. At around 7400 metres on my lead, the appearance of wind slab made the decision to descend easy.

"Are you sure it's wind slab?" he asked.

"Seems hollow beneath me." I kicked my crampons into the snow a bit higher, now doubting my own judgment. "Don't like it – it's got a nasty layered feel."

I remembered reading a report of a fatal accident at about this point on the attempted first ascent of the mountain. We retreated to our bivvy at 7200 metres and spent another night. In the grey dawn, a strong wind promised the arrival of a storm. We hastily packed up, try-ing to keep as much of the windblown spindrift out of our sacks as possible.

I took up the anchor position at the back as we began to descend. After about 500 metres, René, who was leading, turned right down a steep slope.

"Where's he going?" I shouted to Alex.

"We've decided to drop straight down the face. It will be quicker."

"Yes, more direct for sure," I thought, "but what's the icefall going to be like?"

I found myself struggling to match the pace of René and Alex descending steep snow and ice facing outwards. Like Doug Scott on Shisha Pangma, I found myself turning to face in when the slope was above 55 degrees while Alex and René seemed perfectly at ease facing out.

Two-thirds of the way down, we came to a barrier of rock around which the ice separated and fell steeply down to the main glacier, now only 2,000 feet below. A few abseils down the barrier led to an isolated buttress of rock with a small summit. Vertically beneath, the icefall looked like a maze of ribbon candy, but to the right, about 50 metres away and at a 45-degree angle, there appeared to be a much less broken section of the glacier and the promise of escape. We had used the last of our rock pegs so now we hammered a warthog ice peg behind a loose flake of rock. We backed it up with a sling around the flake.

The situation was serious. If the ice peg pulled out and the block failed when René's weight came onto the rope, not only would he fall into a deep crevasse but Alex and I would be left stranded. We watched in a state of tension as René gently eased onto the double ropes and, with crampons sparking on the rock, lowered himself diagonally down until he reached the top of the first big serac. Using a combination of pendulums and acrobatics, he managed to get to the edge of the icefall. Alex and I gave a cheer. René hammered another ice peg into the rock and pulled the ropes tight. Alex safely followed on the abseil-cum-Tyrolean traverse. As I removed the large back-up sling, it occurred to me that I was probably the heaviest of the three of us and if the peg were to pull, I would be lost in the maze of crevasses beneath. I put the fear from my head, carefully checked my connection to the rope and gave the peg a last suspicious look. Had I been thinking, I would have changed my figure of 8 for a configuration of karabiners to act as a brake bar. As I dropped onto the rope, the crampon on my left leg caught in a sling hanging from my rucksack. My leg was now contorted and locked behind me, while the figure of 8 was jammed tight in the diagonal line. I swallowed a scream, half of fear, half of annoyance with my own stupidity, and forced myself foot by foot along the rope. It was painfully slow, but to the other two, I must have looked extremely comical suspended horizontally in space, fighting the rope, trying to prevent myself flipping upside down and losing my rucksack. Twenty minutes later, René and Alex dragged me up onto their stance. I felt like an amateur and a complete idiot.

When I regained my composure, I discovered the good news that from this point a snow slope led off the glacier on the right to ledges traversing beneath the south face, eventually joining the spur René and I had climbed up to the face two weeks before. René untied as soon as we reached the ledges and took off to recce the route. Less happy now we were back on rocky slabs, Alex wanted to stay roped and we soon fell behind. By the time we reached the spur beneath the face, thick cloud filled the Annapurna Sanctuary as it had the day before. There was no sign of René and no possibility of finding the right way down. We had no choice but to sit and hope it would clear.

With only a couple of hours of daylight left, it did. I soon found the right line down. Darkness overtook us when we reached the glacier and we continued by headlamp. René came out with his flashlight to direct us to the top of the moraine and told me off for not being faster. I said nothing. Despite the exertion of the previous few days, the dal bhat presented to us by our reliable cook Pemba was not appealing. I slunk back to my tent and retreated into my dry, base camp sleeping bag. I could hear Alex and René laughing and shouting in the cook tent as they opened a second bottle of rum. As snow began to fall heavily, I sank into an uneasy sleep.

On the final days we shared in base camp, Alex was subdued. Strange things happened at night. Alex and I woke several times, dreaming of stone fall, but when we listened, only the silence of the high mountains greeted us. I was very disturbed, wanting to ask Alex was he sure he was in control? Was the climb now what he wanted, or was it what René wanted? Even if I were not ill, I was convinced I had been manoeuvred out of the team. I knew René was aggressively ambitious. Seeing the same behaviour from Alex in the mountains was a new experience for me.

Three days later, I was still suffering from diarrhea and stomach cramps as I crawled out of the tent to see how they were getting on.

The weather had improved and they were getting ready for the face, which rose majestically with its plastering of snow two kilometres straight up. Alex was pulling the sheath off a 40-metre rope to use as a second rope for abseil. They would only use one rope to climb on. Two ice screws and three rock pegs comprised all the technical equipment they would carry.

"You look like shit," Alex said. "What are you going to do?"

"I think I'd better not go." I was torn with indecision. What I wanted to say was, "Fuck you guys, I'm part of this trip and I'm coming even if you don't want me to." But I didn't. "No. I'd be too slow in this state," I added, half in tears, and uncertain if I really did want to go.

René looked at me and snorted. "John, what has happened to you?"

Perhaps my state of mind had made me ill, given me the shits. I didn't know. I did know that unless something remarkable happened now, the expedition was over for me.

That night, Alex spoke to me as an old friend. "I hope you get better and if we don't do it this time, we'll be back and you can come with us on the second attempt."

"That would be good Alex. I don't know about you, but I have a bad feeling about all this and falling out, letting you down. Be careful up there. We've got lots more mountains to climb."

There was a long pause and then Alex said, "You know, I've been having some scary dreams but I know how to find peace. Did I tell you I'm able to leave my body when I sleep and be with Sarah when I need to? It is the strangest feeling, very real. I can't wait to get home to see if she experienced the same thing."

I didn't know how to respond. Alex was not one for flights of fancy. This was a personal revelation that I had no way of understanding. Why was he telling me this? Was he uncertain and needing an escape? Alex was split in two – one half completely committed, the other deeply troubled and seeking a way out of his own plan. It was a moment when perhaps Alex could conceive only one way out of his momentary depression. Go and do something positive, as he had always done with Sarah. Go and climb the south face of Annapurna.

"Let's just make sure we all get home, kid, so you can ask Sarah for sure."

I walked a short distance up the moraine with them the morning they set off. The alpine flowers were covered in rime and small frozen pools held the grass suspended in time. Two brightly clad figures descended onto the glacier and were soon lost in the maze of humps and boulders.

28

TIME AFTER TIME

After René and I made the decision to leave Alex's body on the mountain, we reached Pokhara in two extremely long days from base camp, well ahead of our liaison officer. We had sworn him to secrecy. I knew I had to break the news to Jean and Sarah. It was my last duty on this expedition. René settled in at a hotel with some French climbers who were going on a high trek to get fit for their winter attempt on Everest. René looked shattered and unhappy, but he would be joining them. I gave him my winter sleeping bag, knowing he would need it, and said goodbye. It was the last time I saw him.

I took an overnight bus to Kathmandu and spent most of the night desperately rehearsing what I would say when I got through. I went straight to the British embassy when I arrived, expecting to be able to use their phone for this awful emergency. I was stunned by the reception I received. The first secretary told me that if we were stupid enough to get one of our friends killed in the mountains, it was no fault of theirs and they had no duty of care. The only thing of value he told me was that we had done the right thing to leave the body on the mountain since there was no facility to repatriate bodies from Nepal. With that, I was told to use the international phone service at the post office. It was the only way to communicate with the outside world. Twice that day I booked a call to Jean and twice the phone system failed during my allotted time. I returned to the embassy to plead for help and was told that unless I could contact Jean immediately, they would be forced to contact her through the police. I managed one more attempt the next morning, which also failed. The embassy then sent the details to London and the first Jean MacIntyre knew of the death of her son was when a local police officer knocked on her door.

Dennis Gray was in town as part of a UIAA gathering, and he and Mike Cheney tried to console me, but I went into a state of total depression waiting for my flight home, knowing how Jean, Sarah and Libby had received the news. A week after I got home, I wrote to the first secretary at the British embassy in Kathmandu, enclosing the full-page obituary about Alex that appeared in the *Times*. I asked if anyone in the embassy expected to get such a glowing tribute when their time came. I never received a reply.

I returned to England after the awful news had sunk in with Alex's family and friends, but I still needed to visit them all. There were no accusations when I told them I had not been with him. Both Jean and Sarah even displayed sympathy, feeling compassion that I had been a witness and survived. But even if they didn't ask, I was asking myself, "What more could I have done?"

Having seen Jean at the family home as soon as I got back, I now needed to see Sarah. I tried to think of what to say, how to make amends. She came up to Millom the following weekend as she used to do with Alex. It was less than a month after the accident. We decided to walk the ridge from the top of Walna Scar onto Dow Crag where Alex and I had stood to watch the sun set over the Irish Sea the year before. I borrowed a friend's collie to come with us, a dog Alex liked to walk with. This was the first time we had found time to reflect. It was just another damp November afternoon, empty of sunshine, yet charged with emotion.

"When you phoned last week John, you said to me something that I really hold true."

We stood on the summit of Dow. "You said the Buddhists believe that big events begin when you throw a pebble into a pond; the ripples expand, and continue to do so forever after the event, less visible but still expanding. I really believe that.

"When I first met Alex, I had never known anybody die. Then a short time later, a mutual friend of mine and of Jim Curran's died and that was when the sequence began, then Joe died, then Alex was killed, then my close cousin died, then my aunt, it went on and on in a short space of time.

"And it was so strange with Alex," Sarah went on. "The night before he died, I was staying on my own in Hayfield. But I just couldn't sleep. All night long there was a shadow on the wall, like a vision." I realised that this experience was perhaps what Alex described as "astral walking," reaching out with his being to be with Sarah.

"You know John, Jean also said to me that perhaps the whole sixth sense thing exists, and possibly Alex knew he was going to be killed. Maybe it is not all that farfetched. To survive in that environment you need to have all of your senses working and more."

Sarah, Jean and Libby were already considering making a pilgrimage to Annapurna base camp as Maria had to Everest. Terry Mooney was going to organize the journey.

"How is Terry taking it?" I asked Sarah.

"Hard. He has a sort of love for Alex, he wanted to be what Alex was, and share some of his adventures. When he gave Alex money, he wasn't buying favours or prestige; it was just genuine good-heartedness. And the same was true of Alex. He wanted to be successful like Terry. Perhaps one day he would have been. Alex liked the good life. You must have seen that he had some of Terry's Jekyll and Hyde nature. He could be all over the place one moment, and then walk into court and be incisive and brilliant. Alex liked contrasts."

I had seen Alex's "Jekyll and Hyde nature" on Annapurna. I wasn't sure which was the true Alex. But now, as we descended back down into the Duddon Valley, I felt better that Sarah seemed so calm. I could also sense her grieving deeply.

We got back to the car in the late afternoon gloom and drove back toward Millom: down the Duddon, across the bridge, through the farm. We were about to discover that the ripples of fate were continuing to expand. A car travelling far too fast came around the corner and hit us head on. The crash pushed us into a ditch. All I could hear at first were the cries of the dog in the back. Then cries from the other car.

"Oh my God, Sarah! Are you alright?"

"I think so, I can't tell yet."

I quickly checked to see if there was any blood and was relieved to see that she seemed okay. We both were wearing seat belts. Even the dog had now calmed down and seemed unscathed. I forced open the door of the car, got Sarah out in case of fire and began to deal with the aftermath. The four young men emerging from the other car, rugby players from Barrow on their way back after a game in Millom, were not as lucky. I could see one was badly cut on the face, having gone through the windshield, and another's arm hung broken by his side. They were all in shock. Within minutes, the local police officer, a climbing friend from the nearby village of Broughton, appeared on the scene.

"Oh it's you again John, is it? Looks like you've been extremely lucky. Here, put these accident signs out for me will you."* The rest of the evening was a blur. We had something else to talk about apart from Alex, at least for one evening.

The crash was a defining moment for Sarah. She wondered what made her put the seat belt on. Was it a premonition? Was there some other force at work?** Maria Coffey recalled discussing the accident with her.

"Sarah said she never put on a seat belt, but something told her to do so. She says she suddenly saw a car coming straight at her and thought, 'this is it; I'm going to die.' But after the smash and the tumult, she real-ised she was okay, and she said for the first time she knew she really wanted to live. Before that, I was really concerned for her. She was in such deep pain, and even though I was just finding a way through my own pain after Joe, I couldn't really help her. After losing Alex, she really didn't care, she just wanted to die."

More than 30 years later, we still talk about those times. Perhaps Alex embraced the ripples and knew that he would have to flow with them. He had a list of big faces in the Himalaya he wanted to climb. Perhaps he felt he had to climb to have a career. Alex MacIntyre told himself – as his own boss – that he had to get his list done; then he could be with Sarah and travel a different path.

---

* A year before, I had rolled another car a few hundred yards further on when I was forced off the road by a car overtaking on a blind bend.

** Maria Coffey describes the many paranormal experiences of climbers and adventurers in her book, *Explorers of the Infinite*.

Sarah has her family and her own life. But it took her a long time to recognize the world needed to start rotating again. "I am always surprised how well I get on with Maria when I see her," Sarah told me recently. "Her life is such a contrast to mine. After Joe died, she managed to recreate herself, to build on her experiences. It took me a long while to get out of the drudgery of having kids and being with someone who I really shouldn't have been with. I was quite resentful. Now I've come out the other side but it has taken twenty years.

"But the truth is I was a young person back then, just twenty-seven. We had only two and a half years together. I've spent a long time since then just burying it all; it was too painful after I had been so happy. But I would love to meet him now, to know what he had done with or without me. I know he would have been hugely successful. I would just love to have carried on that dialogue we had. That is what death is, the end of dialogue."

The end of dialogue is not the end of the story, however.

29

SEARCHING FOR A HEART OF GOLD

Doug Scott believes there are only two reasons people get killed in the mountains: either ambition gets the better of them, or they are unlucky. He thinks Joe Tasker and Pete Boardman died when ambition got the better of them, while Alex was just plain unlucky. Although I see Doug's point of view, I also think you need extraordinary ambition to attempt big peaks in the Himalaya in the first place. This is not an ordinary occupation; this is not your average sport. Alex was unlucky, but his ambition pushed him to extremes.

A friend of mine, a design engineer of immense intelligence, a non-climber but an adventurer by nature in his scientific thinking, put an intriguing question to me: "You say that climbing is mainly about having fun and having life-fulfilling adventures, but it seems to me that you leave on a trip with x members in your team and you come back with y. Assuming y is less than x, what have you gained?"

I thought about it for a week and could not come up with a convincing answer. I eventually emailed him to say: "What we gain is a bit like dark matter. We know it has to be there because we know the universe has mass and energy we cannot see or measure, but we cannot say what it is. But the fact is, we keep on trying to describe it. That's why we write books, give lectures and make films. There is a sum of experiences without which the universe would be ten per cent of what it is. This applies to mountaineering in the same way it does to all experiences that express our unique humanity."

This book took a long time to complete, in part because I could never be quite sure if there was a story to tell. What does a book about an individual and his quest for adventure add to the sum total? About eight years ago, I had a chance to reflect on this after a nasty accident left me laid up in bed for half a year. I decided the book needed to be completed. I phoned Jean to tell her, but she greeted me with sad news.

"I've been diagnosed with terminal cancer, John. It would all be too upsetting for me. There will be things about Alex you may want to say but I do not want to hear. If you have to finish the book do so when I'm gone."

Jean was a feisty, wonderful and very tough lady. She died in November 2012. Many years after Jean's last request to me, I began to find the time and the energy to pull it all together. At times, I asked myself if Alex's legend might be tainted if some of the myths surrounding him were dispelled. But the realities that made Alex the person he was, and ultimately led him to his death on Annapurna, are best expressed through his climbs, his work, his relationships, his foresight and his incredible drive.

He was not alone; he was one leading light in a remarkable generation, the generation that all but climbed itself into extinction. Today, little is known about them. Among our friends who died in the mountains were Peter Boardman, Joe Tasker, Pete Thexton, Al Rouse, Roger Baxter-Jones, Georges Bettembourg, Tobin Sorenson, John Syrett, Jean-Marc Boivin, Jerzy Kukuczka and many others. Is the fact so many died just a run of bad luck? Or did ambition get the best of them? Was dark energy driving us? Or were we simply intoxicated by our adventures, always needing more? Maybe all of these things flowed together through the same veins.

I stood once with Paul Nunn* in the Pan Am check-in line at Heathrow, when a nice old lady asked Paul why we had so many bags piled on our trolleys.

"Because we are on our way to climb in the Himalaya."

Her face lit up: "Oh yes, I've read about you all. You keep on dying but there always seems to be more coming along to take your place."

Paul Nunn's concise explanation of the need to take responsibility

---

* On 6 August 1995, Paul Nunn and Geoff Tier were descending from the summit of Haromosh II (6666 metres), in the Karakoram, when they were overwhelmed by a massive serac collapse and buried.

for "every step we take" is good as a description of a successful expedition, as is Roger Baxter-Jones's mantra I've quoted several times already. But mantras do not protect us either from ambition or bad luck. The principles of self-discipline built on physical and mental commitment are crucial to mountaineering success. Responsibility to yourself comes first and, if it is truly followed, it naturally extends to include everyone else on the expedition. But there are no guarantees. When you add high mountains to the equations of life, then your emotions and the possibilities of fate have many more opportunities to mess you around. There is no final journey back for any of us.

When I was young, I came across the Romantic poet Friedrich von Hardenberg, known more widely as Novalis. Like Alex, he died at 28. Like Alex, Novalis studied law. He passed his exams with distinction, as did Alex. There is little else in common between the long-dead poet, scientist and mystic and my hard-living and hard-climbing friend, except perhaps this quote from Novalis: "I often feel, and ever more deeply I realise, that fate and character are the same conception."

This insight offers an explanation for Alex's premonitions at base camp, not least because Novalis also said, "a character is a completely fashioned will."

Free will. Character. Fate. We all knew the dangers. With every expedition, the odds increase that something will happen. We all knew that. The evidence was there. The characteristics we shared were the will to continue and trust in our own good luck. Each year, the periods between expeditions were punctuated by funerals and the huge piss-ups for lost friends. At one wake, a well-known but very drunk young British climber went around telling everyone that it was good for him because since x had died, he moved up in the pecking order. Can such inane, brutal and disrespectful behaviour ever be forgiven? Perhaps it can, because behind it was a sort of self-realized fear.

Voytek Kurtyka has said many times that those who truly follow the path of the mountains should have no desire to explain the activity in quantifiable results. If we were really in the quantifying game, the lists of failures and deaths would be the only meaningful ones.

Luck in mountaineering, as in war, is a major factor. For success on

the most difficult routes on the highest mountains, the first quality required is blindness to the importance of individual luck. Gaston
Rébuffat once warned climbers, "remember, the mountain does not
know that you are an expert." The mind needs to trick itself into knowing that the mountain will fall to the expert.

The complex set of circumstances that can create or take away luck
means that luck cannot be defined. It is made up of both natural and
human factors – the uncertainties of weather, the exact moment a serac
topples, the accuracy of human observation, the reaction of mind and
body at altitude on a particular day, the right piton and the right plan,
the single stone set on its fatal journey by a ripple of melted snow.

Most climbers begin their interest in climbing by reading a good
adventure story. The first climbing book can shape the reader's view of
what climbing is all about. If that first book is *The Ascent of Everest*
(published in United States under the title *The Conquest of Everest*),
then climbing may seem a matter of teamwork and national pride
overcoming adversity. If the first book is *Into Thin Air*, then one might
question the risks involved and the nature of bravery and sacrifice
without realizing this book has very little to do with climbing. If it is
The Springs of Adventure, then the imagination might be fired by a desire for engagement of all the senses with all that is complex and unpredictable in nature. And if that first book is the parody *The Ascent of
Rum Doodle,* then climbing becomes a metaphor for most pursuits in
life. Climbers tend to read books about their passion not so much to
seek an answer to what it is all about but because they know there is no
answer. It is just a part of life that is wonderful because it is without any
reason to do it.*

There is one personal danger – better described perhaps as a danger
to the person – that can be explained, at least partly. When an individual becomes obsessed with climbing, then it becomes at once the
most dangerous and the most fulfilling of all experiences. That was
our mental state when we climbed Koh-i-Bandaka. We were truly obsessed and did not let our worries about the risk temper our will.

---

* Although if I am allowed a prediction with the same certainty Alex made his, a neuroscientist
will soon have a theory to explain why climbers take risks.

To find a balance in life, we all hope we can see both an entrance and an exit to any situation and make a decision either way. For example, Brian Hall and I had packed our sacks and were just leaving our tent to attempt the unclimbed south face of Shivling when Brian said:

"I'm not going."

I stopped in my tracks.

"Why?"

"Because I am still getting tunnel vision from being hit on the head on Chamlang; it comes and goes but it's not worth the risk."

I understood immediately. Brian still climbs like a demon, with a passion and love that sustain him.

❊ ❊ ❊

In base camp on Annapurna, I believe waves of fear and premonition were washing over Alex; they became one and the same thing. But in Alex's mind, the entrance and the exit to his decision were by the same door. Climb Annapurna and the fear will vanish. The way home will follow and then the next stage of his life with Sarah. An obstacle to that plan – the south face of Annapurna – would have been removed.

It was only one of several such obstacles. There were still a few other great unclimbed faces on his Himalayan list to be climbed, after which a new world would come into view; the path ahead would be level and open with all sorts of new opportunities.

Nick Colton believes that his "tick list" was not entirely self-chosen, that the routes on that list came from research into what had been done and not done. Nick argues that climbing journals, and *Mountain* magazine in particular, were implicated in stoking ambition beyond the limits of reasonable safety. I have some sympathy for this argument. On the other hand, if we read books about drugs, we don't necessarily become an addict. Good and accurate journalism provides the essential homework that should make for a safer trip. It is still down to the individual. Alex had the south face of Dhaulagiri as a possible target but dismissed it as too dangerous. Tomaz Humar, far fitter and faster than Alex could ever have been, took it on solo despite the known dangers.

What if all of those faces had been climbed by the time Alex was born? I believe that the love of climbing still rules both head and heart in some individuals, Alex among them, and that enables all other considerations to be blocked out when the moment comes. Alex belonged to the mountains, even if the mountains did not belong to him.

The 1982 interview between Alex and Ken Wilson in *Mountain* finishes with the familiar "why do it?" discussion. And so, as was often the case throughout the time I knew Alex, I will let him have the last word.

Ken: Given that climbing in general is good fun, physically challenging, spiritually uplifting, cliché, cliché, what is the real pay-off? Is it the competitive instinct, not only that the mountains themselves throw down a challenge but also that in succeeding on them, you gain recognition from your peers?

Alex: I am competitive in that I am always watching other people and trying to learn from them, but I do not think people do this sort of thing just for public acclaim. Basically, I just enjoy climbing big alpine and Himalayan faces. It is something hard that I can do well. I like the whole environment, the going away, the coming back, the contrasts and the constant change from expeditions to civilisation.

Ken: But isn't that putting it too simply? Isn't it true that Western civilisation has given these peaks some quantum of prestige? A whole environment of value has developed around them and without your "civilisation" to return to, to cash in one's chips so to speak, the activity would have less meaning. Obviously climbing mountains has a basic pull, but would people go back time and time again to do harder and more dangerous things if these things didn't have some value in terms of prestige?

Alex: I think I would carry on climbing regardless … If I saw a picture of a big nasty face in deepest Xinjiang or Siberia, and I thought I could sneak in and climb it and never tell anyone, I would be off in a flash.

Ken: Because it's there?

Alex: What else?

JOHN PORTER was born in Massachusetts and started climbing at the age of 12, serving his apprenticeship in the White Mountains, Rockies, Cascades and Yosemite. He moved to the UK in the early 1970s to do postgraduate work at Leeds University, where he joined a team of climbers dedicated to clean ethics, alpine-style, and the fostering of international partnerships.

Ascents of the north face of Koh-i-Bandaka (1977) and the south face of Changabang (1978) with Alex MacIntyre and Polish friends were achieved in the middle of the Cold War. Other climbs include lightweight attempts of the west ridge of Everest in winter, the northwest ridge of K2, the east face of Sepu Kangri, first ascents of Chong Kundam I and V in the Eastern Karakoram, and many other notable climbs around the world over a period of 55 years. In 1980 he founded the Kendal Mountain Festival with Brian Hall and Jim Curran, and in 2011 he and Brian founded the adventure-film website SteepEdge.com.

John is a vice-president of the Alpine Club and has previously been a vice-president of the British Mountaineering Council and secretary to the Mountain Heritage Trust. He lives in the Cumbrian Lake District, UK.